BRACING FOR ARMAGEDDON

BRACING FOR ARMAGEDDON

Why Civil Defense Never Worked

DEE GARRISON

UNIVERSITY PRESS

2006

OXFORD

UNIVERSITY PRESS

Oxford University Press, Inc., publishes works that further
Oxford University's objective of excellence
in research, scholarship, and education.

Oxford   New York
Auckland   Cape Town   Dar es Salaam   Hong Kong   Karachi
Kuala Lumpur   Madrid   Melbourne   Mexico City   Nairobi
New Delhi   Shanghai   Taipei   Toronto

With offices in
Argentina   Austria   Brazil   Chile   Czech Republic   France   Greece
Guatemala   Hungary   Italy   Japan   Poland   Portugal   Singapore
South Korea   Switzerland   Thailand   Turkey   Ukraine   Vietnam

Copyright © 2006 by Oxford University Press, Inc.

Published by Oxford University Press, Inc.
198 Madison Avenue, New York, New York 10016

www.oup.com

Oxford is a registered trademark of Oxford University Press

Library of Congress Cataloging-in-Publication Data
Garrison, Dee.
Bracing for Armageddon : why civil defense never worked /
Dee Garrison.
    p. cm.
Includes bibliographical references and index.
ISBN-13 978-0-19-518319-1
ISBN 0-19-518319-3
1. Civil defense—United States.   2. Nuclear warfare.
3. United States—Military policy.   I. Title.
UA947.G35 2006
363.35'0973—dc22   2005051559

9 8 7 6 5 4 3 2 1

Printed in the United States of America
on acid-free paper

For Jeanne, and for Travis, David Paul, and Marie

Acknowledgments

Over the years I have been writing about nuclear war and reason, many people have generously supported my work. For careful discussions, readings, and critiques of earlier and later versions of sections of this book, I am profoundly grateful to Harriet Alonso, Scott Bennett, Michelle Brattain, John Chambers, Dorothy Sue Cobble, David Fogelsong, Judith Gerson, Phyllis Mack, Art Miller, David Oshinsky, James Reed, Sue Schrepfer, Bonnie Smith, and Deborah White. I also gratefully acknowledge Britt Leggett, Lynn Miller, Carol Petillo and Wayne Cooper, David Swee, Virginia Yans, and my neighbors Barbara Turpin, David Younge, Joy Gianolio, and David Falk for their caring attention to the completion of this work. I am especially grateful to Paul Boyer, Mari Jo Buhle, Lawrence Wittner, and Amy Swerdlow, who believed in the value of this study in its earliest stages.

For providing the supportive atmosphere to follow the truth as each of us sees it, I am grateful to my colleagues in the History Department at Rutgers University, who so generously supported me through several months of a serious illness. Suzanne Lebsock and Mary Hartman ensured that I had copies of the manuscript even in the rehabilitation center and printed versions whenever I asked. Kathleen Casey again and again solved computer problems, both large and small, with great skill and love.

Generous financial support from a John D. and Catherine T. MacArthur Foundation fellowship grant from its Program on Peace and International Co-operation allowed me to travel to important archives and gave me time to write. Rutgers University also supported my research with several sabbatical semesters and research grants during the past six years. My editor at Oxford University Press, Susan Ferber, has provided insightful, critical, and sympathetic editorial assistance throughout.

I am indebted to many archivists and librarians for their kind and enthusiastic help with research problems and questions. I am especially grateful to Wendy Chmielewski at the Swarthmore College Peace Collection, whose knowledge of peace history is as educational as the many peace collections over which she presides. I also give my sincere thanks to the librarians who guided me to key documents in the Dwight Eisenhower, John F. Kennedy, Richard Nixon, and Ronald Reagan presidential collections, in the National Archives, and in the university and state libraries I visited.

My family members—my sister, Jeanne; my sons, Tray and Marty; and my husband's youngest daughter, Shannon—were always there to talk, praise my progress, and urge me on. And as always, John Leggett has listened, responded, and sometimes criticized my thoughts, read and reread my prose, and in so many ways made this book possible through his constant encouragement and his enabling me to find the time and energy to complete the research and writing. I have benefited enormously from his analytic insights, his impatience with formulaic versions of mainstream wisdom, and his inspiring vision of how we might all learn to live together in a sane and just society.

Contents

Abbreviations

AEC Atomic Energy Commission

AFSC American Friends Service Committee

BAS Bulletin of the Atomic Scientists

CD civil defense

CDPC Civil Defense Protest Committee

CND Committee for Nuclear Disarmament

CNI Committee for Nuclear Information

CNVA Committee for Non-Violent Action

CPD Committee on the Present Danger

CRP Crisis Relocation Plan

CSTI California Specialized Training Institute

CW Catholic Workers

DCPA Defense Civil Preparedness Agency

DDCW Dorothy Day Catholic Worker Collection

DDEL Dwight D. Eisenhower Library

DDEP Dwight D. Eisenhower Papers

END European Nuclear Disarmament

FAS Federation of American Scientists

FCDA Federal Civil Defense Administration

FEMA Federal Emergency Management Agency

FOR Fellowship of Reconciliation

GAC General Advisory Committee

GAO General Accounting Office

ICBM intercontinental ballistic missile

INF intermediate nuclear forces

JAMA Journal of the American Medical Association

JCAE Joint Committee on Atomic Energy

JFKL John F. Kennedy Library

KGH Katherine Graham Howard Papers

MAD Mutually Assured Destruction

NAR Nelson A. Rockefeller Archive Center

NETC National Emergency Training Center

NORAD North American Aerospace Defense Command

NRDL Naval Radiological Defense Laboratory

NSC National Security Council

NSDD National Security Decision Directive

NUTS Nuclear Utilization Target Selection

NVAANW Non-Violent Action against Nuclear Weapons

NYT New York Times

OCD Office of Civilian Defense

OCDDOD Office of Civil Defense, Department of Defense

OCDM Office of Civilian and Defense Mobilization

PD Presidential Directive

PPGR Public Papers of Governor Rockefeller

PRM Presidential Review Memorandum

PSR Physicians for Social Responsibility

RSG regional seats of government

SANE National Committee for a Sane Nuclear Policy

SCPC Swarthmore College Peace Collection

SCWILPF Smith College, Women's International League for Peace and Freedom Papers

SDI Strategic Defense Initiative

SIOP single integrated operational plan

TIA Total Information Awareness

WILPF Women's International League for Peace and Freedom

WPA Works Progress Administration

WRL War Resisters League

WSP Women Strike for Peace

Interviews

Leo Bosner
Helen Caldicott
Alfonso Chardy
Kay Clarke
Madeline Duckels
Pam Ford
Jackie Goldberg
Chet Holifield
Anci Koppel
Mark Lane
Edith Laub
Libby Mines
Alexander Pond
Mary Sharmat
Janice Smith
Judy Turpin
Lawrence Vale

BRACING FOR ARMAGEDDON

Introduction

Civil Defense and the Nuclear Dilemma:

The Cold War Tragicomedy

The creation of hydrogen weapons has made a full-scale war of nuclear exchange impossible to win, because it would be catastrophic for all concerned. Yet, even after the advent of "weapons of mass destruction," policy makers in most nation-states have so far found it unthinkable to accept publicly the end of war as a human institution. This thought pattern is akin to that long applied to the institution of slavery, which was considered for centuries an acceptable and permanent feature of organized human society.

But suppose that one nuclear power, or a group of such powers, were to renounce war forever in the name of reason and sanity. How could a "first retreater" be sure that all nuclear powers would do so? How could a nuclear state that has abolished its nuclear weapons find protection from possible nuclear attack caused either by accident or through the act of an enemy madman? Can the good will of our "enemies" be relied upon for survival? And how can one continually create more technologically improved nuclear defenses and possess nuclear weapons by the thousands, while proclaiming that the only purpose of those defenses and weapons is to ensure that they are never used? Since modern political, economic, and military elites seem to have made so little progress in renouncing war as a means of settling conflict, what if one nation wins over another through the use of conventional weapons only? Is the defeated nation then expected calmly to surrender its goals, its sovereignty, its people without making use of its nuclear arsenal? How does one deal with the absurdity that to prosecute nuclear war is to practice suicide, but to renounce nuclear weapons and thus expose oneself to destruction from a nuclear or conventional attack seems equally lethal?

This is the core of the nuclear dilemma. From the mid-1950s to the twenty-first century, it has shaped the foreign policy of every powerful nation-state on earth. This book will focus on analyses of the American governmental and public effort to develop defenses against nuclear destruction and on the relation of changing nuclear strategies to civil defense policies. It will also expose the continuity between the long Cold War years and the development of civil defense ideology and action after the terrorist attacks of September 11, 2001.

●   ●   ●

Since the global controls needed to prevent use of nuclear weapons are not in place, only two prime "solutions" to the nuclear dilemma have been devised by American policy makers to date. One is the nuclear strategy called deterrence, a systematic plan to prevent nuclear war. Deterrence policy has functioned in one of two distinct and opposed forms, both given apt acronyms by strategists.[1] The first has been dubbed MAD, for "mutually assured destruction." The second, a competing form of deterrence often called "counterforce" by its proponents, has been dubbed NUTS, for "nuclear utilization target selection," by its critics. Along with the MAD and NUTS strategies of deterrence, policy makers devised a second possible solution to the nuclear dilemma: the creation of an elaborate federal system of government secrecy about matters nuclear. Each of these two presumed answers—deterrence and government secrecy—is dependent on the other to exist and to operate effectively.

Each of these supposed solutions is directly related to the subject of this book—the changing nature, purpose, and function of civil defense in the nuclear age. The history of civil defense becomes even more complicated given the contradictions between the private beliefs of the highest government officials about the value of civil defense and the rhetorical or declared positions revealed in their official statements during these years. Civil defense was one of the earliest, although almost wholly unsuccessful, government attempts to respond to the organized absurdities and horrors of the nuclear crisis.

This study of the relation of civil defense to both deterrence and government secrecy leads directly to full consideration of the great civil defense dilemma. How can a government accept the possibility of nuclear war without making some effort—real or pretended—to protect its citizens, or at least some of its citizens, from the destruction of blast and fallout? If it does not do so, how can it possibly convince a significant number of its citizens to risk nuclear war? And unless a significant portion of its public agrees to accept the risk of deterrence, then how can a proclaimed deterrence policy be made credible to the enemy? This is the point at which the second proposed solution to the nuclear dilemma—government secrecy—comes into play. How can a government admit the real impact of a full-scale exchange of hydrogen bombs without admitting that, short of permanently moving the society deeply underground into small and separate entities (a solution never seriously proposed by even the most fervent civil defense proponents), there is no known civil defense against thermonuclear war and little possibility that any long-term survivors could recreate, even in small measure, the society they once knew?

Until the mid-1960s, the top federal leaders of both parties could not openly admit that to fight a full-scale nuclear war would be self-annihilation, with no winners, and if fought on a large scale, might destroy most life on the planet. This book will show how they attempted to make deterrence acceptable by assuring the indefensible public that a proper civil defense system would allow a meaningful number of citizens and the basic social structure to survive a nuclear strike without intolerable damage. In the midst of this, another vital factor provided high motivation to top government officials to support the existence of a civil defense program. Government leaders through the Cold War years and beyond found it essential to convince the public to accept and validate—without rancor or militant protest—the existence of billion-dollar bomb shelters. Reserved and stocked for the elite few, these deep underground shelters were funded by ordinary taxpayers, who were forbidden to use them if bombs were to rain down.

Declassified records of Cabinet and National Security Council meetings reveal that, throughout this period, when both Democratic and Republican government leaders discussed civil defense issues, their most detailed analysis was of their own special shelters and escape procedures. Clearly, civil defense for the people was necessary in order to provide the federal government with sufficient justification for the existence of the elite shelters and their supposed provision of "continuity of government" during and after a nuclear exchange. How could the American public otherwise be expected to support a suicidal policy for themselves and at least temporary survival for the privileged few in the government's underground shelters?

It is the insatiable need for a "credible threat" that provides the key to the relationship between the American civil defense program and the nuclear dilemma. Civil defense was first devised by the federal government in the 1950s to persuade American citizens, as well as Soviet leaders, that Americans were ready both to wage nuclear war in retaliation against a first-strike attack and to kill hundreds of millions of innocent people, should deterrence fail. Naturally, few Americans would believe this mad threat. Fewer still would approve this policy of split-second assured mutual oblivion in the event of nuclear release. Therefore it was essential to attempt to enforce a large measure of government secrecy in order to make a civil defense program appear to be wise or useful to the American public. Government secrecy first sought to obscure the actual destructive impact of multimegaton hydrogen bombs. It was necessary to persuade American citizens that, if properly sheltered, a significant portion of the population could survive a nuclear exchange, although the exact details to ensure that supposed durability were left exceedingly vague.

Moreover, to further complicate the great civil defense dilemma, proponents of the two opposing forms of deterrence policy—MAD and NUTS—held very different attitudes toward a program of civil defense. A pure policy of mutually assured destruction promises mutual suicide, and thus concentrates on targeting large enemy cities. Holding populations hostage is the essence of MAD. Both sides are thus supposedly motivated to avoid a strike on the other. The first to attack realizes that it too could be eliminated as a functioning society by the ability of the enemy, in its dying moments, to let loose a strike which would assure the massive destruction of both contenders. The assurance of mutual destruction is designed to prevent a first strike by a nuclear power. Advocates of MAD never consider "winning" a nuclear war. Deterrence will prevent nuclear war only if it rests on the certainty of mutual suicide. It is recognition of this reality that MAD supporters believe will best deter the use of nuclear weapons.

Those who opposed the MAD policy moved to endorse a second, and very different, form of deterrence. The deterrence policy of nuclear utilization target selection first emerged in the late 1950s and again became dominant in the early 1980s. Some argue that it has returned under the George W. Bush administration. Those who promote NUTS realize that the MAD acceptance of mutual suicide when deterrence fails is simply not credible to most people, especially after the United States assured its European allies that if the Soviets attacked Western Europe, Americans would retaliate against the Russians. The notion that the United States would happily sacrifice New York to save Bonn was hardly believable to anyone. NUTS supporters argue that if deterrence is to work, more credible, flexible options must be devised. These include the tactic of "city avoidance," or targeting military targets first when war begins, in the hope that the war might end before the cities are bombed. NUTS seeks to control nuclear war through allowing the elites of both nuclear powers to talk with one another in order to limit targets, and thus end nuclear war before everyone on both sides is dead.

MAD supporters believe that NUTS talk of "controlling" or "limiting" nuclear warfare is mindless bunk. They present several reasons that nuclear war is not likely to end before both sides are destroyed. They argue that state leaders are not always rational and that neither power is likely to accept "defeat" without use of its full nuclear arsenal. Additionally, aiming hydrogen bombs only at military targets would not significantly limit the number of civilian deaths in the population centers, since fallout, the proximity of important military sites to many cities, and the effect of even the smallest H-bombs would inevitably kill millions of urban dwellers as well. Finally, the MAD supporters point out that the powerful electromagnetic pulses released by the explosion of hydrogen weapons would cut off electrical and computer operations over vast distances, leading to the loss of operational and communication controls by the supposed directors of each side's "limited" nuclear war.[2]

These shifting deterrence policies have largely determined the shape of the civil defense program. For example, as a MAD promoter, President Dwight D. Eisenhower gave only rhetorical and limited support to civil defense, while fighting off two major attempts to institute a large civil defense program. A genuine effort to provide civil defense breaks a key MAD rule: each nuclear power must accept mutual vulnerability if deterrence is to work. Any really serious attempt to defend one's population from certain destruction sends a dangerous message that the country with a massive civil defense program might even be planning a first strike.

However, civil defense is an important component of NUTS, an overall strategy based on the concept that nuclear war can be limited and that populations can be protected. Social science strategists, situated in think tanks such as the Rand Corporation or the Hudson Institute, produced dozens of government-financed studies in the 1960s and 1970s on how civil defense could supposedly save millions of lives. Strategists like the famed boy genius Herman Kahn, dubbed the "nuclear priests" by their critics, were NUTS aficionados.[3]

This book will also show how NUTS expanded the discussion of bomb shelters, fallout shelters, casualty estimates, and relocation of peoples from targeted cities to the safer countryside, thus reminding the public of the horror of nuclear war, whereas MAD's talk of mutual suicide made thermonuclear war seem less likely to the average citizen. Only when discussion of civil defense and of the number of people to live or die was left largely invisible could nuclear strategizing proceed relatively free of public attention.

Virtually all of those concerned with nuclear policy—whether official or sideline commentators—admit the terrifying degree of instability found in *both* MAD and NUTS strategies. Deterrence systems require for their successful functioning the existence of mutual distrust, fear, and hostility. Every confrontation carries the risk of a potentially deadly encounter. Every quarrel becomes a crisis, and every crisis a test of resolve. Each side must seek to remain less vulnerable than the other, thus justifying the arms race, as one side or the other reaches a temporary level of nuclear "superiority."

So many have attempted to express the horror of nuclear deterrence. The prominent writer and editor Jonathan Schell noted in 1998:

> Rudimentary moral principle taught us that we must never, even in "retaliation," threaten millions of innocent people, but nuclear strategy required us to do so. Common sense rebelled against offering every person in our country as a hostage to a hostile power and seizing every person on the territory of that power as a counterhostage, meanwhile placing the whole arrangement on a hair trigger; yet policy called this logically necessary. The experience of our century taught us that genocide was the worst of all crimes, but a nuclear "priesthood" taught us that to threaten it, and even to carry it out, not only was justifiable but was our inescapable duty. Every scruple in the human conscience declared that we must never risk extinguishing our species—the supreme crime against humanity, and the only crime greater than genocide—but solemn doctrine declared that it was essential to threaten this act.[4]

Deterrence is the ultimate paradox. It functions well only if each side can convince the other that it is willing to fight a nuclear war, which deterrence is designed to prevent, even though each side knows that to do so would be utterly self-destructive and would fail to reach any imaginable objectives that war is meant to achieve. The logic of deterrence requires that we convince our enemies that we stand ready to risk killing millions of innocent people in their country and to destroy all human civilization as we have known it, all in the name of mutual destruction. Thus, "reliance on deterrence leads to a preoccupation, almost an obsession, with credibility since the continuous task is to persuade the opponent that one's essentially incredible threats are credible," as scholar James Stegenga described the unconscionable illogic of the nuclear dilemma.[5]

In practice, deterrence also meant the accumulation of vast numbers of warheads. The destructive power—measured in millions of metric tons of TNT—reached an almost incomprehensible magnitude of overkill. In 1983, the superpowers possessed 50,000 nuclear bombs and warheads, equaling the lethal power of three tons of TNT for each of the approximately 4.5 billion people on the planet. The 4,800 warheads in the U.S. submarine force alone equaled the power of 18,000 Hiroshima bombings. If one adds the 2,788 warheads located on U.S. intercontinental ballistic missiles and strategic bombers, the United

States could release a destructive force equivalent to 33,400 Hiroshimas. Soviet nuclear forces in 1983 were even larger, their warheads the equivalent of 115,000 Hiroshimas.

And this was a reduction of force. By 1983, the number of American nuclear warheads had dropped considerably since 1967, when the total reached 32,500, the peak of nuclear buildup in the United States. Admiral Stansfield Turner, the former head of the CIA and an experienced military leader, recalled the intense fear he felt at an air force briefing in 1970. He then learned that the air force was lobbying for a return to the peak of 1967 because the number had by 1970 fallen to 27,000 warheads:

> Common sense tells us that 27,000 nuclear warheads, let alone the peak of 32,500, far exceeded any conceivable need the United States could possibly have had. How unrealistic were such numbers? It would take 55 billion aircraft bombs, each bomb containing 500 pounds of TNT, to unleash as much energy as 32,500 nuclear warheads. To put this in perspective, each state in the union could be carpeted with l billion bombs with 5 billion to spare—something quite beyond imagination.[6]

In 1998, the first careful study of the cost of nuclear weapons and weapons-related programs revealed that the United States spent almost $5.5 trillion, in constant 1996 dollars, between 1940 and 1996. If we include the estimated future costs of storing and disposing of toxic and radioactive wastes and of dismantling and disposing of nuclear weapon materials, the cost reaches $5.8 trillion.[7]

Along with deterrence strategy, the second fundamental feature of Cold War policy—a massive government secrecy program regarding nuclear weapons and nuclear strategy—is as unsatisfactory to most observers as is deterrence policy. Our reliance on deterrence and nuclear weapons has generated the ideology of "nuclearism" and eroded the exercise of popular sovereignty so vital to a system that prides itself on being democratic.

Nuclearism is the national security system that aligns nuclear supremacy with the sanctity of the American way of life. Since the mid-1940s, nuclearism has rested on public acceptance of the right of the executive branch and its security agencies to keep nuclear activity secret, on the grounds that if the truth about nuclear planning and operation were known, that knowledge would gravely endanger the very public the security system seeks to protect. Stewart Udall, former member of Congress and U.S. secretary of the interior in the Kennedy and Johnson cabinets, described how "a new, elite group of advisors—nuclear physicists, assorted technologists and 'security experts'—soon emerged as a clandestine government of policy makers who donned robes as unelected legislators with inordinate power to influence policy making."[8] The guardians of nuclear security became an inner circle of "cleared" policy makers shielded from public scrutiny.

Secrecy distorts American democracy. It restricts the participation of Congress and the American people in government decision making, while policy makers are left partially informed. It encourages mendacity among high-level government figures. Government is not held accountable for its actions, and the public cannot engage in informed debate. Nuclearism gravely weakens the base of democracy: the ability of an informed electorate to judge and to choose its leaders.[9] Thus, both "solutions" to the nuclear dilemma—deterrence policy and government secrecy—are recognized by both supporters and critics as highly unsatisfactory in many important ways. But we never really got beyond them. Not even today.

The factors discussed in this book—the nature of the nuclear dilemma, the solutions of deterrence and government secrecy, the attention given by the elite to their own shelters, the lies told to reassure the public that their lives could be protected—all establish the key place assigned to civil defense in the political formulas that have created and sustained Cold War ideology.

•   •   •

The second major finding of this book about the dominant influence of civil defense on American history is the centrality of the protest against civil defense in creating and sustaining the vast antinuclear movement, both here and abroad, during the Cold War period. The unveiling of the American civil defense program—originally created to sanction both deterrence and the elite shelters and with the futility of its existence obscured by government secrecy—sparked the first powerful antinuclear protest in the United States. This study will show how the anti–civil defense movement so expanded popular sovereignty that societal opposition to preparation for possible nuclear war began to threaten the basic doctrines of American nuclear strategy. In retrospect, it is not surprising that civil defense protest became the first mass action of the nuclear era to challenge the national security state. The civil defense program ignited protest because it is the one form of nuclear strategy that cannot be classified "top secret" and cloaked in government secrecy.

Uniquely dependent upon public understanding and cooperation, civil defense was the only Cold War program that had to make serious efforts to win public support. Disagreement over civil defense led to experts debating in public, which increased popular resistance and demystified the government's presentation of the "facts." Indeed, federal leaders had to twice rush to bury civil defense in order to lower growing popular protest. They had learned that public dissent over civil defense threatened not simply deterrence policy, but the very existence of nuclearism itself, and thus imperiled the entire Cold War system of nuclear crisis management.

Popular anxiety about the possibility of nuclear war peaked during the two great government-initiated civil defense hypes, first in the early 1960s and again in the early 1980s. This intense promotion of civil defense occurred during the periods when NUTS was especially prominent in governmental discussion of strategic plans. Just as NUTS advocates had always charged, the MAD threat of mutual suicide had never been credible. Thus the public rarely thought about the effects of a nuclear encounter, for MAD made nuclear war seem remote. But when NUTS supporters talked of fighting and "winning" a "limited" nuclear war, the public was reminded of the horror of nuclear weapons, and war seemed to be a more realistic threat. Moreover, by the 1970s, several accurate studies of the effect of hydrogen bombs, prepared by the U.S. government and by private groups, were made available to the public, greatly expanding popular knowledge and discussion of the effects of nuclear war.

Both John F. Kennedy in the early 1960s and Ronald Reagan in the early 1980s initially put civil defense at the center of their nuclear strategies. Their civil defense hypes strengthened a broad-based social movement that eventually became the largest domestic political effort that Americans had ever experienced. From the mid-1950s through the early 1960s, the movement concentrated on successful resistance to the annual federal civil defense drills and on rejection of the value of fallout shelters. The movement widened to oppose the nuclear bomb tests, which showered deadly fallout over the nation. In the 1980s, the movement centered on the defeat of civil defense plans for the relocation of the populace from target cities before a presumed nuclear attack. Public resistance then expanded into the huge nuclear freeze movement. In both periods, the U.S. anti–civil defense movement was inspired and strengthened by a large anti–civil defense and antinuclear movement in Great Britain and, in the 1980s, in Western Europe. By the summer of 1982, sparked and maintained by widespread public rejection of civil defense plans, the antinuclear peace movement produced the single largest political demonstration in U.S. history. On June 2, 1982, more than 750,000 marched in New York City, while hundreds of thousands more protested in cities large and small nationwide.

The decisive and relatively rapid defeat of the federal civil defense program during the Cold War decades provides a model for modern activists. They can learn from the movement's unique tactics about how to move dissident ideas from marginal groups into the political mainstream. Before the 1960s, state leadership had pursued its nuclear policy largely in secret. By the end of the 1980s, the increasingly informed general public had made clear its opposition to preparation for limited nuclear war, and public knowledge of the actual impact of hydrogen weapons was greatly increased. Public intervention during the nuclear age has resulted in less autonomy for the state in wartime, as was demonstrated during the Vietnam War era and after. The wisdom of even wider democratic control over nuclear weapons policy and the use of other types of weapons of mass destruction are today two of the most vital questions yet to be determined by modern Americans.

This dramatic tale of the powerful proponents of civil defense over the course of fifty years and of their much less powerful but eventually successful opponents is a telling and little-known feature of Cold War history. This project concerns much more than simply an analysis of one phase of the American peace movement. The national debate over civil defense is placed within the larger context of post-1945 American political and cultural history and the history of nuclear strategy. The story involves a number of figures central to the shaping of civil defense history, the best known including Edward Teller, Herman Kahn, Judith Malina, Barry Commoner, Randy Forsberg, Ron Dellums, Dorothy Day, and Oliver North. Also highlighted are those less recognized—the scientists, writers, intellectuals, federal and state officials, reporters, homemakers, and peace activists across the nation who led the anti–civil defense efforts over four decades of organized protest.

Women have been prominent participants in the anti–civil defense effort. They repeatedly emerge as activists and major organizers in the resistance to the annual air raid civil defense drills held from 1955 to 1961; in the crusade of angry mothers and teachers who closed down public school civil defense programs across the country; and in the fight against bomb testing and the crisis relocation program. Their tactics shocked and amused, as they ridiculed their opponents' ideas and denounced the obedient dummy-wives and moronic-mothers pictured in the government's civil defense propaganda materials. The anti–civil defense women deliberately flouted tradition and reversed traditional gender roles. Their successful protest tactics also influenced the earliest antiwar protests of the 1960s.

These women consciously used radical counterrituals to undermine the political rituals embodied in civil defense air raid drills or relocation plans. For example, in 1960 and 1961, more than 1,500 well-dressed women—deliberately costumed in heels, hose, hats, and earrings—brought hundreds of children and tens of thousands of toys to the mass civil disobedience protests in New York City. There they refused to take cover during the federally mandated air raid drills, confident that the police would not arrest the well-groomed mother protesters along with their children and all their trikes, playpens, toy trucks, and dolls. Similar guerrilla theater tactics were employed in the 1980s by those who refused to obey the Reagan administration's order to practice evacuation of their towns in preparation for possible nuclear war. Across the country, women organized scores of "die-ins," where stricken crowds of protesters lay flat on the ground and pretended to be dead, remaining prone as they pondered the loss of their lives and their loved ones after nuclear war.

*   *   *

The social and political history of civil defense is a most serious subject, yet many writers have emphasized the hilarious quality of the American civil defense program, especially in the 1950s and 1960s. Then, schoolchildren were ordered to duck under their school desks and to cover their heads with their loose clothing in order to survive nuclear carnage. Men were urged to tilt their hat brims in order to shield their faces from radiation. Federal propaganda portrayed fresh-faced and confident white, middle-class families waiting patiently in their home bomb shelters for the "all-clear" signal before emerging to wash up and then help with the community cleanup after nuclear apocalypse. Still, to present the history of civil defense as a prominent illustration of public gullibility when the fear of communism presumably ruled supreme is an inaccurate presentation both of the history of civil defense and of public reaction to the nuclear dilemma. The revisionist perspective presented in this book allows us to reconsider some old familiar ideas, such as McCarthyism and the feminine mystique, and see them not as triumphant features of presumed conservative retrenchment, but as final—and ultimately failed—attempts to stave off a massive revolt against the Cold War state and the older gender roles that supported traditional authority. It now seems evident that "the '60s" began in the middle of the 1950s, when the demand for significant social change was first voiced among civil rights activists and antinuclear protesters.

The history of American civil defense over time—from the protest against the Operation Alert air drills of the late 1950s and early 1960s to the fight over the relocation of target populations in the 1980s—is one of the most revealing of Cold War tales. Civil defense propaganda was a massive failed federal effort to control public perception. Presidents continually refused to give more than rhetorical support. Congress repeatedly refused to vote anything more than tiny portions of the requested funds. And from the Truman years to the Reagan era, the vast majority of the American public either ignored civil defense or treated it with derision. In addition, several studies by journalists have accurately pegged the government civil defense propaganda of the 1980s as the wholly unsuccessful attempt by a small rightist group to influence public thinking on the possibility of winning a limited nuclear war.

Civil defense propaganda in retrospect can indeed be seen as humorous, and this study will relate many new examples of its zany composition, from the 1950s through the 1980s. Equally entertaining is the process by which scores of cities reached the decision to refuse to cooperate with federal civil defense plans. Some communities withdrew quietly with little notice, but when whole states refused to prepare for nuclear extinction in the early 1980s, as did Washington and Oregon, they were pelted with government threats of the loss of millions of dollars of federal funds. In these pages are other little-known portions of civil defense history, for example, how during the late 1960s and early 1970s, tens of millions of "upper" and "downer" pills, stockpiled to be given to either pep up or calm down the survivors in the post-attack period, disappeared from the government-run basements where they were stored. But civil defense also excites deadly serious responses. The intense feelings still experienced by those who, as children, were subjected to those frightening school civil defense exercises, for example, is a phenomenon I frequently encountered in the course of writing this history.

The deep emotion aroused by civil defense is best explained as classic tragicomedy. That genre's comic irreverence for society's most sacred and serious subjects—most commonly the omnipotence of death—is the very essence of civil defense propaganda. Sigmund Freud, the great mind explorer and student of the irrational, loved tragic humor. He was especially fond of the tale of the fellow heading for the gallows who asked for a kerchief to cover his neck lest he become chilled. Like the kerchief, civil defense creates comedy to fend off the agonizing horror of avoidable death. Tragicomedy juxtaposes laughter with terrifying chaos, just as civil defense propaganda reflects the on-the-edge daftness of preparation for nuclear war.

Humans now have the power to generate their own earth-ending finale, as technology outpaces ethics, imagination, and intelligence. The relation of civil defense to the casually random extinction without purpose of nuclear war is resplendent tragicomedy. The very concept of civil defense contains within itself all of the dominant themes of dark comedy—the bestial components of humankind, the absurdity of the world, and the ubiquitous negation that is death.[10]

•   •   •

The prologue to this volume describes the actual effects of a one-megaton hydrogen weapon. All of the issues concerning civil defense cannot be understood or properly judged without this essential knowledge of the result of nuclear war.

Chapter 1 of this book discusses President Harry Truman's reluctant creation of the Federal Civil Defense Administration (FCDA) in 1950 and the predominant role it assigned to women; the importance of the Atomic Energy Commission (AEC) to civil defense history; and the content and purpose of early civil defense propaganda. This chapter also describes the reasons that

Congress regularly cut civil defense funds by 80–90 percent during the Truman and early Eisenhower period. The chapter ends with the United States' 1954 Pacific bomb test, called Bravo, which contaminated 7,000 square miles of the Pacific. After Bravo, the secret was out. The whole world was alerted to the effect of hydrogen warfare, despite government denial and downplaying of any danger to the populace from testing.

Chapters 2 and 3 explore the fierce fight to educate the public about the effect of nuclear war in the 1950s. Whistle-blowing government officials, top scientists (in the United States and abroad), academics, reporters, writers, and radical and liberal pacifist groups led this intense effort. One of the most important of these organizations was the Committee on Nuclear Information (CNI), organized by a group of St. Louis women in alliance with Washington University faculty, which proved that strontium-90 in children's bones was rapidly increasing due to fallout from nuclear testing, making an enormous contribution to the fight against nuclearism and to the later passage of the Test Ban Treaty of 1963. Only a few years after Bravo, the antinuclear movement greatly expanded with the formation of the National Committee for a Sane Nuclear Policy (SANE) and of the Committee for Nonviolent Action (CNVA). The remainder of these chapters discusses the 1954–1959 political rituals of Operation Alert—the annual national nuclear bomb drill held in most major cities in the United States—and the arrest of those who protested by refusing to take cover.

Chapter 4 describes John F. Kennedy's time as president, still remembered as the peak of government and media hyperbole in support of civil defense measures. Kennedy advised citizens to build and stock fallout shelters in their homes, creating his civil defense hype to counter the political appeal of his rival, New York governor Nelson Rockefeller, a devoted supporter of civil defense. Rockefeller failed in his effort to require fallout shelters for all citizens of New York, which was partially defeated by hundreds of marching female anti–civil defense protesters in Albany. Meanwhile, housewives, students, Catholic workers, and members of the War Resisters League turned the 1960 and 1961 New York City Operation Alert exercises into the largest mass peace actions since the 1930s. They revitalized the American peace movement, adopting the direct action style of American Gandhism and providing tactical inspiration for the larger revolts that shaped the 1960s. Operation Alert was permanently canceled in 1962, terminated by political elites who had discovered that growing public dissent over civil defense threatened both nuclearism and the strategy of deterrence.

The next chapter shows how, after Kennedy's death, the new and greatly underfunded civil defense agency was moved to the Department of Defense, and the government no longer talked of bomb shelters. During the Lyndon Johnson, Gerald Ford, and Richard Nixon terms, most states and cities, large and small, either drastically reduced or ended civil defense programs. Then, Jimmy Carter reactivated civil defense as a live issue in American politics. Carter set up a new program termed *crisis relocation planning* (CRP), which called for evacuating people from the cities to safer areas in the country during the presumed few days of advance notice the government would have before the Soviet missiles arrived. Carter created CRP partially to mollify the NUTS proponents, who touted a "civil defense gap" between the superpowers. The job of providing secret shelters for the select few was assigned to the new civil defense organization, the Federal Emergency Management Agency (FEMA), which Carter created in 1979.

Chapter 6 analyzes the second great civil defense hype, which peaked in President Reagan's first term, when he announced his seven-year, $4.2 billion plan for an expanded urban evacuation program. The crisis relocation plan was preposterous. Time and again, the press reported that the host rural areas not only knew nothing about the hundreds of thousands of city folk directed their way, but also had no shelter, water, or food supplies with which to assist the escaping urban masses. A huge grassroots movement against civil defense swept the nation. By 1985, twenty-four states and 120 major cities formally refused to participate in crisis relocation planning. As the peace movement rapidly expanded in the United States and Europe, Reagan announced the birth of Star Wars, the greatest civil defense fantasy of all. In 1987, FEMA's eerie contingency plan (operational from 1982 to 1984) was made public by several major journalists. Largely organized by the National Security Agency's representative to FEMA, Lieutenant Colonel Oliver North, this crisis management plan called for suspending the Constitution, turning control of the United States over to FEMA, and declaring martial law, whenever the president proclaimed a national crisis. From CRP for the masses, to the work of Oliver North with commanders, Reagan's bizarre civil defense program provides a fitting environment for the end of nuclear civil defense.

The epilogue discusses the death of civil defense proclaimed by President George H. W. Bush and then by President Bill Clinton, followed by its resurrection in 2001. Comparison of the current Homeland Security provisions to previous civil defense measures is remarkably telling. From duck and cover to duct tape, from deceitful denials to confused assurances, from justification of elite shelters to the closeting of current high officials in secret underground hideaways—once more, the public recoils and the grassroots peace movement builds.

Today, we still face dire nuclear threats, both from our own currently active or stored warheads and from the former Soviet Union's unprotected stockpiles of thousands of nuclear weapons, many of which have already been stolen or sold. Moreover, today there are at least eight nations with nuclear weapons, with other countries likely to follow the path to nuclear proliferation. Although we hear little discussion of nuclear war from American government figures, many of our leaders assure us that "mini-nukes" and small tactical nuclear weapons have uses on the battlefield. We are told that terrorists now threaten American society with suitcase bombs or exploding nuclear reactors or horrifying new types of biological and chemical warfare. How can we best survive the weapons of mass destruction? As we seek an answer to a question that is surely the most important of our time, this history of the rise and fall of American civil defense has much to teach us about the purpose and function of state propaganda and the value of citizens' organizations and demands for peace.

Prologue

The H-Bomb Changes Everything

The first American hydrogen bomb was named "Mike." Built on the Pacific island of Elugelab in the Eniwetok atoll, 3,000 miles west of Hawaii, Mike weighed sixty-five tons and resembled a small oil refinery. After expelling the native residents from their homes on Elugelab in the Marshall Islands, the U.S. government moved in more than 90,000 military personnel and 2,000 civilians. Living on ships or in temporary tent cities, these Americans prepared Mike for detonation. They were the first to observe an H-bomb explosion on the planet earth—the blast that would transform the course of human history.

Mike was detonated on Halloween 1952, two days before the election of Dwight Eisenhower as president. The nearest observers, on ships forty miles away, were shocked to see the size of the mushroom cloud. Within seconds, it swept three and a half miles across the horizon; it was more than twenty times the size of the Hiroshima fireball. No one had expected Mike to be so large—a massive 10.4 megatons, equivalent to 10.4 million tons of TNT, twice as much as all of the explosives used during the entire Second World War. At its farthest extent, the Mike cloud measured more than one hundred miles wide and

FIGURE P.1. H-bomb explosion. Operation Ivy, Mike, 10.4 megatons, 1952. First test of a hydrogen bomb by the United States, at Eniwetok atoll in the Pacific, October 31, 1952. *National Archives.*

twenty-seven miles high. Had it occurred in New York City, the blast would have easily obliterated all five boroughs.

The entire island of Elugelab vanished, completely vaporized by the heat. Mike also tore a hole in the Pacific atoll more than a mile wide, leaving a pit big enough to hold fourteen Pentagon-sized buildings and deep enough to hold the Empire State Building. Eighty million tons of radioactive earth blew into the air and then descended around the world. At Engei Island, three miles from ground zero, a research survey team later found no living animals and only the dry roots of vegetation. The team collected specimens of dead fish that had washed ashore with their skin burned off on just one side, as if the fish had been dropped into a red-hot frying pan just before they died.

The race for the superbomb had begun. After first evacuating tens of thousands of people from the explosion site in eastern Kazakhstan, the Soviets set off their first H-bomb ten months later, in August 1953.[1] The next spring, the United States exploded six improved variants of the new superbomb, including the fifteen-megaton Bravo set off on the Bikini atoll. After Bravo spread radioactivity over 7,000 square miles of the Pacific, the whole world knew about the colossal new weapon. Twenty months later, in November 1955, the Soviets exploded their own superbomb comparable to the U.S. Bravo version. Now both superpowers had H-bombs readily deliverable by airplane or missile. In his 1953 article in *Foreign Affairs*, Robert Oppenheimer, who directed the building of the first atomic bomb, predicted what was to come: "the two Great Powers will each be in a position to put an end to the civilization and life of the other. . . . We may be likened to two scorpions in a bottle, each capable of killing the other, but only at the risk of his own life."[2]

*   *   *

This prologue outlines how the advent of hydrogen weapons transformed the practice of war. The issues surrounding the history of American civil defense—its political purpose and social function, its changing propaganda, its relation to nuclear strategy, its wisdom or futility—cannot be understood or intelligently judged without this initial knowledge of the actual effects of thermonuclear war. Yet even today, few Americans fully realize the impact of hydrogen weapons. In the late 1970s and especially in the early 1980s, partly in reaction to President Reagan's talk of "limited" nuclear war, several widely read expert studies, including some thorough government-sponsored studies, carefully measured the effects of a simulated nuclear exchange. Since that time, however, with the decline of the powerful Western peace movements that had been created by the fear of impending conflict and, most important, with the collapse of the Soviet Union, the whole subject of the effect of nuclear war has largely disappeared from public view. Most Americans realize that a nuclear attack would be catastrophic; few understand the actual destructive power of even a one-megaton hydrogen bomb.

Basic to this understanding is the recognition that modern nuclear weapons cannot be compared with those dropped on Hiroshima and Nagasaki. Anyone who compares the two either understands nothing of nuclear effects or, much more commonly, is equating the atomic bombs dropped on Japan to modern hydrogen bombs in order to mislead others into believing that H-bombs are simply larger than atomic weapons, but otherwise not so very different. The two atomic bombs dropped on Japan in 1945 had explosive yields of about 12.5 kilotons and 22 kilotons, equivalent to 12,500 and 22,000 metric tons of TNT. Today, bombs as small as these are considered quite puny events compared to the megatons held in the arsenals of the nuclear powers. The nuclear materials of a mere one-megaton weapon, for example, equivalent to 1 million metric tons of TNT, is transformed within a fraction of a millionth of a second into a mass of energy five times hotter than the center of the sun. The hydrogen bomb is a vastly different kind of weapon.

The atomic bombs dropped on Japan in 1945 were fission weapons. In the A-bomb fission apparatus, the uranium atom is split, thus releasing neutrons, which split other atoms in a mass reaction, discharging enormous energy within a few seconds. However, the hydrogen bomb operates on the basis of a fission-fusion-fission process. The hydrogen weapon is set off first by an exploding atomic bomb within it, which acts as a trigger. Within millionths of a second, the energy of the atomic bomb explosion causes the deuterium and tritium nuclei within the core of the H-bomb to fuse. This process in turn releases powerful energy, which sets off another fission explosion within the H-bomb's mantle of uranium. The fission-fusion-fission process of the H-bomb produces intense thermal heat and a shock wave that vaporizes all matter within the miles- wide fireball. The H-bomb explosion releases winds moving at thousands of miles per hour and a radioactive death-dealing cloud that most often circles the earth before it falls to the ground. The maximum yield of an A-bomb is approximately 500 kilotons. There is no limit to the possible size of an H-bomb. The synergistic effect of an exchange of multimegaton hydrogen weapons is outside human experience and beyond human imagination.

The creation of the hydrogen bomb changed everything about the process of human violence called war. To understand the effect of a hydrogen bomb is to recognize that if the planet and life as we know it are to survive, a full-scale nuclear war cannot be waged. There is no victory possible in nuclear war, only mutual suicide or, at the least, mutual levels of intolerable destruction. The hydrogen bomb has permanently altered the relational structures of human societies.

Hundreds have attempted to put its horror and its power into words. Specialists in nuclear physics have often been quoted as credible authorities on the power of the hydrogen bomb. Prime among these oft-repeated comments are the words of the most renowned scientist of our time, Albert Einstein. He realized as early as 1946: "Our world faces a crisis as yet unperceived by those possessing the power to make great decisions for good or evil. The unleashed power of the atom has changed everything save our modes of thinking, and thus we drift toward unparalleled catastrophe."[3]

Another famed scientist, the primary designer of the first Soviet H-bomb, Andrei Sakharov, made a decision in 1968 to warn the world about "the real danger, and the utter insanity of nuclear war" by mailing his statement to the *New York Times*. When his views were made public, the Soviet leaders removed Sakharov from his job and exiled him to the closed city of Gorky, where he remained until Mikhail Gorbachev released him in 1986. Sakharov's 1968 manifesto created a sensation. In the face of the peril of thermonuclear war, he warned, any action that increased hostility among humans or any support of the "incompatibility of world ideologies and nations, is madness and crime." Within a few months, more than 18 million copies of his statement had been published in all parts of the world. As the father of the Soviet H-bomb, Sakharov's description of the effects of nuclear exchange was especially convincing:

A complete destruction of cities, industry, transport and systems of education, a poisoning of fields, water, and air by radioactivity, a physical destruction of the larger part of mankind, poverty, barbarism, a return to savagery, and a genetic degeneracy of the survivors under the impact of radiation, a destruction of the material and information basis of civilization—this is a measure of the peril that threatens the world as a result of the estrangement of the world's two superpowers.[4]

* * *

Many expert studies on the nature of nuclear war take for an illustration the effect of the explosion of a mere one-megaton bomb. However, the United States built thousands of bombs of much larger megatonage.[5] By the end of the 1990s, only one or two U.S. hydrogen bombs would be as devastating to world health as the 1986 Chernobyl nuclear plant accident in the Ukraine, and a single U.S. Trident submarine carries warheads equal to thirty times the explosion power of all of the bombs dropped in World War II. At the end of the Cold War, the most common expectation of the American military was that in a full-scale nuclear exchange with the Soviet Union, most bombs fired at the United States would be twenty megatons apiece, thus releasing about 50,000 megatons of explosive power on American soil. Yet for the purpose of example, the following discussion most often addresses the damage done by a single one-megaton explosion.

A mere one-megaton bomb equals the energy released by 1 million metric tons of TNT, the explosive power of seventy-seven Hiroshima-sized bombs. A train carrying the equivalent in TNT of a one-megaton bomb would be 300 miles long, requiring about six hours traveling at fifty miles per hour to pass by an observer. One-half megaton equals the destructive power of all of the bombs used by the Western Allies in Europe in World War II. By the 1980s, one American B-52 bomber could carry more explosive power than had been used in all of the wars in world history.

The first effect of a nuclear explosion is called the electromagnetic pulse (EMP). The EMP is a profoundly important consequence of nuclear radiation. Within fractions of a second after the explosion, an electric current is created that moves upward from the earth and then back to the ground. The EMP generated by one large explosion 200 miles above Nebraska would cause extensive physical damage to electrical and electronic equipment all across the United States. The EMP would produce a total blackout, shutting down every computer and disrupting the entire communicative network. Radios, televisions, telephones, and cars with electronic ignitions would stop functioning. Water stations would stop pumping. Medical help could not be called, even if any doctors or medicine could be found. Repair or replacement of electrical and electronic equipment would surely require many weeks, perhaps months or even years, depending upon the number and size of the nuclear bombs exploded at different heights and the consequent damage to national life. The EMP was at first not understood by American weapon makers because the first nuclear tests took place in the Pacific, where few electrical systems existed. In 1962, Americans noticed the presence of the EMP as a result of a test in the Pacific, because thirty strings of street lights failed on Oahu island, 800 miles from the blast. The next year, atmospheric tests were banned, so direct research on EMP could not continue. However, it seems certain that in the event of nuclear war, the attacker would carefully plan to impose as large and effective an EMP as possible upon the enemy, especially a high-tech one, given the probable damage to military communication systems and to missile systems.

But the first *visible* effect of a nuclear explosion is caused by thermal radiation. When a one-megaton bomb explodes at ground level, about 35 percent of the energy released is in the form of light and intense heat, which precedes the blast wave by a few seconds, like lightning preceding the sound of thunder. This fireball from the detonation of a one-megaton weapon will, within about nine-tenths of a second, radiate as much heat and light as a comparable area of the sun. Traveling at the speed of light, this thermal radiation, within a second of detonation, will instantly ignite materials such as newspapers and dry leaves within a seven-mile radius of the initial explosion. At a distance of six and a half miles from the explosion, anyone with exposed skin will suffer third-degree burns, leaving disfiguring scars. Within four and a half miles, bedding and curtains will burst into flames and anyone exposed will suffer second-degree burns. Within three miles of the explosion, even grains of sand will explode like pieces of popcorn from the heat of the fireball.

In a one-megaton air burst at 2,000 feet, within a five-mile radius, the ignition of clothing will cause even more severe burns. The fires caused by thermal heat will also ignite materials destroyed by the blast wave, such as broken gas pipes, gasoline tanks, and wooden houses. To these must be added the blast-induced fires, igniting seconds later, created by destroyed fuel storage depots and industrial and chemical stockpiles. These fires, in turn, could produce a massive firestorm resulting from rising hot gases, which cause winds of 100 miles per hour to be drawn into its center. Carbon dioxide from the firestorm would sink, settling into basements, subway tunnels, and underground shelters to asphyxiate most remaining survivors. The lethal area of the effects of the bomb blast alone is about 4.4 miles in radius for an air-burst one-megaton weapon.

Even without a firestorm, thermal radiation causes more damage at great distances from the explosion than any other immediate effect of a nuclear detonation. Many survivors with burns will die from lack of medical attention. In addition, flash blindness, the loss of sight for as long as twenty minutes, will affect people who were looking at the explosion. If the weather is clear, a one-megaton weapon exploded at an altitude of 3,000 meters will temporarily blind anyone who looks at the fireball with unprotected eyes from thirty-one miles away during the day and from sixty-two miles away at night. Although flash blindness is not permanent, it can be catastrophic for someone driving a car, for example. Equally ghastly is the damage that thermal radiation wreaks upon the layer of ozone surrounding the earth. A full nuclear exchange would seriously deplete the ozone level, thus allowing a large portion of the sun's ultraviolet light to reach the surface of the planet, causing extensive retinal burns and permanent blindness among diurnal animals of all kinds in both the Northern and Southern hemispheres. Bomb tests by the United States above Johnson island in the Pacific in the summer of 1958 demonstrated that the thermal radiation from a one-megaton explosion occurring at 100,000 feet caused small burn lesions in the eyes of rabbits 345 miles away.[6] Some weather conditions, such as snow on the ground or low white clouds over clean air, can significantly increase the range of dangerous thermal radiation.

An unforgettable description of the haunting effects of thermal radiation was given by a former CIA analyst in the early 1980s to journalist Robert Scheer. Thinking of his observation of a Pacific test of a mere ten-kiloton bomb—much smaller than either of the two bombs dropped on Japan in 1945—the analyst recalled:

> And suddenly I could see all these birds. I could see the birds I'd been watching for days before. They were now suddenly visible through the opaque visor of my helmet. And they were smoking. Their feathers were on fire. And they were doing cartwheels. And the light persisted for some time. . . . Several seconds, it seems like, long enough for me to see birds crash into the water. They were sizzling, smoking. They weren't vaporized, it's just that they were absorbing such intense radiation that they were being consumed by the heat. Their feathers were on fire. They were blinded. And so far there had been no shock, none of the blast damage. . . . Instead, there were just these smoking, twisting, hideously contorted birds crashing into things. And then I could see vapor rising from the inner lagoon as the surface of the water was heated by this intense flash. Now this isn't a primary effect of the weapon, it is an initial kind of effect that precedes other things. . . . you can see evidence of it in the Hiroshima blast and in Nagasaki—outlines of people on bridges where they stood when the bomb dropped. But that initial thermal radiation is a phenomenon that is unlike any other weapon I've seen. I've never seen anything like that.[7]

After the EMP and thermal radiation, the next and most immediate catastrophic effect of a nuclear bomb is the shock wave and blast itself. At the instant of detonation, a nuclear explosion reaches temperatures comparable to the center of a powerful star. Tens of millionths of a second after detonation, a shock wave is formed that moves at supersonic speed and is accompanied by winds reaching hundreds of miles in velocity. The gale-force winds four and a half miles from the explosion will hurl any human bodies still intact against objects with a speed several times the force of gravity. Broken glass, stones, metal, and other objects will fly through the air at speeds over one hundred miles an hour. Most trees will be uprooted and heavy vehicles overturned. Most people will be crushed or wounded by collapsed buildings and flying debris. A twenty-megaton explosion over New York City will destroy all buildings in Manhattan, the Bronx, Brooklyn, Staten Island, and Queens, as well as in nearby Hoboken and Jersey City. Twenty-five miles away, exposed people will receive second-degree burns. An estimated 5 to 10 million people will die in a relatively short time. A mere one-megaton ground burst will crush concrete structures within 6 miles, while a one-megaton air burst at 10,000 feet will reduce all structures to rubble within 4.4 miles of the detonation. Hundreds of mass fires will begin. If the bomb is exploded at ground level, it also will create earthquake-like tremors. If a twenty-megaton bomb is dropped on the ground, it will generate a ground tremor similar to the 1906 San Francisco earthquake.

Within a minute after detonation, then, the thermal pulse can kindle fires over a four-mile diameter and set paper alight as far as twelve miles from ground zero. The shock wave that follows will crush all structures within a four-mile radius and knock out windows and some doors as many as ten miles from ground zero. Buildings will be down, streets filled with debris, water pipes leaking. The air will be full of flying debris traveling at 150 or more miles per hour. Most people within five miles of the blast center will be dead. Twelve miles away, people will have dreadful injuries and burns, ruptured lungs, and ripped or crushed bodies. One minute after the explosion, everything is set for the final, and *most lethal*, stage of destruction to begin.

After the electromagnetic pulse, thermal heat, fireball and firestorms, shock, and blast comes the deadly radiation. The dispersion of radioactive nuclei depends on where the bomb is exploded. In an air burst, radioactive particles of dust and debris are carried to high altitudes of 60–80,000 feet by a one-megaton weapon. They then travel several times around the globe before returning to earth, thus spreading radioactivity over very large areas. The 1986 explosion of the Chernobyl nuclear reactor in the Ukraine created a radioactive cloud that spread over an area inhabited by about 100 million people in the Soviet Union, Eastern Europe, and Scandinavia. The 1,200 square miles next to the reactor are still so contaminated that humans are not allowed to enter the zone without taking protective measures.

If the bomb explodes near or on the ground, vast quantities of radioactive dirt and debris are returned to earth as fallout in the area downwind from the explosion. The lethal area for all life for a one-megaton ground burst is about 665 square miles. Beyond that, many others will die from radiation fall-out exposure up to 600 miles downwind, depending on weather conditions. A one-megaton ground burst in Detroit, for example, given a uniform northwest wind of fifteen miles per hour, would deposit lethal fallout on Cleveland and hazardous fallout as far away as Philadelphia. A one-megaton ground burst will require evacuation of 4,900 square miles for at least a week. The 1,400 square miles near the detonation will not be able to be entered for a month. Where fallout is heavy, people will have to remain indoors for weeks. Many will die from wounds, disease, radiation, or thirst and starvation, since contaminated food cannot be eaten, nor new food produced. Food cannot be harvested from pastures and fields downwind for many months or, if the fallout is heavy, for hundreds of years.

Since radiation cannot be tasted, smelled, or seen without detection equipment, people cannot know when they are entering areas with threatening radiation levels. Nausea, vomiting, diarrhea, lowered resistance to infection, and bleeding disorders result from dangerous radiation. Radiation exposure causes destruction of the mucosa of the intestinal tract, which means those affected literally pass their own intestinal lining. The long-term effects of cancer and genetic defects resulting from the radiation of any survivors are difficult to estimate, although obviously significant. A 1976 government study, prepared by civil defense planners, offered wildly optimistic predictions of the post-attack environment. But even this group envisioned an attack totaling 6,559 megatons aimed at military targets, military support facilities, basic industries, and cities of 50,000 persons or more. They estimated a total of 133 million deaths in the United States within the first few months.[8]

One can hardly imagine life after nuclear war. Estimates from mainstream sources, such as government reports and studies by highly qualified scientists, most written in the 1970s and later, estimate that a nuclear exchange would kill, instantly or shortly after explosion, approximately 65 percent of the urban U.S. population. Counterforce attacks, directed at U.S. military installations, missile sites, or nuclear reactors, would probably kill in the immediate aftermath 5–20 million more. The long-term radiation effects of numerous cancers, birth defects, and genetic damage would haunt the population for generations. There would be virtually no medical assistance or medicine available to most survivors, no clean water, and very little food safe to eat. Additional millions of survivors would soon die of dehydration, infection, communicable disease epidemics, intense emotional stress, and starvation.[9] Radiation weakens the immune system, as do burns, stress, malnutrition, and mental depression. Millions of corpses would rot and spread massive waves of infection. With millions dead and injured, the few if any doctors and hospitals still functioning would surely have to focus on the moderately wounded, leaving the badly injured and those who might be able to recover unaided to fend for themselves.

One might expect the permanent abandonment of the ravaged urban-industrial areas in the North and Northeast. It seems unlikely, however, that the hundreds or thousands of urban refugees would be welcomed into the rural areas of the country, where more residents might survive the initial devastation. The temporarily more fortunate rural dwellers would likely fight off any attempt to deplete their severely limited food resources. It also seems questionable that countries that did not participate in the nuclear war would rush the massive aid needed to help the citizens of the now demolished, radiated, and unproductive United States.

Other nations would have enough worries of their own, aside from the radioactive fallout they may have absorbed on their land, chief among them ozone depletion. This effect of nuclear war would be the creation of oxides that would reduce the ozone layer surrounding the earth and greatly increase the ultraviolet light reaching the earth's surface. Ozone depletion destroys or damages many types of plants, kills many animals, and causes severe sunburn to exposed humans. Perhaps the most severe threat is the damage that ultraviolet light does to the eyes of many living creatures. While insects, nocturnal animals, and aquatic creatures might be unaffected, the massive blinding and death of thousands of species of mammals and birds, together with the death of many plant species, could demolish the ecosystem in the Northern Hemisphere, where most bombs would likely be dropped, and have drastic effects on the Southern Hemisphere as well.

To grasp the effect of a mere one-megaton hydrogen bomb, much less a full-scale nuclear exchange, is beyond full comprehension. In 1983, nuclear physicist Kosta Tsipis, the author of several studies of the effect of nuclear war, may have come as close as any to expressing the unknown:

> [O]ne cannot escape a feeling of apprehension that the synergy of all these effects—the lowering of the earth's temperature, persistent radioactivity, the blinding and death of numerous species of animals, the destruction or shunting of many plant species, and the myriads of ways in which these mutually reinforce each other—will cause some unprecedented catastrophe that is beyond calculation or prediction. There is just no way of accurately estimating these effects. . . . We are simply ig-

norant of the full gamut of the effects of a large-scale nuclear war, and to conceal our ignorance would be not only unscientific but irresponsible. Yet not to admit that we have the power to inaugurate events totally beyond our control represents an equally egregious and ultimately more terrifying error.[10]

Albert Einstein may have said it best. Someone once asked him what kind of weapons he thought would be used in a third world war. Thinking of the new hydrogen bombs, he said he did not know, but he was sure that any wars after that would be fought with stones.

ONE

"Alert, Not Alarm"

The First Ten Years, 1945–1955

In 1950, James J. Wadsworth helped to write the bill that created the Federal Civil Defense Administration (FCDA), the first American civil defense unit in the nuclear age. Blessed with frugal, hard-working ancestors who arrived in the New World in the mid-1600s, Wadsworth was a very rich person descended from very rich people. He was a Yale sports star, as well as a top scholar, graduating in 1926. The party chiefs chose him to run for the Senate in New York, where he served from 1930 to 1941 as a staunch conservative. Next came his wartime job as a top executive in Curtis Wright's Airplane Division. He also had an important brother-in-law, Stuart Symington, then secretary of the air force, who in 1950 steered Wadsworth into the position of deputy administrator of civil defense in the new agency, even though Wadsworth was a Republican. As second in command at FCDA, Wadsworth actually made all of the top decisions, while the political appointee who headed the agency traveled about to make frequent speeches.

In 1950, seated in a camp chair five miles from ground zero, Wadsworth became part of a small, select group who experienced one of the first atomic bomb tests. This moment forever shaped his view of public security. Decades later, he still remembered the "shudder of ultimate fear" at the sight of the "heavenly-horrible colors" that marked the desert air and the shock wave that slammed his chest, as though a football player "had hit me head on with a flying block." Some of his companions were knocked to the ground from their chairs. One of the men near him "could not stop his teeth chattering for nearly half-an-hour." It was here, in the Nevada desert near Las Vegas, that Wadsworth, the high-placed civil defense executive, then adopted a lifetime cause to warn the people of the world that no defense was possible against nuclear attack.

Wadsworth went on to become a deputy representative and later delegate to the United Nations, serving until 1960. He then headed the Peace Research Institute before his retirement in 1962. Until his death in 1984, Wadsworth, like so many other thinking members of his generation and later, longed to believe that "there will survive within the human race an ultimate vestige of understanding that total nuclear war means the end of the human race, and *must* be avoided regardless of apparent creation or acceptance of dishonor." Wadsworth and thousands of Americans made this shift during the first ten years of the nuclear age, recognizing that human history had changed forever and that there was not that much time to grasp the truth.

•   •   •

The development of air war erased whatever remained of the traditional wartime distinction between soldiers and civilians, bringing the fighting to populations distant from the sites where armies fought. Recognition of the consequences of this technical advance brought about a permanent shift in thinking about war. Out of this change came the concept of "civil defense."

American attention to civil defense began during World War I, when German zeppelins bombed England. Even though air attacks were no threat to the United States, the Council of National Defense was created in 1916 to mobilize popular support for the war. World War I civil defense planners immediately recognized the value of women as the symbol for civilian survival in the strange new world of air warfare. The council established the Women's Committee "to obtain greater efficiency in women's defense work and to impress upon women the importance of all methods of economic warfare." Females were needed to ration food, establish home gardens, and encourage loyalty to the war government.[1]

In preparation for the next war, President Franklin Roosevelt created the Office of Civilian Defense (OCD) seven months before bombs dropped on Pearl Harbor. Led by Mayor Fiorello LaGuardia of New York City, the OCD depended on the work of local councils to sustain national morale and to train air-raid wardens and first-aid workers. Probably thinking of a future run for president,

LaGuardia envisioned himself as the head of a civil defense bureaucracy the size of one of the branches of the armed forces. Countering the image that the OCD is "not just community singing, sweater knitting and basket weaving,"[2] LaGuardia insisted that his masculine version of civil defense include panic control, full dress uniforms for volunteers, national air raid drills, sabotage deterrence, home front propaganda, and domestic intelligence gathering. Criticism of LaGuardia's attempts to increase the OCD's power peaked when he directed national religious leaders to preach defense on a scheduled "Freedom Sunday" and when the air raid sirens accidentally went off three times in two days in New York City.

In retreat, LaGuardia turned over the propaganda function of the OCD to Eleanor Roosevelt, appointing the First Lady as assistant director in the fall of 1941. She hired the pro–New Deal actor Melvyn Douglas—husband of the liberal congresswoman Helen Gahagan Douglas—to mobilize writers, artists, and musicians in civil defense work. Roosevelt also employed her friend Mayris Chaney to teach physical fitness. Chaney created a dance called the "Eleanor Glide" and designed "recreative exercises" for those who might be required to remain long periods in air raid shelters.

Congressional and press criticism of the OCD accelerated as anti–New Deal conservatives shifted their attack to focus on the First Lady rather than the president. One critic complained that "under the direction of Mrs. Roosevelt, and certainly with the approval of the President himself, they have taken the old WPA crowd, plus some 'red' recruits and promoted them into the OCD office." Congressmen claimed that Melvyn Douglas made as much money as General Douglas MacArthur and called the organization a massive boondoggle and a "pink tea party."[3] The Bureau of the Budget threatened to withhold funding. When in 1942 LaGuardia and the First Lady resigned, the new director recommended that the OCD be abolished. Ironically, President Harry Truman shut down the agency in June 1945—only six weeks before the beginning of the nuclear age.

But even before the first atomic bombs were dropped on Japan, targeting civilians had become a standard feature of total war. During World War II, Allied commanders, like their German counterparts, directed air attacks against residents of enemy cities. The bombing of Dresden, Hamburg, and Berlin, for example, killed tens of thousands of civilians. A single American incendiary bombing raid on Tokyo leveled one-quarter of the city, created a firestorm, and killed perhaps 100,000 persons. During the spring of 1945, similar obliteration air raids on Japanese cities killed many more people than either of the atomic bombs at Hiroshima or Nagasaki.[4] Civilian massacres on this level became an acceptable hallmark of modern war even before the development of the hydrogen bomb.

In the late 1940s, however, only a few Americans understood that there was no feasible defense against nuclear bombs. Thus a series of government-sponsored reports and a Social Science Research Council study considered the appropriate structure of a new civil defense program. The most ambitious efforts came from the newly created Office of Civil Defense Planning within the newly renamed Defense Department; long called the War Department, the renaming is one of the earliest examples of Cold War doublespeak. Civil defense planners called for a new federal agency to guide the work of a prospective 15 million volunteers and employees. Primary operating responsibility was to be left to state and local governments.[5]

Appalled by the huge expense of such a program, President Truman buried civil defense planning in a small office within the National Security Resources Board. Only six months later, civil defense rose from the grave when the Soviets tested their own atomic bomb in late 1949. Sensing the publicity value of civil defense, the young Congressman John F. Kennedy pressed Truman for a large CD program to avoid an "atomic Pearl Harbor."[6]

Demands for a better civil defense effort against atomic attack were also trumpeted by the congressional Joint Committee on Atomic Energy (JCAE), established as part of the Atomic Energy Act of 1946. Initially led by cold warrior Brien McMahon, the ambitious Democratic senator from Connecticut, the influential JCAE consisted of nine senators and nine representatives with the responsibility to maintain congressional control over the work of the newly formed Atomic Energy Commission (AEC). The JCAE functioned not as a serious oversight committee, but as the major support and shield for AEC activities.

Headed by five civilian commissioners appointed by the president, the AEC was charged with awesome responsibilities—the development and control of nuclear power, the production of nuclear weapons, and all military research and development. Unfortunately, the AEC operated under the most stringent secrecy restrictions, a development that later led to accusations that agency leaders had deliberately misled the public about the dangers of radiation and bomb testing. These suspicions, eventually confirmed, led to the final demise of the AEC in 1975 (to be replaced by the Nuclear Regulatory Commission) and to the abolition of the JCAE in 1976. But during the twenty-nine years of its existence, and especially after the creation of the hydrogen bomb in 1954, the AEC's top managers frequently took the lead in hiding the truth from the American public, not only about the danger of radioactive fallout from bomb testing, but also about the known effects of thermonuclear war.

The then-powerful JCAE held hearings in 1950 on the state of civil defense.[7] Committee witnesses accused the federal government of "buck passing" and of reckless disregard for civilian safety. American Legion spokesmen attacked the inferior leadership of the civil defense program. Seeking "added zeal . . . to make an all-out war effort," Senator McMahon fought for a serious CD program in the summer of 1950.[8] Unlike most intellectuals and scientists, he had few qualms about using atomic weapons. When New Deal liberal David Lilienthal, chair of the AEC from 1947 to 1953, met McMahon, he was shocked to discover that "what he [McMahon] says adds up to one thing: blow them [the Russians] off the face of the earth, quick, before they do the same to us—and we haven't much time."[9]

The outbreak of the Korean War decided the matter. Reluctantly, the Truman administration established a permanent CD organization. The Civil Defense Act of 1950 created the Federal Civil Defense Administration (FCDA) as the umbrella agency designed to guide each state in planning, organizing, and operating its own program for civil defense and to provide each state with matching funds for procuring supplies and equipment. Eventually, civil defense would become one of the most reorganized elements in the history of national government, with five major shifts producing a series of thirteen successive federal civil defense agencies over a period of fifty years—from FCDA, which survived until 1958, to the Federal Emergency Management Agency (FEMA), to the current Department of Homeland Security, which combines FEMA with twenty-one other agencies.

The creation of the FCDA set four important precedents that determined the propaganda and purpose of American-style civil defense. First, the call for military control of civilian defense was defeated, partly by military leaders who had no desire to monitor such an unfocused and ill-funded project. Control of atomic weapons was given to the civilian-dominated AEC, which had begun operation in early 1947, although military influence was still significant, as required under commission rules.

Second, it was agreed that the federal government would assign the major cost of civil defense to state and local organizations, thus virtually ensuring that little would be done despite the verbal support given by some politicians to the importance of civil defense for national security. Federal funds would be saved for weapons production, or "active" defense, rather than for protection against civilian loss, or "passive" defense. Moreover, the generally poor quality of civil defense planning, most often based on data that ignored the real effects of nuclear blast and fallout, further underlined the peripheral importance of civil defense to most political leaders. Most important, the central role assigned to women in civil defense propaganda ensured the low status of the effort, thus increasing public skepticism and derision of the program. High-level federal support for civil defense would remain chiefly rhetorical, with the exception of two short-lived efforts during the Kennedy and Reagan administrations.

A third aspect of U.S. civil defense development was the role of the federal civil defense agency as propagandist. State and federal civil defense archives demonstrate how civil defense planners have continually bemoaned—with great intensity and at much length—the supposed general "apathy" of the citizenry regarding survival in nuclear war. Despite all of the media hype encouraged by the FCDA, the public simply would not take civil defense seriously. Some citizens chose to believe that nuclear war would not occur. Most quite rightly realized that civil defense measures would not provide adequate protection from nuclear carnage.

The public disregard and frequent ridicule of civil defense programs led to the planners' focus on "education"—the production of propaganda to convince the public that civil defense was not just necessary, but actually *possible*. In the Truman years, proponents often spoke of civil defense as a primary means of building the public will to fight a nuclear war if it became necessary to do so. In 1956, Val Peterson, head of the FCDA, described this propaganda production as "the greatest mass educational effort ever undertaken in this nation."[10] The dominant function of the CD bureaucracy was to ease widespread public anxiety about the destructive nature of nuclear weapons. How could the majority of the public be expected to risk probable death and certain destruction of society as they knew it, much less support an ineffective civil defense program, if they fully understood the impact of nuclear war? Could the public be trusted to uphold the often-heard 1950s slogan "I'd rather be dead than red"? Might not the public settle for temporarily red rather than permanently dead?

In the 1950s, civil defense propaganda thus emerged as a focused attempt to legitimize the policy of deterrence. Deterrence strategy rested on public willingness to risk nuclear war, in the mythical belief that the national population could absorb and survive a first strike, in order to eliminate the enemy in a second strike. By the 1980s, civil defense would also be used to justify the concept of "limited war." In the beginning, however, the Truman administration most often defended, albeit in somewhat hazy terms, the use of civil defense as humanitarian insurance to save lives—the message least likely to elicit instant public dissent.

The fourth and final precedent established by the FCDA civil defense program is the centrality of women's contribution to civil defense. Truman's first civil defense agency, the National Security Resources Board, had depicted civil defense as a series of circles centered on the family as the basis for protection.[11] In 1951, President Truman, in an introduction to an FCDA training film, likened civil defense to American frontier settlements attacked by Indians. Just as on the frontier, mothers and children needed to cooperate in defense of American homes. By 1955, the FCDA boasted that females headed its program of women's activities in forty-two states. The decisive role of the family in civil defense planning was partly a reflection of the national decision to save money for making weapons, rather than to assume expensive provisions for civilian protection. It was much cheaper for American families to take care of themselves in their shelters at home. But something more was at stake in the stress placed by civil defense planners on the importance of housewives and mothers to the survival of the populace during and after nuclear attack.

The role of women, especially mothers, is such an obvious feature of civil defense propaganda that many scholars, as well as peace activists, have puzzled over the deep meanings signified by this popular connection of femininity to nuclear survival. Historian Elaine May emphasizes the symbolic value of civil defense measures as assurance that not only nuclear holocaust, but the changing nature of women's role itself, could be controlled and contained within time-honored traditional values. Other commentators have noted the age-old association of women and domesticity to reproduction and the continuity of culture. The traditional position of the mother is as a self-denying and preserving protector. As scholar Gillian Brown notes, "domesticity is repeatedly invoked as the stay against extinction" in civil defense propaganda and even in antinuclear literature. In this framework, the domestic conservative project and the mother's devoted protection of life blended to comfort those in the underground shelters that life, culture, and even the species would go on after a nuclear exchange. Historian Laura McEnaney focuses on the use of gender and family by civil defense strategists as a legitimating premise for privatizing civil defense. Home shelters and self-help are designed to make the illusion of surviving a hydrogen bomb attack seem possible and hence to make government policy seem realistic and reasonable.[12]

It is perfectly logical, then, that in 1956, for the first time, a knowledge of CD became one of the official requisites in the judging for the Mrs. America contest. But the ultimate symbol of motherhood is that of grandmother. Thus, one of the most publicized civil defense propaganda coups was the FCDA advertisement highlighting "Grandma's pantry," a fully equipped collection of emergency foods, medicines, pet food, and other supplies made ready for postwar endurance. Like Grandma, American women could provision their home bomb shelters in order to solve unexpected problems, even nuclear attack.[13]

In civil defense movies and pamphlet illustrations, women appear as calm mothers, often wearing high-heeled shoes, quieting their happy children in home bomb shelters, secure in their knowledge that they have earlier provided their families with the food, water, and children's games that will make the wait underground enjoyable and safe. As one FCDA pamphlet advised, "Make a game out of it: Playing Civil Defense." Equally calm fathers, often holding shovels, are shown seated beside their wives as they await the all-clear signal. The families pictured are invariably white and middle class; no poor, working-class, or minority Americans are depicted. By the mid-1950s, more flexible gender

GRANDMA'S PANTRY WAS READY

FIGURE 1.1. Grandma's pantry. The Federal Civil Defense Administration emphasized the role of women in preparation for nuclear war, as in the 1950 booklet *Grandma's Pantry Was Ready: Is Your Pantry Ready in the Event of Emergency?*
National Archives.

roles appear in civil defense propaganda booklets. Apparently because after the hydrogen bombs have fallen, men are presumably off somewhere else, women are shown in films and pamphlets serving in traditionally male jobs, working as emergency ambulance drivers, police officers, firefighters, and medical doctors.

Katherine Graham Howard, a tireless proponent of the crucial role of women in civil defense, became deputy administrator of the FCDA in 1953, the first woman in any federal department or agency to become second in command. A southerner, heiress to the R. J. Reynolds tobacco fortune, and wife of a proper Boston lawyer, Howard concentrated on speeches to women's gatherings, on radio and television talks, and on cultivation of the women's press corps.[14] Howard gave upbeat talks, outlining in cheery terms the commonsense activities that the women of the family must perform in order to survive nuclear attack. She assured American women that the "hydrogen bomb was neither particularly new nor particularly astonishing." She urged them to monitor both their families and their neighbors' families after a nuclear attack, to ensure that no one spread demoralizing rumors that might induce panic or terror in the local community.[15]

In early 1953, Howard observed at first hand a Nevada bomb test, another first for a woman. Along with fifteen congressional representatives, she awaited the blast just a few miles from ground zero and, as always, hoped that her dress was appropriate for the occasion: "I was comfortably clothed in a tweed sport coat, scarf, Davidow wool suit, yellow slip-on sweater, wide red belt, and under all this a dark green cotton dress. I was wearing a small red hat. On my feet were my trusty red loafers as protection against sand and cactus." The next day—clad in a special white duck uniform of overalls, hat, and gloves, with high rubber boots—she toured the mangled and radiated interior of a demonstration house destroyed by the blast. To her astonishment, she then was measured for radiation exposure and "saw the indicator move like the speedometer on a car, going up and up." Always the naive and cheerful optimist, Howard probably really did believe AEC officials who assured her that she had nothing to fear.[16]

Howard resigned from the FCDA in 1954 to return to her more important duties as "housewife." At her farewell party, she explained, "Husbands won't wait, while wives administrate!" It is not known how she felt about the farewell gift she received from the agency in honor of her service there. She was awarded a radioactive hubcap from one of the automobiles exposed to atomic blast in a recent Nevada bomb test.[17]

•   •   •

With these four precedents established—civilian management, state and local control, propaganda production, and the central role of women—the 1950 creation of the FCDA also began the battle that would dominate all future civil defense planning. What was the best method to protect the populace—disperse, evacuate, or shelter? Although dispersion of people and industries over a wide area was presented as a logical solution in the late 1940s, such a displacement would cost billions and require legal force to move people and businesses into designated areas, vastly disrupting family life as well. Dispersion was soon discarded as a possible option for civil defense planners. In the early 1950s, most citizens knew that, in addition to the enormous cost and urban disruption required to institute dispersal, widely spaced targets would be vulnerable anyway, due to the rapid increase in the number, speedy delivery, and accuracy of nuclear bombs. In addition, dispersion would counteract the most fundamental government goal: to offer civil defense as a means of survival to the white middle class in their suburban homes. This group was perceived to be the constituency most vital to the survival of the Cold War political consensus.

The second civil defense method, evacuation, is equally problematic. Evacuation, or "relocation," as it was sometimes called, requires advance warning time, immense expenditures, careful transportation planning, and preparation of a receiving site. But this location, especially after the development of the ability to quickly retarget missiles, could easily become the new target of the attacker. Later, as the dangers of radioactive fallout became more apparent to the public, the question of how to protect and treat evacuees complicated the issue, as did concerns of class and race. How could white suburbanites or rural white families deal with the hordes of hungry, thirsty, and frightened urban poor streaming into their communities from the target cities?

Evacuation supposedly required at least four to six hours of warning time in order to empty the cities of people. As weaponry improved, the actual warning time shrank to a few minutes. Moreover, evacuation was centered upon the possibility of each family escaping in the family car, an impractical plan from any number of perspectives. Another major problem with evacuation is that the enemy can fake an impending attack and then actually attack the urban population after they have returned to the cities, when few citizens would be willing to accept government directives to evacuate a second time. It also seems possible that once the urban population has been evacuated, the government might feel political pressure to begin a nuclear war, rather than lose credibility with its citizens. Further, evacuation had one overwhelming defect. It made even more obvious to the average citizen that Americans in the city had little chance of survival. If nuclear war broke out, large cities and industrial areas were the prime targets. Protection for the soon-to-be-vaporized urban core was too expensive or logistically futile to provide. Hence, evacuation was quickly judged impossible by most, especially after the effects of hydrogen bomb warfare became better understood.

The third alternative, bomb shelters, frequently emerged among civil defense leaders as the most popular option. This policy elicited less ridicule than the dispersal and evacuation/relocation options. Yet a shelter system was also unreliable—even if it were radiation-proof and the occupants did not die from suffocation or burns within the structure. The last outcome seemed more and more certain for those persons within fifty miles of the explosion, as CD planners confronted the true nature of hydrogen bomb warfare. On the other hand, if the enemy exploded an H-bomb in the air rather than on the surface, people in shelters for many miles surrounding the blast might be incinerated or suffocated. Moreover, if chemical or biological weapons were dropped in the wake of the nuclear bombs, pumps drawing in air for the shelters would simultaneously draw in poison.

But most important, even a relatively adequate shelter system—one well stocked and buried far underground—was incredibly expensive. What other projects would need to be cut in order to finance a somewhat effective shelter system? How could the government convince residents of major cities to calmly and reasonably accept that they would have no need for shelters because the area of the city for several miles around the impact area would simply become a very deep pit when the H-bomb hit? Where and what kind of shelters should be built? What conflicts might arise among the sheltered, given the country's current race and class issues? How should community shelters be devised within the Jim Crow reality of the South? Since shelter for all seemed impossible to finance, who would be left unprotected and who would make that selection? Who would pay for the storage of provisions and medical supplies? And how could one survive after emergence into a charred and radiated world?

Besides, as Senator McMahon noted in 1950, there was something un-American, and certainly unmanly, about hiding in holes: "[W]e are not going underground for anybody . . . [to] make moles of ourselves." Twelve years later, even the man who seemed most obsessed about the need for financing a large civil defense program, the renowned nuclear physicist Edward Teller, could not overcome his suspicion that fear of nuclear war threatened the very existence of virile American males: "If we listen to those who wrongly state that a next war will necessarily be lost, we might easily end up living on our knees and perhaps later dying in a war that others fight over our impotent bodies."[18]

Given the overwhelming problems of adopting either dispersal, evacuation, or shelters, the unfortunate bureaucrats at the FCDA during the last years of the Truman era became the first of many to struggle to solve the unsolvable. The newly established FCDA first adopted a shelter policy. And then not one penny was voted to finance this program for the next three years.

Why this congressional disdain? First, the immediate Korean crisis seemed to be over, and President Truman did little to push shelter defense, preferring instead to save money for weapons production. Second, the first FCDA director, Millard Caldwell, a former congressman and former governor of Florida, was uninformed and arrogant. He first told Congress that $300 billion was needed for minimally adequate shelter protection, and then openly admitted that he did not know how the FCDA might spend the $250 million start-up fund it requested. African Americans took the lead in fighting Caldwell. As governor of Florida, Caldwell had refused to address members of the National Association for the Advancement of Colored People (NAACP) as "Mr." in his correspondence with them. In 1950, Harry Moore, head of Florida's NAACP, publicized Caldwell's tacit approval of vigilante violence. The next year, Moore was murdered by a band of racists. The NAACP's strong but unsuccessful protest against congressional approval of Caldwell's appointment to head the civil defense agency, followed by a call for his impeachment, embarrassed Truman and many in the Democratic party.[19]

Finally, two powerful congressmen opposed the FCDA budget. Clarence Andrew Cannon of Minnesota, chair of the House Appropriations Committee, was one of the first to understand that short of permanently moving the entire society thousands of feet underground, no feasible civil defense program could provide significant protection against a full-scale H-bomb attack. He believed the money was best spent on arms. Texan Albert Thomas, chair of the Independent Offices Subcommittee, the House committee reviewing the FCDA budget, also recognized that for most urban areas civil defense was nothing more than a useless boondoggle. Congressmen Cannon and Thomas became the two men on whom presidents could rely to block federal monies for civil defense.[20]

Refusing to support any shelter program during Truman's era, Congress cut 92 percent of the total funds requested by FCDA in 1951, 86 percent in 1952, and 93 percent in 1953, with the FCDA receiving each year a lesser amount in actual dollars than the year before.[21] This was achieved with no public outcry of any sort. Yet the FCDA was still allotted almost $120 million between 1951 and 1953. Much of the funds went toward the production of propaganda, what historian Paul Boyer has called "the reassuring message of civil defense."[22] The chief marketers of this material were typically public relations experts in the Public Affairs Office of the FCDA, advertising specialists, and the many top-level FCDA officials with patronage appointments, who promoted the propaganda program in order to strengthen their own job status and security.[23]

The FCDA "public education" effort began when 20 million copies of the little booklet *Survival under Atomic Attack* were distributed by 1952. A movie with the same title was produced under government direction with private funds and narrated by Edward R. Murrow, reportedly selling more copies than any government film ever had before. These early efforts to explain nuclear war assured the public that except for radiation effects, nuclear bombs were no different from conventional arms. Radiation was compared to a sunburn. The booklet even claimed that radioactive dirt was harmless "if you keep scrubbing with warm water and soap."[24] Another widely distributed booklet called *How to Survive an Atomic Bomb*, written by radiologist Richard Gerstell, pronounced radioactive fallout to be no more dangerous than sunlight if absorbed in moderation. Protection against nuclear bombs could be achieved if one dropped to the floor, kept car windows rolled up, and wore a wide-brim hat to avoid radiation burns. After the attack, Gerstell advised citizens to "avoid panic," turn on the radio or TV for "instructions," and visit a doctor or hospital if that seemed necessary. To steady the nerves, "reciting jingles or rhymes or the multiplica-

FIGURE 1.2. Tilted hat brim. The first civil defense manual sponsored by the U.S. government assured readers in 1950 that if people took simple precautions, radioactivity would not hurt them and that the experts had everything under control. *National Archives.*

tion table" would help "to make sure you've got hold of yourself by the time the all-clear sounds."[25]

The FCDA also sponsored the Alert America campaign, which began in late 1951. Ten thirty-two-foot trailers carried portable exhibits to eighty-two cities across the country. The patriotic pageant provided ideological and moral guidance, along with information designed to calm public fears while teaching the value of civil defense. In addition, the FCDA ran conferences, sponsored studies, and as a trial, gave every resident of Allentown, Pennsylvania, a metal identification tag to be worn around the neck. Just like a GI dogtag, it could be used to identify the wounded and dead.[26]

The media was generally cooperative with FCDA initiatives in the early 1950s. Indeed, the CD public policy campaign was the first such major effort in a society increasingly attuned to mass media, especially television.[27] NBC-TV put out the FCDA message in a seven-part series in 1951, reportedly watched by 12 million people. The mass magazines touted civil defense in dozens of articles. A 1950 *Collier's* piece even found "really hopeful" evidence that a family could emerge from an air raid shelter within 300 feet of ground zero with realistic expectations of continuing a normal life only temporarily disrupted by nuclear war.

Encouraged by the FCDA, a number of professionals of all types—educators, architects, morticians, hospital administrators, physicians—joined the official bustle to popularize civil defense preparation. Ministers planned for mass burials as well as Bible study for children who felt upset after experiencing nuclear war. Psychiatrists considered pre-attack national organization of the public into small therapy groups, led by specialists trained to deal with natural fears about the future. Morticians instructed their colleagues to wear lead-lined clothing when handling radioactive corpses and to refuse cremation since radioactive particles might be released in the smoke. Viewing of the radioactive dead before burial was judged possible, but only if family members promised not to linger near the bier.

The American Medical Association (AMA) seemed particularly eager to help with the emerging civil defense program and with the nuclear aftermath. The early years of the Cold War were also the time when the conservative leadership of the AMA became obsessed with the need to defeat Truman's proposal for a national health insurance program. This need to resist "the creeping paralysis that is socialism" influenced even the AMA's view of radiation disease. The *Journal of the American Medical Association* (*JAMA*) observed in 1947 that reports of radiation sickness by British atomic energy workers could not be trusted, because it "has to be remembered that, with a Labour government in control of the country, workers have every opportunity to exploit real or alleged grievances."[28]

The FCDA made a special effort in the 1950s to draw medical professionals into the creation of civil defense propaganda. In those years, *JAMA* frequently published reports on medical civil defense activities. Medical advisory committees at the federal, state, and local levels were devised to help the AEC downplay the effects of radiation and reassure the public that adequate post-attack medical care would be available. At a time when the AMA so feared the initiation of a national medical care system, the support of civil defense could be used to show the profession's devotion to Cold War patriotism and civic responsibility.[29]

But it was the educational establishment which embraced civil defense with the greatest enthusiasm. Federal civil defense officials recognized that educational institutions were the logical place to focus their massive propaganda campaign. A large proportion of FCDA publications were directed to school-children and, indirectly, to parents. The AEC also published school materials in cooperation with the National Educational Association. Educators could use civil defense to justify federal aid to education. In addition, conservative and anticommunist postwar attacks on progressive education—charges of "*reduc*ation" or "why Johnny can't read"—could be countered by the schools' patriotic support of civil defense.[30]

Even before the end of 1951, civil defense programs had begun in one-quarter of the country's schools. Educators concentrated civil defense activities on two efforts: the provision of necklace identification tags and the establishment of air raid drills. By 1950, atomic air raid drills had already been adopted by the school systems of many major cities. Los Angeles schools held surprise weekly drills in late 1950. Children were told to kneel with their backs to the windows, their faces buried in their knees in fetal positions, their eyes closed, and their hands clasped behind their necks. As one New York teacher later remembered this "atomic head clutch position" of his childhood: "the teachers would tell everybody to get under the desks. You could feel the tension in the air, fear. The kids are fidgety and jumpy. . . . then there would be absolute silence. You never knew if it was a drill—a test—or the real thing."[31]

The New York City schools spent $159,000 by early 1952 to provide 2 million identification tags for public, parochial, and private school children from kindergarten through fourth grade. A 1951 Bead Chain Manufacturing Company advertisement in the *School Executive* showed one child displaying his dogtag proudly to a uniformed soldier. Another ad pictured a happy, protective mom in uniformlike dress awarding a dogtag necklace to her thrilled son. The caption read: "From New York to Redwood, California, many cities . . . are ordering Identification Necklaces as a safeguard for their school children. . . . Bead Chain has long been accepted as standard by our Armed Forces, for whom we have made identification necklaces for many years."[32] The advertisement did not elaborate on the sort of "safeguard" the necklaces provided for children: the tags were to enable more accurate identification of the dead—or of the wounded, charred, or mangled bodies of the youngsters who survived the initial blast. In contrast, Chicago's 1950 preparation for nuclear war might be judged a bit more thoughtful: the city's civil defense planners suggested a program "to tattoo its citizens with their blood types—underneath the armpits because arms might be blown off—in case radiation sickness called for quick transfusions."[33]

The most notorious and best-remembered civil defense publication designed for use in schools was the FCDA-produced comic book featuring Bert the Turtle. Bert, who ducked into his shell when danger appeared, was also the main character in a 1951 film seen by millions of schoolchildren. The movie's long-remembered catchy tune gave Bert's advice to youngsters:

> He'd Duck and Cover. Duck and Cover.
> He did what we all must learn to do.
> You and you and you and you.
> Duck and Cover![34]

FIGURE 1.3. Duck and cover. Schoolchildren duck for cover under their desks during an H-bomb drill, 1954. *Courtesy Ollie Atkins Photography Collection, George Mason University.*

Subsequent studies, as well as oral histories, have recognized the long-lasting trauma that many children experienced in the 1950s and early 1960s as a result of school air raid drills.[35] Sociologist Todd Gitlin remembered his experience as a young child taking cover in school bomb drills, "the first American generation compelled from infancy to fear not only war but the end of days":

> Every so often, out of the blue, a teacher would pause in the middle of class and call out, "Take Cover!" . . . Sometimes the whole school was taken out into the halls, away from the windows, and instructed to crouch down, heads to the walls, our eyes scrunched closed, until further notice. . . . Whether or not we believed that hiding under a school desk or in a hallway was going to protect us from the furies of an atomic blast, we could never quite take it for granted that the world we had been born into was destined to endure.[36]

It was the school civil defense drills that more than any other factor would later ignite angry opposition to civil defense programs nationwide. Most protesters were angry mothers of young children, but sometimes the protesters were students themselves. Singer Joan Baez's first act of civil disobedience was as a California high school student in the mid-1950s who refused to obey instructions during a school air raid drill. As a result, she remembered, "the next day I was on the front page of the local paper, photograph and all, and for many days thereafter letters to the editor streamed in, some warning that Palo Alto had communist infiltrators in its school system."[37] Jackie Goldberg, a leader of the free speech movement at the University of California in the early 1960s, began her Berkeley revolt by organizing other students to march in protest against the existence of the university's bomb shelter. As another student recalled those school-sponsored drills much later, "In many ways, the styles and explosions of the 1960s were born in those dank, subterranean high-school corridors near the boiler room where we decided that our elders were indeed unreliable." In the late 1970s, a California cab driver, remembering his youthful experience in school drills, said it all: "If it happens, it happens. They drop it, then we are blown away, and that's it. Only the young, the naive, and the school teachers were fooled by the drills."[38]

In the public schools, a generation of children was exposed to the idea that nuclear holocaust was just another problem of modern life. Most important, as historian JoAnne Brown notes, school civil defense programs attempted to teach American families "to equate emotional maturity with an attitude of calm acceptance toward nuclear war." Perhaps no better illustration of this effort exists than the proud report of Dr. Jean A. Thompson, acting director of the New York Bureau of Child Guidance, in the summer of 1951. Thompson cited the twelve psychiatrists employed by the New York Board of Education, who assured her that "well-adjusted," psychologically secure children did not exhibit signs of nuclear terror. As an example, she told the story of the twelve-year-old boy who heard an explosion, looked out the window of his home, and comforted his mom with the remark "no mushroom cloud" before "he returned to his homework, with a pleasant and reassuring smile at his mother."[39]

The civil defense propaganda of the early 1950s was a deliberate and conscious effort by government to bring public thought into line with national security policy through shaping public attitudes toward nuclear war. This plan relied on a system of emotion management that would suppress an uncontrollable terror of nuclear bombs and encourage in its stead a more pliable nuclear fear. In light of the destruction of nuclear exchange, how could the American public come to believe in the wisdom and legitimacy of the central role of nuclear deterrence in national security policy and thereby fulfill the moral requirements of American Cold War policy?[40]

The logic of deterrence demanded that Americans must be willing to respond to Soviet aggression with nuclear weapons, to fight and believe they could survive in a postwar society. Making a suicidal foreign policy appear to be a wise choice to ensure national survival became the crucial concern of civil defense proponents during the earliest phase of the Cold War. Pacifist scholar Alva Myrdal pointed out a central paradox of this period: "People rightly should have become more startled and fearful as the nuclear arms race went into swing. It is a psychological riddle how people everywhere conditioned themselves to live with fear without mobilizing vigorous opposition."[41] The shimmering cascade of civil defense propaganda released upon the American public during the early Cold War era goes a long way toward explaining how that strong and wholly rational opposition to nuclear war was first countered in the 1950s. The complex reality of the consequence of nuclear war, a situation no sane person could willingly accept, was announced by the self-proclaimed political realists in and out of government as not only mentally sound but essential to national survival. Such was the limited understanding of how the discovery of nuclear energy had forever changed the history of human beings and their practice of the organized violence called war. Much like the White Queen in the children's classic by Lewis Carroll, *Through the Looking Glass (and What Alice Found There)*, those national figures who touted deterrence after the appearance of the hydrogen bomb seemed to be saying, "Sometimes I've believed as many as six impossible things before breakfast."

●   ●   ●

Throughout this period, when civil defense propaganda was widely distributed by government agencies, the immediate postwar peace campaign nurtured by world federalists, ministers, pacifists, and atomic scientists was growing slowly. Norman Cousins's influential 1945 essay in *Saturday Review* was one of the first explanations of the cataclysmic result of atomic weapons. His book on the subject reached an estimated 47 million readers. In 1946, a group of prominent atomic scientists, including Albert Einstein, Niels Bohr, Robert Oppenheimer, Leo Szilard, and Hans Bethe, wrote a widely read pamphlet entitled *One World or None*. It warned that nothing less than human survival was at stake.[42] John Hershey's article "Hiroshima," published in 1946 and later as a bestselling book, convinced more readers that no preparation could protect many victims from nuclear attack.

The Federation of American Scientists (FAS), formed in 1945, committed itself to educate the public about the unparalleled horror of atomic warfare. The cover of the major publication of the nuclear scientists' movement, the *Bulletin of the Atomic Scientists* (*BAS*), held a drawing of a Doomsday Clock, which became world famous as an indicator of the danger of the outbreak of nuclear war. Created in 1947, the Doomsday Clock displays the time that the human race has left before the clock strikes midnight and humanity is destroyed by its inability to control atomic weapons. In 1949, the hand moved from seven minutes before destruction to three minutes. The closest it has ever been is at two minutes, where it remained from 1953 to 1963. Reset fifteen times in fifty-eight years, whenever the hands of the Doomsday Clock move, the world takes notice.[43]

As the public's strong fear of nuclear war persisted, heightened by the Soviet test of an atomic bomb in 1949, Cold War proponents were justly concerned by 1950 that widespread nuclear terror threatened both deterrence policy and its necessary component—the popular will to risk nuclear war. The first important official response to this concern was worked out in 1951–1952 by civil defense theorists—social scientists, engineers, physicists, and chemists—and published in an initially secret study entitled *Project East River*.[44] It was produced by the federal government and undertaken by Associated Universities, one of the first Cold War think tanks, which was sponsored by several Ivy League universities. The advice offered in *Project East River* provided the canonical text carefully followed by CD planners.

Project East River recommended that the government frame information on the effects of nuclear war to achieve two objectives. First, propaganda should attempt to convince Americans that nuclear weapons were essentially no different from conventional ones and thus prompt people to adopt individual defense measures against nuclear blasts. The second recommendation of *Project East River* was that the public be taught to think of themselves as disciplined military personnel trained to resist fear during and after attack—just "like trained soldiers under fire."[45] Properly prepared, the militarized American family could avoid debilitating and dangerous panic, perform its civil defense duties, survive nuclear war, and emerge to help with the cleanup.

In 1950, the *Bulletin of the Atomic Scientists* devoted a whole issue to a discussion of civil defense. It included an article by the young Yale psychologist Irving L. Janis on how to create public attitudes supportive of national security policy. The 1950 *BAS* article was written under contract to the Rand Corporation, which was originally financed by the air force and later was the major think tank employing nuclear strategists—those who would later be dubbed by critics the "nuclear priesthood."[46] Janis regarded civil defense as training that would enable Americans to "build up a tolerance for insecurity" in the pre-attack period, while also developing "realistic expectations" for post-attack survival. Janis recommended that public address systems be installed "in every major target area" so that immediately after the nuclear explosion—and before survivors of nuclear attack reacted with "inappropriate, disorganized, and maladaptive responses"—citizens could hear a "calm, authoritative voice of a familiar radio announcer" giving "reassuring announcements . . . about the arrival of rescue and relief teams."[47]

Janis added a Strangelovian twist to the message. He recognized the need for government construction of a massive underground shelter program to preserve the political, military, and industrial elite—along with a number of essential industrial workers (including, no doubt, a sufficient number of secretarial staff to handle the paperwork).[48] This elite shelter would allow those inside to prosecute a "defensive" war and to provide political and economic guidance to American society after the war ended. He recognized that the enormous expense of shelter protection would forbid the construction of public shelters for the majority of the civilian population, even those "in the most vulnerable urban centers." This situation could lead to a serious national crisis, he warned. The public at large would have to be informed about the provision of shelters to only a favored stratum of the society, mostly because a sizable portion of the urban work force would be needed to build them. Janis feared that the urban masses might "become increasingly alarmed by the fact that no attempt is being made to provide them with protection from direct exposure to an A-bomb attack. If the potential danger of such attack becomes more and more apparent, the demands for public shelters may become a critical political issue." In other words, the imminent threat of nuclear war might set off a pre-attack civil war between the preselected leaders designated for the government-built shelters and everyone else. The hapless masses might fight to gain access to scarce shelter space—rather than accept their fate with patriotic docility and soldierlike adherence to the wishes of their commanders. Thus Janis proposed that the public be encouraged to build private or neighborhood shelters at their own expense.

His analysis is straightforward in its understanding that private shelters will not save many lives. The real objective of a private shelter program was to provide the public not with security, but with the illusion of security.[49] A private shelter program, he predicted, would give citizens the sense, no matter how false, of having done something to save the lives of their loved ones. It would minimize social resentments among the masses of the population and help to avoid a last-minute conflict between the people and their protected rulers. It would reduce mass anxiety over the prospect of nuclear destruction.[50] The aim of private shelter construction was to lessen panic and thus to increase the willingness of the American public to accept deterrence as the core of national security policy. Deterrence was not defended because it would prevent war; it was best defended by the assumption that, when it failed, the dire consequences would be tolerable and possible to overcome.

Like the vast majority of serious studies of civil defense, Janis's Rand-financed analysis revolves around the central question of why most Americans, despite the avalanche of pro–civil defense federal propaganda, either rejected civil defense or simply refused to think about the possible consequences of nuclear war. Janis reported the widespread skepticism about civil defense as ranging from only "lukewarm" acceptance, to the assumption that nuclear war "would be a totally inescapable, uncontrollable form of mass annihilation." He suggested several tactics to increase the effectiveness of government propaganda: explain how relatively few people died in Hiroshima and Nagasaki as a result of the blast; provide information about Russian capabilities; advise insecure Americans that their hair will grow back in a few months if they suffer radiation poisoning; and initiate civil defense propaganda campaigns not when war seems imminent, but "at the time of a comparatively limited, cushioned crisis . . . rather than in a full-blown crisis."[51] The federal prescription to fool the urban masses into believing that they could protect themselves during a nuclear attack in their pitifully inadequate backyard or basement or public shelters and, especially, the open respect it was accorded in the early 1950s by top policy makers, seems incredible today. Nevertheless, this position as well as the *Project East River* assumptions upon which it rested became an essential component of civil defense planning beginning in the late Truman era.

By the mid-1950s, it was apparent that civil defense had become therapy in the service of national security policy and of those leaders and workers who were preselected to take cover in the hugely expensive government shelters. The family, the neighborhood, and the local community had been reconceptualized as quasi-military formations by civil defense theorists and administrators. This propaganda strategy fell far short, of course, of full realization, then and in the future. Still, as civil defense officials often stressed, the decision to "Alert, Not

Alarm!" remained their slogan throughout the Truman and early Eisenhower eras.

. . .

This entire propaganda structure suffered a fatal collapse on March 1, 1954, when the hydrogen bomb code named Bravo exploded near Bikini atoll in the Marshall Islands. The fifteen-megaton Bravo, the largest hydrogen bomb ever detonated by the United States, was far more powerful than scientists had predicted. After Bravo, radioactive fallout encircled the world. The claim that hydrogen bombs were not really so different from atomic bombs was no longer credible. The 1954 Bravo explosion marked a major transition in nuclear history. As the world better realized the nature of thermonuclear war, the peace movement expanded, and civil defense propaganda assumed new forms.

After World War II ended in 1945, a hotly emotional discussion of the development of a fusion, or hydrogen bomb, had begun at once.[52] A major impetus behind the H-bomb was physicist Edward Teller, an immigrant from Hungary. This forceful, bushy-browed scientist—consumed by his fear of communist attack—fiercely worked to encourage development of the Super, as the hydrogen bomb was called. He said he could see no moral difference between the fission and the fusion bombs.[53] The pressure was growing on Truman to approve the production of the Super. Edward Teller, the future AEC chair Lewis Strauss, Senator Brien McMahon, the JCAE, the Joint Chiefs of Staff, and Secretary of State Dean Acheson felt it must be done, since the Russians were believed, correctly as it turned out, to be building an H-bomb of their own.[54] Robert Oppenheimer, chief scientist of the Manhattan Project that built the first A-bomb, was one of the majority of members of the General Advisory Committee (GAC) of the AEC who decided in October 1949 that the development of the H-bomb was immoral:

It is clear that the use of this weapon would bring about the destruction of innumerable human lives; it is not a weapon which can be used exclusively for the destruction of material installations of military or semi-military purposes. Its use therefore carries much further than the atomic bomb itself the policy of exterminating civilian populations.

GAC members judged the H-bomb to be a weapon of genocide and advised that it not be produced. The radioactive effects of the H-bomb, the GAC majority also argued, represented an "intolerable" threat to the future of the human race.[55]

But President Truman approved development of fusion nuclear weapons in early 1950. Asked to comment on Truman's decision, Albert Einstein replied:

> If successful, radioactive poisoning of the atmosphere and hence annihilation of any life on earth has been brought within the realm of technical possibilities. The ghostlike character of this development lies in its apparently compulsory trend. Every step appears as the unavoidable consequence of the preceding one. In the end, there beckons more and more clearly general annihilation.[56]

Massive nuclear construction projects began at once. Within a few years, about 10 percent of the nation's electricity was consumed by the American nuclear program.[57]

The decision to make a Super was based on the assumption that the Soviets were unalterably intent on the destruction of the United States. That conclusion marked the beginning of a major shift in American strategic policy. Embodied in the National Security Council study paper of 1950 known as "NSC-68," the change committed the United States to containing communist expansion or influence anywhere in the world and also produced a great increase in military spending to support a massive peacetime military establishment and its weapons. The arms race was on. By the end of Eisenhower's term in 1960, the number of warheads in the United States numbered more than 18,000; if properly placed, they were enough to destroy all life on the planet several times over. By 1962, during the Cuban crisis, warheads numbered 27,100.[58]

The battle over the Super was an important factor in the cancellation of Robert Oppenheimer's security clearance in 1954, an event which enraged many leaders of the scientific community and must have intimidated others from speaking out against the nuclear strategy of the period.[59] Some blamed Lewis Strauss, chair of the AEC, and especially Edward Teller, for the McCarthy-like attack on Oppenheimer, whose opposition to development of the Super was well known. President Kennedy, in his last official act, decided to give Oppenheimer the Enrico Fermi Award, the highest award bestowed by the AEC. But even after the positive attention and exoneration awarded to Oppenheimer, the split among scientists over the moral and political issues raised by the Teller-Oppenheimer debate would not heal.

In March 1954, three months after Oppenheimer's security clearance was suspended, the Bravo nuclear test exploded in the Pacific. It would have required a freight train stretching from Maine to California to carry Bravo's equivalent in TNT. The AEC then announced that 26 Americans and 236 Marshall Islanders had been "unexpectedly exposed to radiation." For hundreds of miles around the blast, sea birds died by the tens of thousands because their wings were set afire by thermal heat. The 1954 Bravo contaminated 7,000 square miles of the Pacific with radioactive fallout. If the bomb had been dropped on Washington, D.C., with the winds blowing in a northeasterly direction, the entire northeastern seaboard would have been decimated, while lethal to serious fallout would have covered all of New England.

The Bravo fallout affected twenty-three crew members on a Japanese fishing vessel called the *Lucky Dragon*. The eventual death of one of them set off a massive protest against bomb testing among the Japanese people. More than 400,000 people attended the funeral of the *Lucky Dragon* fisherman. His dying words were "Please make sure that I am the last victim of the bomb." Meanwhile, boats fishing in the Marshall Islands area brought more than 600 tons of contaminated fish to Japan. In the next six months, 30 million Japanese signed a petition calling for the end of nuclear testing.[60]

Lewis Strauss at first simply lied. He denied in public the widespread contamination of fish, theorized that some unknown chemicals in coral had sickened the hapless crew members of the *Lucky Dragon*, and privately declared his belief that the *Lucky Dragon* was really a communist spy ship. A self-made businessman and hard-line political conservative, Strauss had made a fortune as an investment banker. He insisted on being called Admiral Strauss, although his only military service was as an administrator in the office of the secretary of the navy. His willingness to sacrifice public truth to his version of national security, as well as his rigid arrogance during the Oppenheimer case and his controversial support of the nuclear power industry, would finally force him from further public service. In 1959, the Senate denied his appointment as secretary of commerce, the first time since 1925 that a Cabinet nominee was not confirmed. This dramatic political bloodletting focused on his denial of the truth and obsessive secrecy about nuclear issues.[61]

After Bravo, however, the old lies would not hold. Even Strauss soon admitted publicly that an H-bomb could eliminate the entire metropolitan area of New York City. Newspapers worldwide discussed the horror of the new nuclear weapon, in excited analysis of how many miles from ground zero the fireball could consume and how many deaths, then and years later, would be caused by radioactive fallout on the planet. After Bravo, the exclusion area around future American bomb tests in the Pacific was expanded to cover an area almost equal to 20 percent of the continental United States. After Bravo, many informed Americans realized that the fallout from a thermonuclear bomb far exceeded the danger from the explosion itself.

The AEC was now the prime defender of the Super and bomb testing, as its leaders attempted to obscure the danger of radioactive fallout. In the process, the AEC created a major public debate over the wisdom of government secrecy and the trustworthiness of AEC spokesmen. But Edward Teller had the most bizarre assurance to offer the public about the lack of danger from fallout. He announced that since the chance of deformed births is reduced if one keeps the sperm cool, Americans could do more to cut down deformities by forcing all men to wear kilts than by stopping nuclear tests.[62]

Still, despite Teller's efforts, the facts were now known to many throughout the world. An exchange of H-bombs could bring near-annihilation to the people of both superpowers and, depending on the drift of the radioactive particles, to millions of people elsewhere. A U.S. attack on the Soviet Union could kill by fallout hundreds of thousands, maybe millions, of Western Europeans as well. By 1955, even most AEC officials acknowledged that the hydrogen bomb was something radically new in human violence. Although many politicians and military men continued to pursue traditional goals through warfare, many others were beginning to grasp the new reality.

TWO

The Battle to Inform the Public, 1952–1957

In 1951, Eastman Kodak Company officials reported to the Atomic Energy Commission that its Geiger counters at the Kodak film plant in Rochester, New York, had detected high levels of radiation from the bomb tests in Nevada, some 2,700 miles away. The radiation was coming down in the heavy snow that covered the Rochester area. Kodak executives, fearing that the radiation might destroy company film stocks, warned that they might have to sue the government for damages if the fallout recurred. At that point, the AEC secretly began to provide Kodak with advance notice of bomb tests and to delineate areas of potentially heavy fallout. Yet citizens in Nevada and Utah much closer to the test sites were never given such early warnings. Instead, in the early and mid-1950s, the AEC assured them that if they stayed indoors or dusted off their clothes after a test explosion, they could avoid harmful contamination. For many of those "downwinder" civilians showered by fallout and for the military personnel assigned to serve near ground zero during the nuclear bomb tests, information about radiation crucial to their health was deliberately withheld, and, for many, this ultimately proved fatal.[1]

Between 1946 and 1963, first in the Pacific and then in the American West, the United States exploded 124 atmospheric and 4 underground or underwater nuclear bombs. As a result, millions of downwind people, and other living things, in the United States and elsewhere were exposed to radioactive fallout. The U.S. government also exposed at least 200,000 men and women in uniform, later dubbed the "atomic soldiers," to various levels of radiation and fallout in a series of atmospheric nuclear bomb tests held in the Southwest in order to find out how soldiers might react to nuclear war. Thousands of these atomic veterans were condemned to miserable bouts with cancer.[2]

Through most of the 1950s, despite the increasing fears and doubts expressed by many top scientists, the AEC leadership denied any real danger to the populace from fallout. Lewis Strauss, AEC chair from 1953 to 1958, was convinced that the Soviets were bent on nuclear destruction of the United States. He believed that testing had to be done to ensure nothing less than "the security of the nation and of the free world."[3] Strauss thought that the trade-off of the "slight" risks from tests was worthwhile in order to save the millions of Americans whose lives would be lost in a Soviet attack upon the United States, which was sure to happen if the United States did not maintain its formidable nuclear superiority. Strauss, known as the "father of the nuclear industry," was so incapable of accepting criticism that he questioned the patriotism of anyone who opposed his views. Despite all of the arguments presented to refute the need for testing, he always held fast to his conviction that testing was necessary in order to improve weapons and to maintain American nuclear defense. Not until after Strauss departed the AEC in 1958 did the truth about the effects of nuclear explosions begin to reach the American public in reasonable quantities from government sources. The first fight against the government, chiefly led by scientists, was to expose the effects of nuclear bomb tests, followed by the longer struggle of others to bring awareness first to the scientific, intellectual, and political elites and then to the general public.

The period from 1954 to 1961—from the Bravo H-bomb test to the time when civil defense received its highest support from government—was also one of the two peaks of anti–civil defense protest. And it was these dissenting protesters of the late 1950s who won the day, springing from marginal status to mainstream importance, they achieved a decisive and amazingly rapid victory by 1962. This chapter describes the first stage of that growing protest, from the Bravo test to the major expansion of the antinuclear movement in 1957. That increase was enormously strengthened by the national civil defense drills called Operation Alert, the federally sponsored, annual nuclear air raid drills held in the major cities of the United States from 1955 to 1961. The existence of Operation Alert fired the peace movement into action, and the public reaction to Operation Alert convinced many top federal officials that the annual bomb drill posed an intolerable threat to nuclear strategy.

•   •   •

President Dwight Eisenhower was elected in 1952 shortly before the explosion of Mike, the first H-bomb. Despite his occasional public lip service to the need for civil defense and his public indications that the United States would respond with "massive retaliation" to communist aggression, President Eisenhower recognized earlier than most of his top advisors that H-bombs had made nuclear war unthinkable. In July 1954, less than six months after the Bravo explosion in the Pacific, Eisenhower expressed this understanding with furious conviction to the South Korean leader Syngman Rhee. In a meeting in Washington, D.C., Rhee told the president that the United States must be willing to fight the communists if democracy were to survive. Even as Secretary of State John Dulles sought to defuse tensions, President Eisenhower angrily exploded at Rhee:

> When you say that we should deliberately plunge into war, let me tell you that if war comes, it will be horrible. Atomic war will destroy our civilization. It will destroy our cities. There will be millions of people dead. War today is unthinkable with the weapons which we have at our command. . . . The kind of war that I am talking about, if carried out, would not save democracy. Civilization would be ruined, and those nations and persons that survived would have to have strong dictators over them just to feed the people who were left.[4]

Eisenhower understood that the Super had changed the nature of warfare. A thermonuclear war had no purpose except mutual extinction. In case of war with a nuclear superpower, he noted, "you might as well go out and shoot everyone you see and then shoot yourself." He also rejected the concept of limited war. He was "dead sure," he announced at a January 1956 meeting of the National Security Council, that "No one was going to be the winner in . . . a nuclear war. No one would surrender with still powerful weapons at hand. The destruction might be such that we might have ultimately to go back to bows and arrows."[5]

Eisenhower could not publicly acknowledge that a nuclear war would destroy American society. To confess this would create a massive debate, even with some of his closest advisors, would produce confusion and chaos at home, and would shake the international alliance system, which partially rested on the belief that the United States would fight a nuclear war to save Western Europe from Soviet attack. Since his only goal was to avoid war against the Soviets, he decided to adopt the pretense that if the Soviets threatened American interests in any serious way, he would respond with a total nuclear attack. Eisenhower chose to create this pretense as the most sane and reasonable solution to nuclear devastation that he could achieve. He reasoned that if everyone thought he would initiate a massive nuclear attack against the Soviets, then the Soviets would be careful not to do anything that might elicit that deadly response. Hence, the unthinkable—nuclear conflict—would be avoided.

When Eisenhower assumed the presidency in 1952, he gave the states major responsibility for American civil defense and cut back federal funding for programs, necessitating a shift from a shelter policy to a cheaper evacuation policy. He understood the futility of wasting money on civil defense for the masses. He knew that provision of even a minimal measure of protection to a limited number of Americans would require billions of dollars of expenditures and that a more adequate system of protection would also require a complete reorientation of society to a life of survival underground. A veteran strategist, he realized that neither of these options were acceptable to the American public.

The president appointed a like-minded official as director of the Federal Civil Defense Administration, former governor of Nebraska Frederick "Val" Peterson. Serving from early 1953 to 1957, Peterson first stressed evacuation as the best means of saving lives during nuclear attack. But as the American public learned more about fallout effects from H-bomb tests, evacuation of unprotected millions through open areas outside the cities became even more difficult to sell to a suspicious Congress and a skeptical public. Peterson was then forced to switch back to the need for shelters as an adjunct to evacuation, but this time as a defense against radioactive fallout, not against heat and blast. It was becoming more and more difficult for government strategists to avoid the knowledge that urban dwellers had little hope of surviving a direct hit.

Peterson had first blamed the shelter program of his predecessor for "all of its talk about going underground" at a cost of billions of dollars. He assured Congress that "there will be no digging holes . . . in the new civil defense program" for "the vast improvement in the destructive power of nuclear weapons could [now] turn such shelters into death traps in our large cities."[6] Still influenced by *Project East River* recommendations, however, Peterson argued the desirability of small home shelters built with private funds. He did not explain why privately financed basement shelters would save lives while government-funded shelters would not. Indeed, no one publicly questioned the obvious contradiction, other than the usual "idealistic but well-meaning" pacifists, who could always be found by mainstream newspaper reporters to provide comic contrast to the "tough" thinking required from "realist" establishment figures.

In early 1955, the Senate Armed Services Committee, alarmed by fears that the AEC might be deliberately hiding evidence from the Bravo test about the dangers of fallout, appointed a subcommittee, headed by Senator Estes Kefauver (D-Tenn.), to examine FCDA policies and operations. This was the most extensive federal investigation yet of the civil defense program. At the time of the hearings, the FCDA had moved to a combination evacuation/shelter policy, whereby people were to be evacuated from cities and sheltered elsewhere. Details were exceedingly vague.

In the Kefauver hearings, FCDA director Peterson revealed a startling new variation on the evacuation plan. He announced his intent to dig miles of trenches two feet wide and three feet deep along the public highways leading out of targeted cities. People in the open when the bombs hit could then hide in these trenches, which could be quickly covered with boards and a foot or so of dirt. Peterson felt that tar paper might be a better cover than boards, because "a person standing in one of those trenches could flap that thing [tar paper] every 20 or so minutes and shake that stuff [fallout] on the ground." An incredulous Kefauver noted that there was no provision for food, water, or sanitation in the trenches. Peterson replied: "Obviously, in these trenches, if they are built on an emergency basis, there would be no provision for sanitation."

Another option being considered at the FCDA, Peterson continued, was to lay concrete pipe four feet in diameter along the highways, rather than digging trenches, and to bury these pipes after they had filled with people in hiding. Peterson assured the senators that the trench plan was cost effective. The bill would be only twenty-five cents a foot, or seventy-five cents a person, allowing three feet per person, and was thus much less expensive than the pipe plan, judged to cost $40 per person. Pondering millions of evacuees sitting inside pipes for days at a time, without fresh air, light, sanitation, water, or medical care, led Senator Leverett Saltonstall (R-Mass.) to conclude that he would rather take his chances lying on his face on the ground "than get into a concrete pipe a mile long, with no exit, with some people coming this way and some that way [in a four-foot-high space]." To no one's surprise, the Kefauver committee concluded that FCDA plans for evacuation were less than adequate.

The media—and Congress—seemed not to know how to report Peterson's views. What was to be made of an FCDA director—appointed by a popular and respected ex-soldier president—who first argued that only evacuation would save the people in the cities, and then urged that fallout shelters also should be constructed to protect those unable to leave the suburbs near target cities, and next advocated a system of trenches or pipes to provide haven for those city refugees unable to reach safe areas in time? Meanwhile, Peterson also testified before Congress that after a nuclear exchange:

> I think the best we will be able to do in the United States is to run soup kitchens. We can't eat canned foods, we won't eat refrigerated foods. We will eat gruel made of wheat cooked as it comes out of the fields and corn parched and animals slaughtered as we catch them before radioactivity destroys them. . . . if this kind of war occurs life is going to be stark, elemental, brutal, filthy, and miserable.[7]

Throughout his tenure, Peterson continued to make ambiguous statements that showed his basic uneasiness with either evacuation or shelter plans. As early as 1953, Peterson told the National Women's Advisory Committee of the FCDA that "the only alternative I can see for the great cities in the United States are to dig, die, or get out."[8] In 1955, he reported that "the cities are finished" if hit by an H-bomb.[9] Even after the FCDA issued an "advisory bulletin," which stated that the Bravo explosion demonstrated that no one in a downwind strip 140 miles wide and 20 miles from ground zero could have survived more than twenty-four or forty-eight hours without protective measures, the agency did not order a reevaluation of its evacuation policy.

Congress and the public continued to be mightily unimpressed by an evacuation scheme, even when shorn of its trench/pipe options, that did not seriously address vital questions. How much warning time would be available for emptying target cities? The FCDA had admitted that as ballistic missiles became operational, the idea of moving millions of people within fifteen to thirty minutes, or even two hours, of probable warning time was nonsensical. Even supposing there were sufficient warning, how and where would the people be sent, and what preparations would need to be made to receive them? How could people be persuaded to leave the city promptly when ordered to do so unless they had first located their children and other loved ones to go with them? And even if evacuation were feasible, how much would it cost? The *Philadelphia Inquirer* spoke for many when it noted in 1955:

> Philadelphia ... has two million inhabitants. Officials talk glibly of evacuating the city on anything from one to six hours warning. No staff officer in his right mind would undertake to move two million disciplined soldiers any considerable distance in under three days. How will things go in the case of a heterogeneous crowd in haphazard vehicles, bearing the halt, the lame, the sick, infants and children and aged pensioners, in addition to all the able-bodied: What happens when cars break down and run out of gas? Isn't mass evacuation an infallible prescription for a colossal catastrophe ... ?[10]

Public skepticism about continued government efforts to legitimize a civil defense program was reflected in the congressional response to civil defense budget requests. In 1954, Eisenhower greatly reduced Truman's civil defense budget proposals and asked for only $125 million. Congress cut that to $46.5 million. The next year, the administration requested $87.5 million and received a little over $48 million.[11] As before, the FCDA spent much of its effort on "public education" or, in other words, the production of propaganda.[12]

• • •

Widely accused after the Bravo explosion of hiding vital facts about fallout, the AEC habitually responded with more cover-ups and soothing assurances. Sparked by the publications of Ralph E. Lapp, a number of protests by scientists became a major factor in forcing the AEC to reveal more facts about fallout in the mid-1950s. A nuclear physicist who had worked at Los Alamos, Lapp could write with convincing authority on the effects of the Super. His widely reported pieces in the *Bulletin of the Atomic Scientists* (*BAS*) in 1954 and 1955 accused the AEC of advancing nuclearism by sponsoring an "official drought" of information that could kill freedom of expression and gravely damage democracy.[13] Lapp provided detailed estimates of fallout and blamed the AEC for "sanitizing" the public reports of radioactive danger. He showed that a fifteen-megaton Super exploded near the ground could release radiation in doses high enough to kill everyone in the open within 250 square miles. Within three hours of the blast, he predicted lethal or highly dangerous radiation doses over 1,200 square miles. Lapp stressed that accurate knowledge of fallout effects would "kill civil defense [programs] in the country." AEC director Lewis Strauss was particularly furious about Lapp's efforts to expose the AEC's attempt to play down the danger of fallout and did what he could to discredit Lapp with the media. As historian Lawrence Wittner noted, Strauss secretly read Lapp's private mail, an intrusion made possible only with the assistance of the FBI.[14]

The AEC, forced to deal with Lapp's exposures, gave one of its commissioners, Willard F. Libby, the job of providing information to reassure the public. In unconvincing, indirect answers, Libby presented the AEC line that although radiation after a nuclear explosion was extensive, its effects disappeared very rapidly. A few years later, when Libby's own homemade fallout shelter accidentally burned down in a brush fire, Leo Szilard—the famed nuclear scientist and postwar agitator for peace—remarked gleefully that the fate of Libby's shelter not only proved "that God exists, but that He has a sense of humor."[15]

In 1955, a series of nuclear detonations in Nevada were held with army soldiers placed in trenches as close as 3,000 yards from ground zero. One blast, felt seventy-five miles away in Las Vegas, leveled most houses in a government-built mock city. Officials later announced that all inhabitants of the city would have been killed. But no need for concern, the AEC assured the public once again, for nuclear tests were supposedly necessary events if Americans were to avoid all-out war. Still, many citizens were unconvinced, especially after the Pope Pius XII, in his 1955 Easter message to the world, warned of the dangers of "the horrors of monstrous offspring" created by nuclear testing. As Robert Oppenheimer commented in Paris, when asked to judge the danger of bomb tests, "Physicists don't know. Specialists in genetics don't know. Nobody knows, and we must take account of this ignorance."[16]

One of the first publicized studies to contradict the government's reassurances that fallout was not a serious problem in the western states came from two scientists from the University of Colorado Medical Center. In early 1955, Dr. Ray R. Lanier, the director of the university's radiology department, and the biophysics department head, Dr. Theodore Puck, announced that a great upsurge in radioactivity had occurred in Colorado after one of the Nevada tests. They were also among the first to point out the falsity of the AEC's frequent claim that fallout from tests was no more dangerous than medical X rays. Lanier and Puck showed that the analogy—comparing X rays with fallout from nuclear fission—was not valid, for minute quantities of radioactive alpha and beta particles produced by nuclear explosions are inhaled or swallowed and settle in living tissues, where they radiate the body from within, whereas medical X rays do not contain these alpha and beta "internal emitters." In the *New York Times*, Strauss blasted Lanier and Puck as "irresponsible." Colorado governor Edwin C. Johnson stated that the two scientists "should be arrested" and implied that they were dupes of a communist plot to stop bomb testing. The media quickly picked up the red-baiting theme, no doubt causing other scientists to pull back from further criticism of the testing program. At the same time, AEC commissioner Willard Libby wrote a *U.S. News and World Report* article that claimed that bomb fallout would "not likely be at all dangerous."[17]

By 1955, the AEC was worried about its faltering public front in the world. That year, the English mathematician and philosopher Bertrand Russell and Albert Einstein issued their manifesto warning that a large nuclear war could mean the extinction of life on the planet earth. The statement, endorsed by Einstein on his deathbed and publicized throughout the world, called for the abolition of war. Their words were memorable: "Shall we, instead, choose death because we cannot forget our quarrels? We appeal, as human beings to human beings; remember your humanity and forget the rest." Less than a week later, fifty-two Nobel Laureates issued a similar alert, proclaiming that "all nations must renounce force as a final resort of policy. If they are not prepared to do this they will cease to exist."[18]

AEC chair Strauss was caught red-handed in his successful effort to prevent a paper by Nobel Laureate Hermann Muller from being presented at a UN meeting in Geneva in the autumn of 1955. Muller's paper outlined the serious genetic effects of fallout on the population. Strauss's deceit and dishonesty caused a furor and led the president of the Association for the Advancement of Science to write an angry article blasting Strauss, which appeared in the October 1955 issue of the prestigious journal *Science*.[19]

Two other internationally recognized scientists—American Linus Pauling and Russian Andrei Sakharov—also warned that millions would die worldwide because of nuclear tests. In what he called a "conservative" estimate, Sakharov said that testing had caused 500,000 human deaths worldwide by the mid-1950s, and that each year of continued testing increased the toll by 200–300,000 persons.[20]

In addition to the scientific denial of the value of civil defense, Congressman Chet Holifield, a New Deal Democrat from California and member of the Joint Committee on Atomic Energy for twenty-eight years, in 1956 held the first of five hearings that were designed to further discredit the inadequate civil defense provided by the FCDA. Holifield, known as "Mr. Atomic Energy" during his thirty-two years in Congress, was a consistent supporter of the nuclear power industry. As chair of the Military Operations Subcommittee of the House Committee on Government Operations, he began an investigation of the national civil defense operation. The 1956 Holifield hearings lasted six months and included 211 witnesses, whose testimony filled 3,145 pages. They comprised the most thorough investigation of civil defense ever undertaken.[21]

Holifield first noted the "widespread belief in this country that civil defense is either futile against sudden massive assaults with nuclear weapons, or is hopelessly inadequate under present arrangements." He certainly did not want to "contribute any further to the apathy and indifference and fatalism which are now so extant among the American people that as we go from city to city we find a hearing room without a citizen present in many instances, unless they are witnesses, to hear the discussion and to hear the questions and answers of the committee." Holifield sought to educate the absent hordes of disbelievers as to why an expensive, but necessary and feasible, shelter system should be created to protect American citizens during nuclear war.[22]

In the 1956 Holifield hearings, the FCDA programs and leaders were thoroughly denounced. Again and again, witnesses targeted the agency for its bumbling failures and its responsibility for the public's general ridicule and dismissal of civil defense options. Merle A. Tuve, chair of the Committee of Civil Defense of the National Academy of Sciences and the National Research Council, expressed the common view when he testified that he regarded the FCDA leadership "to have been so fumbling and inconsistent as to have lost public confidence and made a difficult situation more difficult."[23]

At this point, the Holifield hearings produced two of the most remarkable statements ever recorded in the long history of congressional consideration of civil defense. The testimony by Peterson and by Major General Otto L. Nelson, director of a 1955 review of the *Project East River* report, are noteworthy for the stunning clarity of their truthful presentations. General Nelson emphasized the calculated ineffectiveness of the civil defense program. First, he said, Congress and the administration had judged civil defense protection to be "so difficult, complex and expensive that there is no practical or effective solution. However, this is not to be admitted publicly but instead an ineffective phantom program is to be set up with appropriate individuals and agencies to serve as scapegoats." Nelson guessed that the "justification for such an attitude is the feeling that for political reasons something must be done, so you make a gesture in the absence of any effective programs or the knowledge of how to undertake them."

Committee members were surprised that Peterson was quite willing to acknowledge the basic truth of this criticism. But, unlike General Nelson, he went on to admit and pinpoint the reason that civil defense was so inadequate: the terrible nature of nuclear weaponry meant that "we haven't developed that capability" for civil defense. "When I say 'we,' Mr. Chairman, all mankind stands before you deficient in this respect." Peterson also admitted that most FCDA post-attack planning was merely "academic." In the bleak postwar wasteland, all resources would be shared in collective misery, which he described as a kind of "disaster socialism."[24] The FCDA and Peterson never recovered from this outburst of truth telling. He was replaced in 1957. The agency struggled on until 1958.

The words of another 1956 Holifield committee witness, the representative of the Women's International League for Peace and Freedom, are equally memorable. She attacked civil defense as nothing more than a mean fantasy to fool the public into believing that many Americans could survive a multimegaton nuclear attack. Her prescient call for sanity reads like poetry: "It is for us, too, to recognize finally that civil defense, however conscientiously devised, is a cruel delusion, an expense of spirit in a waste of shame, and a relic of wars already passed into history."[25]

Another committee witness, Willard Libby from the AEC, drastically understated the destructive capacity of thermonuclear weapons. Yet even his scaled-down version of the impact of a twenty-megaton weapon was terrifying. Many other witnesses, including Ralph Lapp, corrected Libby's report and made clear the almost inconceivable destruction of a nuclear exchange. Peterson summed it up: "I do not want to be a party . . . to any make-believe, that by delegations and by planning and by thinking, that . . . you [can] get America ready for this kind of attack. . . . it would be very questionable . . . that we will ever be prepared. We are just not going to be prepared for that kind of hell."[26] But Holifield refused to accept that "in a nation as great as this nation is, and with the resources, the skill, and the ingenuity of its people," there could not be developed an adequate civil defense against hydrogen bombs.[27]

Amazingly, the hearings did reveal such a plan—devised in 1956 by the U.S. Naval Radiological Defense Laboratory (NRDL)—for a national shelter program that could provide some long-term postwar protection to millions of Americans. Presented by NRDL official Walmer Strope, who would become a lifelong activist for civil defense, the proposal influenced the subcommittee more than any other document. According to the plan, the United States would be divided into a hundred or so "city-states," called Metropolitan Target Area Authorities. The city-states would be underground and each would be self-sustaining for an indefinite number of years, independent of central control. They would be equipped with nuclear power generators, complete air-purifying systems to filter out germs and poison gas, and huge underground systems of tank farming to produce their own radioactive-free food. In short, the only sure way to protect significant numbers of persons from thermonuclear war would be to create separate and independent segments of the society and plunge them underground. There the subpopulations would remain for perhaps decades if necessary.

Understandably, the NRDL underestimated the cost of this venture, claiming that it could be achieved with only $20–40 billion. Other witnesses, however, noted that an adequate attempt at civil defense would probably cost about $250 billion, the amount of money then being spent on military forces and on the development and stockpiling of fusion bombs and missiles. Holifield downplayed the cost and nature of a more sufficient shelter system. He could easily predict the average citizen's response to a survival plan to spend much of life underground in a nation controlled by a hundred independent governments. Besides, as one later commentator dourly remarked, this option, even if judged to be politically and financially acceptable, would no doubt surface an underground shelter race, to accompany the arms race, as each superpower sought superiority in the nuclear world.[28]

Near the end of the 1956 hearings, a mightily flustered Holifield accused Peterson of sounding as though he did not even believe in civil defense. Peterson replied: "I don't believe in kidding anybody about what is going to happen to the world and the people of the world in the event of a thermonuclear war, and I have contempt for anybody who attempts to minimize the sheer destructiveness and death and desolation that will befall mankind if these weapons are dropped."[29] As both FCDA director Peterson and Congressman Holifield well knew, those most active in minimizing the effects of the H-bomb were the official spokesmen for the AEC.

The final report of Holifield's subcommittee recommended that the federal government assume primary responsibility for civil defense, that a Cabinet-level Department of Civil Defense be established, and that its director be authorized to construct group shelters, whether the president supported the plan or not. Yet the hearings had no real effect, largely because the president had no intention of increasing the money spent on civil defense through adoption of a costly shelter policy or even a strengthened evacuation plan. Secretary of State Dulles also continued to oppose an expanded civil defense system, on the grounds that it was inadequate, frightening to American allies, and provocative to the Soviet Union. Eisenhower did make FCDA director Peterson a member of the Cabinet, while Congress cut the 1957 FCDA budget from the requested $134.8 million to $93.5 million, its largest appropriation ever. Holifield refused to give up. He began to organize his next congressional hearing designed to force an expensive shelter policy upon the nation.

In 1956, two other events dramatically advanced public knowledge of the effects of nuclear explosions. One was the presidential campaign of Democratic candidate Adlai Stevenson, who cited the genetic damage done to downwinders and promised to work for a test ban if elected. His call for an end to testing gave strong new momentum to his campaign and won him the support of many prominent scientists. But this advantage was lost when the Soviet government praised him publicly. Still, more and more people learned the truth about the H-bomb as a result of Stevenson's campaign efforts.

The other event was the major scientific discovery by British physician Alice Stewart that low-level fetal X rays increased the risk of cancer by a factor of ten. Prior to the presentation of Stewart's evidence, the AEC and other nuclear advocates had been able to argue the "threshold" theory of radiation, which held that radiation was perfectly safe below certain thresholds. (This had allowed the advocates of testing simply to raise the current "threshold level" whenever radiation levels became higher than expected.) But Stewart showed that there was no safe level of radiation, especially for the young, and her research also made clear that the amount of radiation absorbed is cumulative over time.[30]

In the mid-1950s, the danger of radiation was taught to millions of Americans by a grassroots group based in St. Louis, Missouri, which eventually organized into the Committee for Nuclear Information (CNI) in early 1958. The origins of CNI came in late 1956 when Gertrude Faust, from the St. Louis Consumers Federation; Marcelle Malamas and Virginia Brodine, organizers for the International Ladies Garment Workers Union; and well-to-do leading local reformer Edna Gellhorn, a former suffrage leader and president of the St. Louis League of Women Voters, then in her mid-seventies, joined forces. Together with twenty-four other prominent St. Louis women, they organized into the Greater St. Louis Women's Committee for Ending H-Bomb Tests. The group included Helen Nash, an African-American physician; Mary Rider, an advocate for the homeless and vice president of the St. Louis Trades and Labor Council; and Doris Wheeler, a former Socialist party activist.

This remarkable collection of educated and socially concerned women pressured the city health commissioner to test local milk for the presence of the radioactive isotope strontium-90, which had been deposited worldwide by fallout. Prior to the explosion of nuclear bombs, the substance had not existed anywhere in the world. Released into the atmosphere by nuclear explosion, it eventually fell back to earth and lodged in the topsoil, where it was absorbed by plants and eaten by cows. Strontium-90 is rapidly passed on to humans via cow milk. The substance, which is similar to calcium, lodges in human bones and can cause cancer sometimes decades later. It is especially threatening to children, who absorb far more strontium-90 in their growing bones than do adults.

When the city health commissioner replied that he had no facilities to measure the substance, the women demanded action. Aided by St. Louis congressman Frank Karsten, the women wrote highly publicized letters and met with senators and congressional representatives. Within weeks, the U.S. surgeon general agreed to include St. Louis with four other cities to be tested for strontium-90 contamination of milk. The tests showed positive results, which were predictably downplayed by the AEC and the U.S. Public Health Service.

The St. Louis women's appeal to measure strontium-90 was supported by the St. Louis chapter of the Women's International League for Peace and Freedom; Ralph Abele, a prominent local minister who led the Metropolitan Church Federation; and 130 faculty members from Washington University in St. Louis, including physicists Michael Friedlander, John Fowler, and T. Alexander Pond. Described by Gertrude Faust as "so bright he scares you," Pond had helped to write Adlai Stevenson's campaign speech on the threat of fallout and the call for a nuclear test ban.[31] Along with Walter Bauer, a member of the medical school faculty, Pond and Fowler produced a widely read report in October 1956 that highlighted the amount of dangerous fallout from testing. In response, the Senate Foreign Relations Subcommittee on Disarmament, chaired by Minnesota senator Hubert Humphrey, also collected widely reported testimony from concerned St. Louis scientists, physicians, and reformers.

The Washington University physics department was uniquely active against nuclearism under the leadership of Nobel Prize–winner and university chancellor Arthur Holly Compton and department chair E. U. Condon, hired in 1956. One of the best known scientist dissenters, Condon suffered several professional setbacks due to his opposition to government secrecy about nuclear policies and his support of civilian control of atomic weapons. In 1951, Condon had lost his job as director of the National Bureau of Standards, a post he had held since 1945, and was denied government security clearance at his new job at Corning Glass in 1954. Branded by the House Un-American Activities Committee as "one of the weakest links in our atomic security," Condon had become a national symbol of governmental persecution of political critics.[32] Also at Washington University during the 1950s was the brilliant contrarian and organizer Barry Commoner, a member of the biology department.

This union of progressive male faculty and St. Louis women taught their fellow citizens one overwhelming message: democracy was gravely threatened because voters were being deliberately misled about the effect of fallout and about the real damage caused by a multimegaton H-bomb. The CNI stressed three reasons that government "experts" were not providing accurate scientific information: they used inaccurate data; they held views determined not by scientific opinion but by sociopolitical factors; and they often deliberately gave insufficient information in order to convince the public that testing was not harmful to living things. The grassroots effort organized by the citizens of St. Louis was intent, above all, on challenging American nuclearism in its formative years. They concentrated on the establishment of a speakers' bureau, organizing scores of scientists and other specialists to give thousands of public speeches about nuclear danger. The creators of the CNI taught that democracy required independent sources of nuclear information that were formed outside the government and disseminated outside official channels. As Condon argued in 1956, "public discussions should not be hushed up by military or political leaders taking a 'this is too difficult for you to understand attitude.'"[33]

The national debate over fallout, strontium-90, and the wider threat of nuclearism had begun and could not be stopped—despite the facile claims of the AEC that the amount of radiation released by bomb testing was harmless to human health. Ahead lay the various projects of the St. Louis activists, including the famed Baby Tooth Survey, that were to become some of the most widely publicized accounts of the truth about nuclear dangers.

Despite the growing level of dissent among scientists and groups such as those in St. Louis, in the mid-1950s older sectors of the established peace movement were still somewhat demoralized and scattered. For a brief time after the nuclear attack on Hiroshima, newly organized groups of atomic scientists and world federalists had called for international sanctions against nuclear war. But these liberal elements had succumbed to the growing power of anticommunist Cold War ideology that followed the Soviet production of the atomic bomb and the beginning of war in Korea. Only two camps of the major organizations within the prewar peace movement survived into the early 1950s.

One remaining peace camp, attracting mostly liberal pacifists, was composed of the American Friends Service Committee (AFSC), founded in 1917, and the Women's International League for Peace and Freedom (WILPF), established in 1919. Both organizations opposed Cold War militarism, nationalism, and attacks on civil liberties.[34] They sought to educate the public about the need for peace, but had little immediate interest in building a mass protest movement. Their favored tactics were letter writing to politicians, conferences, and publication of materials in support of disarmament and conciliation.

The other major peace camp—the radical pacifists—was much smaller in size than the liberal side of the organized peace movement. Radical pacifists included many World War II conscientious objectors. They favored nonviolent direct action and took a "third camp position," which opposed both capitalist and communist forms of nationalism. Many followed a distinct pacifist lifestyle, often living in groups and renouncing the acquisition of material wealth. Centered in New York City, radical pacifists were based in the War Resisters League (WRL), the Catholic Workers (CW), and the Fellowship of Reconciliation (FOR). In this era of muffled but rising rebellion, radical pacifists felt increasing despair over their failure to raise a massive public alarm over the dangers posed by the Cold War nuclear buildup and Senator Joe McCarthy. By the mid-1950s, a number of radical pacifist leaders had become convinced of the need for a stepped-up program of nonviolent civil disobedience.[35] They would take the lead in the revitalization of the American antinuclear movement.

Formed in 1933 on New York's East Side by that tough-minded pilgrim of social justice, Dorothy Day, the Catholic Workers ran "houses of hospitality" for the poor and hungry. By the 1940s, the Catholic Workers had become the leading voice of the religious wing of radical pacifism in the United States. In what she called "loving disagreement" with the Church, Day criticized the failure of the Catholic hierarchy to live up to its teachings of peace, love, and charity. As one of the nation's leading advocacy journalists, she preached absolute pacifism and nonviolent resistance in her influential monthly paper, the *Catholic Worker*. Many liberal Catholics and nonreligious radicals all across the country read the *Catholic Worker* faithfully, as one of the few progressive publications available in the days of the early Cold War. Day espoused a libertarian socialism that fiercely denounced Soviet-style communism, even while she and the Catholic Workers defended the civil liberties of all, including American communists.

The WRL, the U.S. affiliate of the War Resisters International, founded in 1921 with members in twenty-four countries, was the largest secular radical pacifist group in the United States. The religious counterpart to the WRL was the FOR, established in 1915 and also an international group. Like the Catholic Workers, the WRL contained a vitally strong component of women activists. In the mid-1950s in New York City, male leaders from the WRL and the FOR included A. J. Muste, Jim Peck, David McReynolds, Ralph DiGia, and Bayard Rustin, all of whom would be among the first arrested for opposition to civil defense. Peck and Rustin would also be among the first civil rights activists. Following Gandhian principles of nonviolent resistance, the small band of radical pacifists supported democratic socialism, denounced communist dictatorship, and called for disarmament, civil rights for all, and democratization of the global order.

Because radical pacifists in New York City were beleaguered, isolated, and fully committed to social change, they knew each other well and communicated frequently. The Catholic Worker House in the Bowery functioned as a spiritual and intellectual mecca for creative young people drawn to New York City from across the country. Novelist and journalist Dan Wakefield remembers the *Worker*'s famous Friday night lectures: "There were old and young, men and women, graduate students and Bowery denizens, eager to talk about the night's speech, whether it was given by a priest or a politician, a migrant worker or a Yeats scholar, and no one was squelched or snubbed or shushed; anyone could have a say."[36] After the Friday night sessions, talk often continued at the White Horse Tavern. Here, soon-to-be-famous writers, artists, journalists, poets, pacifists, civil rights activists, musicians, and assorted leftists discovered one another in one of the most significant intellectual and political communities in the mid-1950s United States. The radical journal *Liberation*, founded in the winter of 1955–1956 by Muste, Rustin, David Dellinger, and others, provided another forum to stimulate the new ways of thinking.

These radical pacifist groups came together in 1955 in New York City in opposition to the first federally sponsored, nationwide air raid drill, Operation Alert. This was the beginning of the Gandhian-inspired, nonviolent, mass civil disobedience movement in the United States. It first surfaced in 1955 in anti–civil defense protest and in the black civil rights bus boycott in Montgomery, Alabama, and quickly grew to become a central organizing principle of the civil rights movement and the antiwar movement that followed.[37] It began when the civil defense establishment expanded its alert, not alarm, concept to new dimensions in the initial dress rehearsal of the macabre exercise called Operation Alert.

● ● ●

From 1954 to 1962, federal and state civil defense agencies worked together with the mass media to produce the giant annual sociodrama named Operation Alert—an enactment of an imaginary nuclear attack on the United States. This massive political ritual took place each summer in more than sixty major cities across the nation. During the simulated nuclear attack, millions of urban residents were required to take cover for fifteen minutes, while the simulated dropping of hydrogen bombs ravaged the nation. The staged drama was complete with special costumes, siren sound effects, and set scripts enacted by the powerful and poor alike. While local civil defense officials practiced preparations for nuclear war, the highest federal officials were evacuated to secret government shelters. The air raid drill was consciously shaped by its directors into a national epic designed to demonstrate governmental mastery of a potential

FIGURE 2.1. Civil defense protest, 1955. Twenty-eight people are arrested in City Hall Park, New York City, for refusing to take shelter during the Operation Alert civil defense drill.

Swarthmore College Peace Collection.

nuclear crisis through the flawless operation of civil defense and to present an image of order amid uncontrollable and terrifying events.[38] The films, images, and symbols produced to accompany Operation Alert also created a post-attack scenario that featured white, middle-class, suburban families, all exceedingly clean, emerging from the holocaust with calm resolve, carefully combed hair, and freshly laundered clothes. In good spirits and apparently untroubled by blast effects or fallout, they awaited orders via radio from the calm and efficient men in the new underground White House.[39]

The reality of the public response to Operation Alert was entirely different from that described by federal propaganda. Most citizens ignored the Operation Alert exercise, or if they thought of it at all, laughed at its preposterous images and rhetoric. Some cities openly refused to participate: Peoria, Illinois, was one of the earliest.[40] And as everyone well knew, and quickly repeated, "If it won't play in Peoria . . . ," there was little hope for success elsewhere.

Federal officials first ran a dress rehearsal for Operation Alert in 1954, without public participation or much media attention. It was largely a trial run for the political and military leaders to make sure their own shelters were tested and that their public relations plan to sell the public on the need for elite shelters was in place. The concept of the construction and maintenance of nuclear shelters for the elite—"command posts" to ensure "continuity of government" during the post-attack era—first appeared during Eisenhower's term in office. Besides the bomb shelter under the White House, which would not survive a direct hit, three great underground shelters were created for top political and military leaders in the 1950s.

The Raven Rock underground bunker in Pennsylvania, six miles north of Camp David, was built between 1950 and 1953 on round-the-clock construction shifts, at a cost of about $1 billion. Another billion dollars was required for maintenance, until at least the late 1990s, when it still had a secret staff of 500. Within the bunker, a trio of three-story steel buildings was erected as operations centers for the president and his closest advisors. Buried inside a mountain of green granite, with the equivalent of walls 1,000 feet thick, the bunker could hold 3,000 people. It contained a water reservoir, medical and dental facilities, a barber shop, and a chapel.

Another haven, aptly named High Point, was built between 1954 and 1958 on Mt. Weather, in Virginia, forty-eight air miles from the White House, at a cost of more than $1 billion. Its entrance protected by a thirty-four-ton blast door five feet thick, it consisted of twenty-nine three-story office buildings. It contained enough water, food, and living space to support several thousand people for ninety days, including secretaries and stenographers, although only the president, Cabinet members, and Supreme Court judges were assigned private rooms. The government officials destined for evacuation to High Point in an emergency were not allowed to bring their families with them. From the beginning, it was deemed questionable how many would actually flee to High Point and hence abandon their families. It was also questionable whether the air could be purified sufficiently after a nuclear holocaust to ensure survival for those inside High Point. This shelter also had a hospital, crematorium, and sewage plant. In the underground TV studio, the surviving elites could pose before a wall-sized picture of the Capitol and broadcast assurances that government leaders were on the job and in charge to anyone who had survived the attack and also had a working TV and electrical system.

Construction of a third site, the Greenbrier in West Virginia, began in 1959. This enormous underground shelter, built to house 1,153 members of Congress and their staffs, lies beneath a five-star resort hotel in White Sulphur Springs. Staffed from 1962 to 1992, Greenbrier held an elegant dining room, with "picture window" murals, which seated 400 people at circular tables. So well equipped was this shelter that fresh supplies of all prescription medicines used by members of Congress, including birth control pills, were always kept ready in the event that nuclear war brought Congress to the underground sanctuary. Throughout three decades, only a few members of Congress knew about the elite shelter at Greenbrier, for it was decided that most could not be entrusted with this information.[41] It was not until the existence of Mt. Weather was exposed in 1992 by the *Washington Post* that representatives learned that the shelter's fresh-air supply was only good for seventy-two hours. After that, those inside would have been exposed to airborne radioactive particles.

In a late January 1954 meeting of the National Security Council (NSC), careful consideration was given to all of the possible ramifications and problems of providing effective elite shelters. The group agreed that after nuclear war very little would be left of Washington, D.C., or other major cities. As the NSC pondered the issue of how many cities might be totally "shalacked," Eisenhower expressed his concern with the possible adverse psychological impact on public opinion, and the moral issues raised, if the public knew that key officials were going underground. The NSC ran a full test without public participation in 1954, with an emphasis upon the emergency "relocation centers," as the shelters for the privileged few were now dubbed.[42]

Katherine Graham Howard, the female leader at the FCDA, recorded her own thrilling forty-two-hour-long participation in the 1954 dress rehearsal. On Sunday, she went to her "secret emergency headquarters" with her assistant, Miss Parker, and with FCDA administrator Val Peterson, who arrived with his assistant in preparation for the Operation Alert rehearsal set for Monday morning. A military guard was posted outside her window throughout the night to "guard against saboteurs," Howard reported, but the only danger he encountered was from a marauding snake. The next morning, the scripted reports estimated that in her hometown of Boston, a four-mile radius was wiped out, and a total of 442,000 people were killed at once. There were 315,000 survivors, 13,000 of them seriously injured, the rest in shock and without food or shelter or clothes. A two-way TV connected her and Peterson with the Eisenhowers, who were ensconced in the shelter under the White House. Mamie Eisenhower and Howard chatted for a few minutes about topics other than the obliteration of millions of American lives. Howard insisted that she would remain at her post throughout the evening for, as she reminded Peterson, women are accustomed to taking care of children all night.[43]

As government leaders enacted their retreats to secret shelters, radical pacifists felt increasing despair over their failure to raise a public alarm over the dangers posed by the nuclear buildup and the new hydrogen weapons. Independently and together, a number of radical pacifist leaders had become convinced by the mid-1950s of a need for a stepped-up program of nonviolent civil disobedience.[44] Dorothy Day was more than ready for a shift to direct action. In 1954, her receptivity was enhanced when an FBI agent who visited the Catholic Worker office to query her about one of her friends drew out his gun and brandished it before her. This event so appalled and angered Day that she became convinced that a new effort must be made to confront J. Edgar Hoover's political police. When she learned that compliance with the Operation Alert air drill would be made compulsory by New York state in 1955, with penalties of up to a $500 fine and one year in jail, she and Catholic Worker Ammon Hennacy, also an active member of the War Resisters League, helped to organize a small group who would refuse to take shelter when Operation Alert began on June 15.[45] They notified the Federal Bureau of Investigation, city authorities, and the media of their intent to defy the new law.

Even before the June 1955 Operation Alert drama, federal authorities staged a great media extravaganza in early May in Nevada. Civil defense officials and volunteers from all over the country were invited to observe the atomic bomb test explosions, which were given the reassuring name of Teapot Apple-2. The Upshot-Knothole series of tests in 1953, which had dumped fallout over much of the country, some of it detected by nongovernmental entities, had resulted in many sheep deaths in the West. Due to growing public protest, the AEC decided to move the tests to the Pacific during 1954, an election year, but tests returned to the American Southwest the following year. Teapot was a series of fifteen explosions to test the use of tactical nuclear weapons on some future battlefield, to teach the thousands of atomic soldiers about how to fight a nuclear war, and to show the public that nuclear war could be exciting as well as survivable. The AEC published a booklet especially for the Teapot tests to assure America that each bomb "is justified by national and international security needs and that none will be fired unless there is adequate assurance of public safety."[46] The twenty-nine-kiloton blast came at daybreak, with a force more than twice as big as the Hiroshima explosion.

A doom town had been constructed, just as in 1953, but this time it was more complicated in structure and better advertised. It contained paved streets and two-story frame houses, complete with furniture and mannequin "families." When the bomb went off, remote cameras broadcast on national TV the walls of the houses being blown in, roofs being sent flying, and resident dummies losing their heads or bursting into flames. Thousands of soldiers, many of whom were later gravely affected by the radiation they absorbed, were assigned to trenches less than 4,000 yards from the bomb explosion. Civilian guests were placed in trenches two miles from ground zero.

Jean Fuller, director of women's activities at the FCDA, was one of six women who volunteered to get into a trench 3,500 yards from ground zero. They were among the several hundred women at the test site that morning who had come from all over the country: representatives of public relations firms, newspapers, local civil defense offices, businesses, nursing organizations, large women's clubs, and veterans groups' women's auxiliaries. Caterers were brought in from as far away as Chicago to set up grills on the sand at the test site and to feed the enthusiastic and excited observers. Fuller later exulted over the memory:

It was rugged, but I am sure that those of us who were privileged to participate will always profit from the experience . . . of the tremendous white light, the seismic quake of the ground all around, the loudness of the noise of the blast, and then the tremendous blast effect, first from the positive side and then the after-shock, or negative phase. Of course those of us in the trench missed the "beauty" of the spectacle because we were completely engulfed in the dense cloud of dirt from the blast.[47]

Arthur Landstreet, who was in the civilian trenches two miles from the blast, was less sanguine. He wrote: "It felt like someone had taken a sandbag and struck me in the middle of the back. . . . tons of dirt were whirling and there was dust everywhere. We had nothing but a brown, drab sight as our only reward."[48] The dust curtain enveloped the whole eight-by-twenty-mile expanse of the bomb test area and lasted hours. Fuller, and perhaps others, remained lighthearted, convinced by authorities that the highly radioactive dirt would do them no harm. Meanwhile, the nuclear cloud encountered rain as it moved across the country and dropped fallout in Colorado, Missouri, Illinois, West Virginia, and Texas.

A few weeks later, the first Operation Alert was staged. The government drama planned for the bombs to hit sixty critical target cities, some with seven megatons, but most with one megaton per city. Headlines across the country described how President Eisenhower and 15,000 top executive officials successfully fled Washington to secret "control" centers. Meanwhile, Congress and the Supreme Court remained in session, and attendees at a baseball game in Yankee Stadium also remained in their seats when the sirens went off. Perhaps in response to Eisenhower's fear of public resentment of elite shelters, the feds made clear to the press that one of the vital "highlights" of Operation Alert 1955 would be to study how best to move people into temporary relocation sites to assure continuity of government.

The media production of Operation Alert 1955 featured pictures of the president and his highest advisors, all garbed in spotless suits and shirts, relaxed on folding chairs in front of large tents at their hidden destinations, as they smoked pipes, read documents, jotted notes, and calmly carried on the process of government after major cities were destroyed and millions killed. As the federal planners of Operation Alert soon learned, a great many citizens found these ridiculously posed pictures impossible to take seriously. The public extravaganza of that year's Operation Alert was never repeated.[49]

In New York City, the protesters who had resolved to refuse cover ate lunch at a local church. Seasoned dissenter Bayard Rustin from the WRL advised them to hold their protest signs high above the crowd so as to give the press cameras a better shot. When the sirens sounded, they waited quietly in prayer and meditation on park benches in City Hall Park. Flanked by television and newspaper reporters, they calmly restated their opposition to the government-manufactured pretense that the nation could devote major resources to preparation for nuclear war and at the same time shield people from its effects, short of taking the whole society underground and equipped with supplies to last many years. A pamphlet distributed by Dorothy Day read: "We will not obey this order to pretend, to evacuate, to hide.... We know this drill to be a military act in a cold war to instill fear, to prepare the collective mind for war."[50]

The police loaded twenty-seven pacifists (and one shoeshine man mistakenly arrested) into vans for booking. Ranging in age from twenty-two to seventy years, most of the protesters were affiliated with the Catholic Workers, the Quakers, or the War Resisters League. Among those arrested were Day and Hennacy, Muste, Peck, and Rustin. Seven of the eleven women arrested were Catholic Workers; two described themselves as anarchists. Another, Orlie Pell, also the president of the New York Metropolitan ("Metro") chapter of WILPF, identified herself as a member of the WRL. Members of the WILPF chapter and the radical pacifist group immediately formed a provisional defense committee. They collected more than $35,000 within a few days, another sign of public hostility toward civil defense. They later obtained another $150,000 for appeal to the U.S. Supreme Court.[51]

On the evening of the arrest, the protesters were brought before Judge Louis Kaplan. He called them murderers, holding them responsible for the mock deaths of almost 3 million New Yorkers killed during the air raid drill, according to government announcements of the assumed carnage. He set bail at an exorbitant $1,500 each. After a heated exchange with twenty-nine-year-old actress Judith Malina, who would go on to Living Theater fame, Kaplan set off a small riot in the courtroom when he spitefully ordered her to Bellevue Hospital for psychiatric observation. Malina was held there for several days. A few protesters in Boston, Philadelphia, Chicago, and elsewhere also refused to take shelter and distributed leaflets. Civil defense officials in these cities paid no attention to them.

Eisenhower listened carefully to the top-secret reports of what had been learned from Operation Alert 1955. All states but Idaho and Nevada had participated in the exercise. (Perhaps some government official had realized that the less the population of those states heard about radioactive fallout, the better.) Three cities—in New York and Massachusetts—were told that bombers were on their way, but each city government conveniently assumed that the bombers were shot down and thus did not participate in the civil defense drill. The president mentioned the need to declare martial law after a nuclear attack. Did anyone have a better idea, he thundered at a government meeting, to deal with the chaotic disaster of a postnuclear world? No one did. The meeting continued. Each year, the discussion of Operation Alert by the presidential staff focused more and more on the elite shelter problems and the continuity of government until this issue all but dominated the White House's connection to civil defense.

Outlining the results of the 1955 exercise, Val Peterson explained that 8.5 million Americans had died, with another 8 million badly injured. Fallout casualties were conveniently not known, but Peterson noted that the fallout was presumed to have covered 63,000 square miles. Federal stockpiles would only feed about 2.5 million people for three weeks after the blasts; 25 million people were in need of food and water.[52] These figures were extremely low in light of what was known in 1955 about the effects of thermonuclear war. But even these understated statistics sobered Eisenhower, who had only one comment: "Staggering." He did have one heartening thought, upon reflection. The mock casualties would have a deterrent effect on the Soviet Union, he predicted, but only if the Soviet Union would run a test like this of its own.

On June 17, Eisenhower heard a recital of other problems realized during Operation Alert. The initial "substantive problem" chosen for discussion was how to provide indemnification for damages during a nuclear attack. The decision was made to give to whomever needed it a government guaranteed credit of $50 "from any established banking organization." A high official from the Agriculture Department brought as an example of such a problem the situation of a farmer who could not sell his lettuce if his highly perishable crop could not find transport to market in time, and therefore would be lost. It is astounding that a presidential advisory group was even discussing the possibility of a lettuce crop remaining in an unpolluted state after a full-scale nuclear war. Once again, as he did so often in the late 1950s, Eisenhower stated softly but firmly the nuclear reality. After a nuclear war, he interrupted:

[W]e will have to run this country as one big camp—severely regimented. . . . Millions of homeless people would have to be sustained and helped and fed in soup kitchens, and, compared with this responsibility, the objective of indemnifying property loss seems rather insignificant. People will be lucky if their losses are only property—and not their own lives.

Ike reminded his advisors that all of the ordinary processes in American government would no longer work in the post–nuclear attack world: "We must be very much bolder in our whole approach [to postwar recovery]. We must stop depending on things that sustain usual life in a State."[53]

Five months later, the trials of the accused civil defense protesters took place in New York City. The pacifists were represented by attorney Kenneth Greenawalt, assisted by Conrad Lynn, a civil rights lawyer, and Harrop Freeman, a

Cornell University law professor. Displaying his evident hostility toward pacifists, Judge Hyman Bushel inquired if the defense attorneys planned to call the Soviet official V. M. Molotov as a witness and asked long-time pacifist leader A. J. Muste if he had ever read Marx. Bushel dismissed the cases of two defendants, one who was pregnant and another who had been arrested by mistake. He pronounced the rest guilty and then suspended sentences, claiming he had no wish to create martyrs. This judicial concern led columnist Murray Kempton to note the "collective threat to our insanity" posed by the convicted men and women.[54]

National press coverage of the protest and trial was limited, but generally accurate and supportive. *Harper's* and several progressive national magazines wrote highly positive stories. New York newspapers and CBS television gave fair coverage, including the report that civil defense protesters in Boston, Chicago, and Philadelphia were ignored by the police, while citizens in several cities chose to ignore the drill completely. Except for *Commonweal*, major Catholic publications blasted the Catholic Workers for disobedience to authority. The FBI hastily compiled many new pages for its files. J. Edgar Hoover made another unsuccessful attempt to persuade the Justice Department to prosecute the Catholic Workers movement for sedition.[55]

White House preplanning for the 1956 Operation Alert was much more extensive than in earlier exercises. Several months before the event, a fifty-nine-page report, "Briefing for Operation Alert," with detailed test procedures, was sent to forty top officials within the Cabinet, National Security Council, and intelligence and military groups.[56] Major emphasis was again placed on the efficiency of the secret shelters operation. The prime goal of the exercise was described as "the maintenance of the Federal government and its administrative machinery." The plans cited that the president "on D-Day" would also issue orders to pick up dangerous persons, establish a censorship office, and issue a call for Congress to reconvene at a "relocation site." Then came detailed plans for land transportation and mail service between the sites. Also spelled out were the plans for naming those responsible for getting workers back into factories, feeding refugees, and restoring the readiness of the land and air military forces—all within a week of the nuclear attack.

These plans ignored reality, in light of the operation being predicated on fifty megatons landing on major cities, plus another eighty-eight somewhat lesser bombs being dropped on smaller cities. Nine major military bases and the Atomic Energy Commission office were slated to receive another twenty-two megatons.[57] Yet the document predicted only 12 million fatalities and 8 million injured, with only 24.8 million irradiated during the first seventy-two hours after the massive attack. Still, these impossibly low estimates were an improvement over those of 1954, which the document notes as having been criticized by government officials as being too low.

At a meeting on July 13 of the Cabinet, presided over by Vice President Richard Nixon, members of the White House staff proposed that the publicity given to the 1956 Operation Alert be deemphasized given the previous year's negative public reactions. A lengthy Cabinet discussion ensued as to whether to continue Operation Alert in 1956. Several Cabinet members had "grave apprehensions about going ahead." Secretary of Defense Charles Wilson said it scared people (and "whom are we trying to scare into doing what?"), accomplished nothing of value, exacerbated interservice rivalries in the Pentagon, and strengthened and confirmed the weapons makers—"what might be called the fear lobby"—who then made huge new budget requests. Secretary of State John Foster Dulles said that the dramatization of Operation Alert "alarmed our friends abroad, especially countries wherein we had bases, and which considered themselves as very likely targets." Another official argued that war preparation drills played into the propaganda needs of the communists. The counterarguments stated by the civil defense authorities focused on how they would all be laughingstocks in the press if they canceled the 1956 drill and that thousands of people planning and preparing for the drill would be furious.

Nixon summed up the discussion and announced that, from that point on, no national casualty and damage figures would be announced. Only local casualty estimates would be given, and only to the local civil defense authorities. Cabinet members were also told not to talk to the press nor to issue any press releases. Meanwhile, Admiral Strauss at the AEC would give his usual reassurance to the public about how controllable fallout really was. No one mentioned the 1955 anti–civil defense protest and the publicity it received, but surely it must have been on their minds. They specifically agreed, however, that the main problems had been too much media attention and the announcement of casualties, which excited the public and encouraged peace protests and refusals to cooperate.[58]

A week after the Cabinet meeting, Dorothy Day spoke at a pacifist meeting held right before her next defiance of Operation Alert. Day told her audience that, like the Poles and the Germans who had recently revolted against their Soviet oppressors, those who would refuse to take cover during the Operation Alert drill had little chance of success. Yet they were bound by honor and conscience to bear witness to the futility of defense against nuclear war. On July 20, six of those arrested the year before and twelve others—Quakers, anarchists, and WRL members—once again refused to take cover. Dozens of photographers and reporters covered the drama. Almost seven months later, the protesters were sentenced to either five days in jail or a fine of $25. Day and three

FIGURE 2.2. Civil defense protest, 1956. Civil defense demonstrators are arrested in Washington Square Park, New York City. Dorothy Day is at the far end of the bench. *Swarthmore College Peace Collection.*

other Catholic Workers chose to spend the time in jail.[59] The political ritual had created a counterritual.

Meanwhile, the top secret debriefing on Operation Alert 1956 to a large meeting of federal leaders from the Cabinet, intelligence agencies, the NSC, and the Joint Chiefs of Staff reported that the final estimate of 15 million casualties (still absurdly low) was not released to the public. Minor problems in internal communications and transportation to and from the elite shelters were mentioned. Eisenhower once again cautioned his planners that, after nuclear holocaust, there would be no way to prevent general hysteria, panic, and confusion. Even the president and top officials are bound to be "completely bewildered," he said. Who would bury the dead? he asked, and where would workers find the tools for the mass burial? The president ended the meeting with his own view of what he had heard about the plans for continuity of the government. Don't worry so about details, he said. Keep it simple, for merely to function at all will be a grand achievement. Any sort of "government which goes on with some kind of continuity will be like a one-eyed man in the land of the blind," he reminded them yet again. The last words of the minutes reported: "The President stressed that not all of the casualties of such a war will be lives. Among those casualties will be justice. . . . War is the antithesis of justice and fairness."[60] Throughout his second term, Eisenhower would hold firm to his belief that nuclear war was not an option for the United States.

THREE

Holding the Lid On, 1957–1960

During his second term, Eisenhower successfully opposed the National Security Council's call for a $40 billion shelter system. He also resisted other demands for improved shelters, including the recommendations of the presidentially sponsored Gaither Report, one of the most fervent calls yet for a mammoth increase in civil defense. Galvanized by the militaristic fever that swept the United States in reaction to the Soviet Union's launching of the world's first artificial satellite in 1957, the antinuclear peace movement enormously expanded in this period. Several powerful new pacifist groups sprang into action in the United States and in Great Britain, and older groups launched new activist projects in opposition to nuclear war and the civil defense system, while the Operation Alert protests of this time were the biggest and most powerful peace actions since the 1930s. Many government officials realized that it was impossible to ignore the growing public recognition of the catastrophic effects of thermonuclear weapons.

●　●　●

In August 1957, the Soviet Union fired the world's first intercontinental ballistic missile (ICBM). The United States had failed to launch an ICBM two months before, and would fail again in September. Then came Sputnik, the first manmade satellite, launched into orbit by the Soviets in October. A few weeks later, the U.S. attempt to send up its first satellite exploded in humiliating failure a few feet off the ground. The United States would finally succeed in January 1958 and sent up another satellite two months after that. By that time, however, the Soviets had launched their Sputnik II, weighing a massive 1,120 pounds, completely dwarfing the 2-pound U.S. satellite then in orbit. The American pose of military and scientific superiority was gravely damaged.

This was all a terrible shock to many citizens who had believed that communists were incapable of creating advanced technology. Edward Teller announced on television that the United States had lost a battle "more important and greater than Pearl Harbor." Senate majority leader Lyndon Johnson was among many top political figures who issued frenzied warnings. He claimed that "control of space means control of the world," that the Soviets might soon be able to control the water of the earth, raise the sea level, cause drought and floods, and even freeze the world over.[1] The "missile gap" myth was beginning to build. Many American leaders proposed crash programs for more missiles, bombers, bombs, and bomb shelters. Ike spent much of his second term responding to the increased calls for militarization.

But even before Sputnik cracked the nation's confidence, Ike was forced to deal with another congressional inquiry led by Representative Chet Holifield. The 1957 hearings featured the presentation of a three-stage civil defense plan to be run by federal, rather than local or state, officials. In the first stage, various styles of shelters, at a cost of $20 billion, would provide protection for a supposed 80 percent of the population. Then, during the two years after a nuclear attack, decontamination procedures would be undertaken, at an undisclosed cost. In the third year, people would emerge from the shelters and begin to develop a safe food supply, free of the effects of fallout. The means to achieve these goals were undefined, but the chief planner assured, "Our research indicates that all of the above problems can be solved with a reasonable and concerted effort."[2]

At this point, Val Peterson was replaced as head of the FCDA by a recently defeated governor, Leo Hoegh of Iowa. Again, the military made clear its unwillingness to assume any responsibility for civil defense. Once more, Congress refused to provide funds. The FCDA request for fiscal 1958 of $130 million was cut by Congress to $39.3 million. Meanwhile, Eisenhower noted in early 1957 his belief that, as the nuclear powers' understanding of nuclear weapons grew, it would become less likely that they would be used, "because as I see it, any such operation today is just another way of committing suicide."[3] The president's position put Hoegh in the same spot Peterson had been, leaving him unable to push for either evacuation or shelters. Evacuation had been so ridiculed that it had come to be seen as unfeasible, and Eisenhower had made it clear he would not support an expanded shelter system.

Still, Eisenhower felt the need to respond to Holifield's campaign to spend billions of dollars on civil defense. In April 1957, he appointed a committee to advise him on the need for an expanded shelter program. It was composed of more than a hundred scientific and technical experts, nuclear strategists, and top businesspeople, including Jerome Weisner, later the science advisor to President Kennedy, nuclear strategist Herman Kahn, and Paul Nitze, then head of policy planning in the State Department. Known as the Gaither Committee, under the chairmanship of H. Rowan Gaither—also chair of the boards of the Ford Foundation and of the Rand Corporation, a nuclear strategy think tank—the group deliberated for several months.

Nitze, essentially the chief author of the Gaither Report, was very good at devising alarmist rhetoric, having in 1950 drafted "NSC-68," which established as U.S. policy the great expansion of U.S. military force in order to block Soviet expansion anywhere in the world. Indeed, as Strobe Talbott has noted, much of Nitze's life "had been a kind of Paul Revere's ride to warn his government and his fellow citizens that they were in jeopardy from a Soviet attack." Born in 1907, Nitze, the son of a famous academic, married the heir to the Standard Oil fortune and worked twelve years as a successful investment banker before he entered government work. For forty years, he played a major role in the development of Cold War strategy, serving five presidents. Nitze did not accept that there was no defense against nuclear weapons. His chief concern was that the Soviets might use military superiority as a basis for nuclear blackmail.[4]

Influenced by Nitze, the 1957 Gaither Committee expanded its mission far beyond a study of civil defense, calling for a massive military buildup in order to match the perceived growing threat of Russia's missile capabilities. The report noted the vulnerability of the Strategic Air Command to destruction on the ground by a Soviet attack and recommended a great increase in American intercontinental missiles and in conventional military forces as well—all at a cost of $19 billion over the next five years.[5]

Although Eisenhower had appointed the committee solely to study the issues of civil defense, the Gaither Committee members gave considerably less attention to the discussion of "passive" defense. They agreed that civil defense would save lives, but more important, it would "augment our deterrent power in two ways: first, by discouraging the enemy from attempting an attack on what otherwise might seem to him a temptingly unprepared target; second, by reinforcing his belief in our readiness to use, if necessary, our strategic retaliatory power."[6] Civil defense would show the Russians that the United States was ready, if necessary, to use nuclear weapons and symbolize to the American public the urgency of the Soviet nuclear threat. The report called for a $25 billion program designed only for those outside the major target areas who were able to survive the blast and go to a fallout shelter, where they would spend two weeks. The political and nuclear strategists who devised the Gaither Report put together a system of civil defense primarily designed not to save lives, but to pretend to save lives and to show Americans that their government was concerned about their safety.

The Gaither Report was delivered to one of the largest National Security Council meetings to date.[7] More than forty people, including the Joint Chiefs of Staff, gathered to hear the president's response in November 1957. The committee issued a warning that by 1959 or 1960 the Russian nuclear force of ICBMs would be able to destroy the Strategic Air Command with a first-strike attack so powerful that it would prevent the United States from retaliating. The Gaither group advised the United States to prepare to fight a limited war and to vastly increase the defense budget. This was the beginning of the "missile gap" myth that the Democrats, and many conservative Republicans, used to discredit Eisenhower's lowered military budgets and to help win a Democratic victory in 1960.

Eisenhower was appalled by the recommendations to increase the defense budget by more than $40 billion a year. Only a few days earlier, in a meeting with some of the Gaither Committee members, he had pointed to their report and snorted: "But do you know how much a billion dollars is? Why, it's a stack of ten-dollar bills as high as the Washington Monument." He refused to follow up on their recommendations and insisted that the report remain top secret. It was quickly leaked to newspapers by some of the men who produced it. The "military industrial complex," about which Eisenhower would soon warn the nation, moved into high gear to frighten the public into approving increased spending for nuclear and traditional weapons. The military establishment, especially the air force, attacked the ceilings on defense spending, while corporations and groups of organized labor, contractors, scientists, and technicians involved in weapons manufacturing called for more funding. The major newspapers touted the horror of the supposed missile gap.

While Eisenhower did bend a bit in the last years of his term to call for a larger defense budget and several hundred more U.S. missiles, he remained firmly opposed to vastly increased expenditures on weapons or civil defense. Partly this was because he knew that the secret U-2 spy plane flights over Russia showed that the Soviets were not producing any significant number of ICBMs, despite the beliefs of many top members of the Gaither group. Just as important was his private fear that military-related expenditures would strengthen the tendency of the nation toward becoming a garrison state. He refused to give in to what seemed to be widespread and growing hysteria, at least among media sources. The president had the last word. After he thanked the Gaither Committee members for their efforts, he reminded them firmly that all-out nuclear war was not an option for him. "You can't have this kind of war," he said. "There just aren't enough bulldozers to scrape the bodies off the streets."[8] Eisenhower's opposition to the calls for large increases in weapons and civil defense in 1957 saved billions of dollars and perhaps even a war. His view of civil defense was central to his larger understanding of the thermonuclear revolution.

•   •   •

Mass consciousness of the possibility of human extinction was enormously strengthened by the controversy over civil defense addressed by Eisenhower. By 1957, many American scientists, intellectuals, and activists shared the president's realization of the power of hydrogen weapons. That year marks the major turning point, as the antinuclear movement exploded, emerging in force on several levels, among a number of groups, and in several countries.

Norman Cousins, liberal editor of the *Saturday Review of Literature*, was intent on teaching the public about the suicidal result of nuclear war. In the summer of 1956, he had met with the St. Louis women, lay advisors, and scientists who would later form the Committee for Nuclear Information (CNI), and learned from them the growing danger of strontium-90 fallout. Cousins also helped to write some of the widely discussed calls for the end of testing featured in Adlai Stevenson's 1956 presidential campaign. In January 1957, Cousins traveled to Africa to visit Albert Schweitzer, the famed humanitarian, just voted by a Gallup poll as the fourth most admired man in the world. Cousins convinced Schweitzer to speak out for peace. In April 1957, Schweitzer arranged for his "Declaration of Conscience" to be read over Radio Oslo and then to be transmitted in various languages around the world. His call for an end to the terror of nuclear testing and of nuclear war had a major impact upon world opinion, from India to Italy, from West Germany to Norway and Japan, and was endorsed by the pope. Despite the fact that no American radio station broadcast Schweitzer's appeal and most American newspapers refused to discuss it, another Gallup poll at the end of 1958 reported that Americans now judged Schweitzer not as the fourth, but as the third most popular man in the world.[9]

At this time, the eminent American scientist Linus Pauling, recipient of the 1954 Nobel Prize in chemistry, was even more successful than Schweitzer in teaching Americans the truths about fallout, which the AEC leadership was attempting to cover up. By 1956, Pauling was spending half of his time studying and speaking about nuclear weapons and fallout. Pauling's crusade also began with the activist women and physicists in St. Louis, where Barry Commoner, Edward Condon, and others convinced him in 1957 to organize scientists to demand an international agreement to stop nuclear testing. In less than a month, Pauling released his "Appeal by American Scientists," signed by more than 2,000 persons, to the press and to Eisenhower. This outcry against nuclear weapons by important scientists, including several Nobel Prize winners, was a dramatic challenge to government nuclear policy, especially after Pauling announced on an ABC television program that, in the next twenty generations, 200,000 children would suffer from mental and physical defects due to fallout, and 1 million people would lose five to ten years of their lives. Pauling presented to the secretary general of the United Nations a list of more than 11,000 scientists from forty-three nations who had endorsed the American antitesting petition. They included thirty-seven Nobel Laureates, and high percentages of members of the U.S. National Academy of Scientists, the Fellows of the Royal Society of London, and the Soviet Academy of Scientists.

For his courageous and effective crusade against nuclear testing, Pauling was publicly and privately denounced by several leading American government figures, including Lewis Strauss and J. Edgar Hoover, head of the FBI. Pauling was portrayed as the dupe of a communist conspiracy and perhaps even a communist sympathizer himself. After 1958, he received no federal funds for research for twenty years. The FBI continued to track him for years to come, although they never found any evidence of his alleged communist connections.[10]

The AEC was also feeling pressure from public concern about nuclear war. In 1957, the AEC received so much mail expressing fear of nuclear testing that it had to develop a new form letter to reply to the inquiries. That summer, Nevil Shute's novel *On the Beach*, a story of how fallout from a nuclear war ended life on earth, sold 100,000 copies in six weeks, and approximately 8 million people read it in serialized versions in their newspapers within three months. When the movie version of the novel became a colossal hit, ways to lessen its public appeal were discussed at a Cabinet meeting, along with an AEC briefing on what to say and not to say when questioned about the film. The AEC urged Cabinet members to make clear to the press that radiation effects only lasted a few days, that civil defense procedures could reduce the number of casualties after nuclear attack to about 3 percent of the population, and that the film lent itself to extreme pacifist and "Ban the Bomb propaganda."[11]

In St. Louis, the fight against nuclearism took off. In 1957, a faculty speakers' bureau at Washington University informed local citizens about the deadly power of nuclear war and radioactive fallout. Professors Barry Commoner, Alexander Pond, Walter Bauer, and John Fowler organized widespread support for the Pauling petition, the speakers' outreach program, and the warnings against strontium-90. In early 1958, the WU faculty and St. Louis activist women officially joined forces in the formation of the Committee for Nuclear Information. After a major debate, the founders approved Commoner's recommendation that the group not take a partisan position, but rather concentrate its efforts on providing extensive information on nuclear matters to the public, in order to elicit free and open discussion. As the anthropologist Margaret Mead noted, the CNI refutation of government propaganda was "setting a pattern for the proper relationship between citizen responsibility ... and decision making" and was counteracting the excessive governmental secrecy which so threatened democratic procedures.[12]

In 1957, the American peace movement experienced a major reorganization and revival. Much of the energy came from Lawrence Scott, an ordained Baptist minister and civil rights activist, who had just resigned from his job as peace education director of the Chicago branch of the American Friends Service Committee. Scott had encountered criticism from AFSC officials and supporters for his leadership of the civil defense protest in Chicago during Operation Alert 1955. He expressed his disillusionment with "middle class pacifists . . . [who] have alienated themselves from any non-violent movement possibilities of a truly revolutionary character which would furnish the dynamic spark in [this] revolutionary era."[13] Scott brought together leaders of the radical, liberal, and traditionalist pacifist camps for a historic meeting in Philadelphia in 1957. Because these groups could not agree on a common strategy, a decision was made to split into three units. Each would employ different tactics, but they would be united in their opposition to bomb testing and the Cold War preparation for nuclear war. One group, the liberal pacifists, soon became the National Committee for a Sane Nuclear Policy (SANE). The overwhelming response to SANE's call for members, placed in a *New York Times* ad in November, made it a powerful national organization within weeks. By the summer of 1958, it had 130 chapters and more than 25,000 members. The second group, the radical pacifists, were joined by a new direct-action group, Non-Violent Action against Nuclear Weapons (NVAANW), that would soon become the Committee for Non-Violent Action (CNVA). The more cautious third group, a coalition of older peace organizations, including the Women's International League for Peace and Freedom (WILPF), pledged to focus on opposition to nuclear bomb testing.[14]

• • •

In preparation for the next clash with militant pacifists, government preplanning for Operation Alert 1957 was even more detailed than in previous years, with more sophisticated objectives and a greatly lengthened timetable. A full six weeks before the drill in mid-July were devoted to federal planning and instituting "partial activation of relocation sites." Perhaps it was this concentration on saving the elite that led Eisenhower to interrupt the July 19 briefing on Operation Alert to note his concern about a letter to the editor he had seen. It carried the complaint of an ordinary citizen with regard to the "fat cats" being rushed out of Washington while the ordinary citizens stayed behind. The president saw a worrisome "morale factor in all of this."[15] The debriefing report noted that the First Lady joined the president in "his mountain hideaway" to which he had been evacuated by helicopter during the 1957 drill.

The FCDA newsletter on women's activities focused on the action of those females who supported the 1957 Operation Alert. Participants in the Northeast region were said to have come from women's clubs, churches, and reserve officers' women's auxiliary leagues to provide volunteer service during the drill. These women served as "stenographers, typists and file and logging clerks." Meanwhile in Jacksonville, Florida, more than a hundred wealthy female civil defense supporters boarded their own boats to escape from the simulated holocaust on shore, and "practically every boat carried a woman as co-pilot."[16]

In May, Scott went west to prepare for NVAANW's first direct action: a civil disobedience demonstration at a Nevada bomb-testing site. Because A. J. Muste, Bayard Rustin, and several other civil defense protesters were in Nevada, the July 12, 1957, demonstration in New York City in defiance of Operation Alert was sponsored solely by the Catholic Workers. This time, the court handed down the heaviest sentences yet imposed. "You are a bunch of heartless individuals who breathe contempt of the law," the judge told the protesters.[17] Each of the twelve demonstrators received thirty days. Among them were twenty-five-year-old Richard Moses, an Eastern Airlines reservation clerk, and his twenty-two-year-old wife, Joan. Of the dozen, four were women—called "the air raid ladies" by the other female prisoners. In addition to Joan Moses were Judith Malina, a young actress, and Deanne Mower, a shy, nearly blind ex-teacher who had joined the Catholic Workers. Sixty-one-year-old Dorothy Day was arrested for the third time in as many years, and like the others, she was stripped, then bloodied by a rough vaginal search, supposedly performed in order to find hidden weapons or drugs. The Catholic Workers and the WRL conducted daily picketing of the Women's House of Detention until the civil defense protesters were released in August.[18]

The American antinuclear protests of this period were greatly strengthened by similar resistance to nuclear weapons and testing that erupted in Great Britain at this time. In 1957, 2,000 women wearing black sashes marched in torrential rain through central London to protest continued British nuclear testing. The Campaign for Nuclear Disarmament (CND) was formed in early 1958 in response to the first British H-bomb tests. So widely publicized and influential was the action of CND that its disarmament symbol—a broken cross within a circle—quickly became known to millions throughout the world as the international peace symbol.

CND's 1958 Easter march, from London to Aldermasten, the British nuclear weapons facility, received worldwide publicity as 5,800 well-dressed citizens marched for four days over fifty-two miles in pouring rain, the last mile in complete silence. Bayard Rustin, who was in England at that time, was asked to speak to the assembled crowd. He was so impressed by the event that it became a chief inspiration for his organization of the 1963 Civil Rights March on Washington. The Aldermasten march grew to 20,000 in 1959 and swelled to 100,000 in 1960. The growing popular militancy against nuclear weapons and tests in Britain was thoroughly known and studied by the rising antinuclear movement in the United States. American pacifists in the WRL, CW, CNVA, and SANE kept in close contact and frequently exchanged information with British activists, the connections increasing the determination of antinuclear protesters on both sides of the Atlantic.[19]

In the United States, the federal mobilization training process for Operation Alert continued in 1958 in even more organized fashion. The primary purpose of the drill was intended to be "examining the adequacy of Federal Guidance and Mobilization to meet the attack situation." Special attention and detailed information were given to those entering the newly built elite shelter at High Point in Mt. Weather, Virginia. Those evacuated to High Point were assured that they would have barber, beautician, and tailoring services. The ladies—that is, the secretarial and clerical help—were told to wear low-heeled shoes. Maids were provided at High Point but all had to make their own beds. The families of those sent to elite shelters were only to be told that their relatives were at "work at a field unit."[20]

In the summer of 1958, Eisenhower closed down the FCDA and placed the small civil defense program that survived into the new Office of Civilian and Defense Mobilization (OCDM), under presidential control and with the malleable Leo Hoegh as director. Holifield's crusade was once again defeated. His latest committee announced in June 1958 that "civil defense is in so low a state that nothing could make it worse and something [almost anything] could make it better."[21] What Eisenhower did endorse was known as the National Shelter Policy, created in late 1958. This was in reality no change at all. The policy concentrated on the provision of public information about how to construct shelters to protect against fallout.

Operation Alert 1958 marked the nadir of the civil defense protest movement, because so many CNVA and WRL direct-actionist members were then involved in support of another civil disobedience test, the voyage of the now-famed *Golden Rule*, a boat staffed by four pacifists who attempted to sail into the U.S. nuclear testing zone in the Pacific in early May. After the wide publicity given to the arrest and imprisonment of the *Golden Rule*'s crew, an American anthropologist and former AEC employee, Earle Reynolds, along with his wife, Barbara, and their two children suddenly decided to complete the *Golden Rule* mission by sailing their boat, the *Phoenix*, into the Pacific nuclear testing zone on July 1. Barbara and Earle Reynolds's arrest and subsequent imprisonment set off a huge support movement for the crews of both boats by thousands of Americans. Most of the protesters had never been in a demonstration before, and few were pacifists. In San Francisco, 432 people petitioned the U.S. attorney to arrest them for being guilty of "conspiring" with the boat crews. Long picket lines around federal buildings and AEC offices formed in large cities across the nation. While out on bail, Earle Reynolds spoke on twenty-one radio and eight television programs and to some 10,000 people in live audiences at high schools, colleges, and churches throughout the country. Initially, the crew of the *Golden Rule* had hoped their "effort and sacrifice" would "say to others: Speak Now." Their call was heard, eventually, by millions.[22]

Because the CNVA and the WRL were so heavily involved that summer in the events following the *Golden Rule* protest, it was left to Dorothy Day and only eleven other protesters to refuse to take cover during the 1958 Operation Alert. A black judge, Kenneth Phipps, was more sympathetic to their cause than previous judges had been. He gave most of the protesters suspended sentences. Five Catholic Workers, including Dorothy Day, served ten days in jail. After her fourth arrest for defying Operation Alert, Day was deeply discouraged, fearful that her protest had so little impact upon public opinion or government policy. She was unaware that her years of lonely defiance of the civil defense drills would reap a massive return during the next year.

Strengthening that continuing revolt, the St. Louis citizens' coalition achieved two more breakthroughs in educating Americans about nuclear danger—one in a story format read by millions and the other in the famed Baby Tooth Project. The first effort was created indirectly by Holifield's 1959 government hearings, which had provided expert testimony about the destructive impact of thermonuclear war. Using the government's own data, the CNI produced a 1959 article-length piece of fiction entitled "Nuclear War in St. Louis: One Year Later." As described, the war lasted one day, during which 7,000 megatons hit the United States. St. Louis was nailed by two bombs with a combined 18 megatons of destructive power, creating a crater one mile wide. A firestorm finished life in the city, and spontaneous fires erupted thirty miles away. More than a half million in the St. Louis area died the first day. The 200,000 survivors from the St. Louis area were taken to South Dakota, since no one could eat the crops in Missouri for at least a century. In South Dakota, the survivors endured cancer, starvation, blindness, and infections. Many simply went insane, no longer able to endure the daily struggle.

The St. Louis article was an enormously powerful document, reprinted in dozens of magazines and newspapers, including the *Saturday Evening Post*.[23] By the early 1970s, 45,000 copies had been distributed worldwide, including to American government and military personnel. "Nuclear War in St. Louis:

One Year Later," alongside the movie *On the Beach*, proved to be one of the most intellectually and emotionally devastating, yet effective, ways that large numbers of people were informed about the unavoidable consequences of a nuclear exchange.

CNI's second major effort was its Baby Tooth Survey. Based on its appeal to mothers nationwide, CNI eventually collected more than 65,000 baby teeth, categorized by each child's age and geographic location, which were mailed in by worried mothers from across the nation. Each tooth was independently tested by nongovernment experts—mainly those at the Washington University dental school and local dentists—for the presence of strontium-90, at no cost to the parents.[24] The teeth were sorted and cataloged by hundreds of local women, including volunteers from the Council of Catholic Women, the Council of Jewish Women, and the Junior League, librarians, members of the women's auxiliary of the St. Louis Dental Society, and many other individuals and groups. Tens of thousands of grant dollars were provided by several foundations. Community participation in the project was overwhelming. Collection was assisted by the county and city public school systems. Even stroke patients at the local hospital exercised their muscles by printing collection envelopes. Similar, if not quite as dramatic, cooperative coalitions formed in many other cities, including New York, Boston, Philadelphia, Montreal, Toronto, and San Juan.

The data gathered in the survey clearly showed that strontium-90 in American children's teeth was rapidly increasing, much of it deposited by Soviet tests. If above-ground testing continued, strontium-90 would reach dangerously high levels within a relatively few years. Even before the popular and respected magazine *Consumer Reports* published these and its own results of the study of strontium-90 in 1961 and 1962, the Baby Tooth Survey had made news worldwide. Demonstrating the effectiveness of CNI's threat to advocates of bomb testing, Edward Teller accused the organization of being led by communists in 1958.

* * *

The expanding protest against Operation Alert in New York City was reflected in the new publicity it received from the *Village Voice* in the spring of 1959. A picture of David McReynolds of the WRL appeared on the front page a week before the drill with the notice "This Man Will Commit a 'Crime' on Monday Morning." One of the first advocates of gay rights in the period, McReynolds had worked under civil rights leader Ella Baker, joined the staff of the new radical journal *Liberation* in 1957, and become field secretary of the WRL in 1960. McReynolds called for volunteers to join him in defiance of the April 17, 1959, national air raid drill. That year, resistance also spread to Jamaica, Queens, and

Haverstraw, New York, although the protesters there were not arrested. Dorothy Day and eighteen other protesters in New York City were taken to jail. First offenders received suspended sentences, and Day again served ten days.

One of the most significant new developments of the 1959 civil defense protest was the entry into the fray of two young mothers, Mary Sharmat and Janice Smith. On April 17, these two women intentionally left their homes with their children to break the law. They expected to be arrested for refusing to obey Operation Alert requirements to take cover for fifteen minutes. The civil defense drill seemed ridiculous and even obscene to Sharmat and Smith, who knew that in the event a nuclear bomb hit their city, most of New York City would be pulverized. Twenty-four-year-old Sharmat was the daughter of a Republican naval officer killed in World War II and the granddaughter of Hilda Brungot, an outspoken feminist who served many years in the New Hampshire legislature. Twenty-one-year-old Smith was the granddaughter of Samuel Aaron, the founder of the Bakers' Union.

Before setting out to break the law, Mary Sharmat had taken money from her savings account to be used for bail. With her six-month-old son, Jimmy, snug in his stroller, she sat down on a bench by the civil defense truck at the center island of Broadway and 86th Street:

> I pushed Jimmy's stroller back and forth to keep him happy and gritted my teeth in determination not to become a coward and return home. . . . The sirens started blowing. I sat. . . . then a man came to me and Jimmy. He demanded that I take shelter. I said, "I cannot take shelter. I do not believe in this." He said, "You are nuts." . . . Another Civil Defense man came over to argue sense to me and he screamed over the sirens and I just kept repeating, "This is wrong, I refuse to take cover." He was terrified of me and I of him. . . . I gave Jimmy his bottle but nothing would stop his crying. Then a policeman got out of his car. He walked over and said, "Lady, we are going to give you a ticket." I said, "Give me a ticket." That was the least of my worries. He threw up his hands and got back into his car. Both he and the other policeman waved and smiled at me. The Civil Defense men were furious. By this time . . . there must have been several hundred people lining the streets all watching the incident. . . . The men from the local stock exchange office left the stock tapes and came out from Loew-Neuberger. This is most unusual. The Civil Defense men ran and took cover. Jimmy cried and I sat. The "all clear" signal sounded. Commerce commenced and people continued their interrupted shopping. I picked up a pair of shoes at the repair shop and ran a few other errands and then went home. My husband was surprised to see us. He had anticipated a call from the jail. He went up to the bank and returned the bail money to our

savings account. I unpacked the overnight case and put back the extra diapers and baby foods. Jimmy fell asleep in his crib.[25]

That same morning, Janice Smith's husband told her he had heard of a group of Catholics who were to seek arrest in City Hall Park. When she arrived at the park, she heard the sirens wail and sat with her small children on one of the park benches. At the far end of the park, she could see police officers and television camera crews surrounding a small group of protesters. Spotting Smith and her children, the reporters surged over to her park bench. "I refuse to act like a desert rat and run," she told the police. "All this drill does is frighten children and birds. I will not raise my children to go underground." Smith and her children were arrested and forced into a police car, where she encountered sixty-two-year-old Dorothy Day, of whom Smith had never heard. On their way to the police station, Day gave twenty-one-year-old Smith "a great hug and kiss" of approval, as Smith remembers. At the police station, Smith struggled to corral her gleeful four- and two-year-old children, while she listened to the police lecture her about obeying the law. The police, happy to be rid of the boisterous children, eventually released Smith without charges.[26]

The embrace in the police car between Dorothy Day and Janice Smith on April 15, 1959, is a powerful historical symbol. It represents the bridge between the small band of radical pacifists who had kept civil defense protest alive in the 1950s and the hundreds, and finally, thousands, of civil defense protesters who would be energized by Smith's and Sharmat's brilliant new organizing tactics, which focused on angry parents. During the next year, prior to the 1960 Operation Alert drill, the leadership of civil defense protest expanded from the older group of radical pacifists to include young women, who relied on the image of enraged motherhood to produce the political counterritual that won public sympathy for their cause.

The day after Smith's arrest, Sharmat read about it in the New York papers and set out to call every Smith in the New York City phone book until she found her. Delighted to make contact, the two young women could hardly stop talking. If there were two women who independently decided to defy the drill, they reasoned, perhaps there were three or even four more in the New York area. Perhaps others had defied what they believed to be a bad law." Of course, the two women knew that most New Yorkers had simply continued about their business and ignored the drill. Sharmat and Smith pledged to devote one hour a day on the telephone during the next year to finding eight mothers who would refuse as a group to take cover during the 1960 Operation Alert. Then, they met Pat McMahon at the playground where Sharmat often took Jimmy. McMahon had four children, was a follower of Gandhi, and belonged to the WRL. Together, the three women located two other mothers in the Bronx who had refused to take shelter. One of them, Adrianne Winograd, took over recruitment efforts on the Central Park playgrounds.

In six months, they were fifty women—and growing. They began a vigorous public relations campaign and, with the encouragement and help of the older group of radical pacifists, moved to strengthen the Civil Defense Protest Committee, which worked out of the office of the WRL. Most of the young women recruited had full-time jobs as wives and mothers, but they gave all of their spare time to preparation for the big day—the next Operation Alert to be held on May 3, 1960. The women gathered by Smith and Sharmat strengthened the new direction of civil defense protest. Thinking of themselves as nonpolitical in comparison to the old pros whom they met at the WRL, the young women emphasized and strengthened a publicity strategy that would appeal to a wide group of citizens unwilling to seek arrest but able to come to the park before the 1960 drill and participate in other ways. Some would merely pass out literature to the people who had taken shelter underground. Others would remain in the park until the police told them to take cover in the designated shelters. A third group, expected to be much smaller, would remain and risk arrest. The appeal would thus be addressed to concerned but nonradical persons who were not politically active and especially to young mothers, whose main concern was protecting their children from nuclear catastrophe.

A few of the old pros were at first unenthusiastic about the wisdom of a strategy that encouraged persons to come to the park and then take cover if they chose not to defy police orders. They feared that this might threaten the creation of a militant band of purists engaged in nonviolent confrontation with authority. A second group of experienced organizers interested in joining the civil defense protest, called the "politicos" by Sharmat and Smith, had recently left the Communist party after Premier Nikita Khrushchev's revelation of Stalin's crimes. The politicos too had some doubts about the validity of the tactic of appealing to the political center. During two lengthy meetings of the CDPC, Sharmat and Smith persuaded the old pros and politicos to give a place in the movement to all brands of political beliefs. According to Sharmat, at first only Day, Rustin, McReynolds, and

FIGURE 3.1. Civil defense protest, New York City, 1960.

Photo by Charles Solin, Committee for Nonviolent Action, Swarthmore College Peace Collection.

FIGURE 3.2. Civil defense
protest, New York City,
1960.

*Photo by Charles Solin,
Committee for Nonviolent
Action, Swarthmore College
Peace Collection.*

Muste strongly supported the young women. But none of the radical pacifists or
ex-members of the Old Left took a firm stand against the young mothers—especially since the women had already energetically assumed major responsibility
for organizing protests at the next annual drill, to be held on May 3, 1960.[27]

The women found eager recruits in the New York metropolitan branch of
WILPF and collected several thousand dollars in small contributions. Probably
unknown to the national office of WILPF, this sudden revival of the chapter was
partly the result of the entry into Metro of several energetic and organization-
ally talented women who had recently left the Communist party. One member
of WILPF, Bess Cameron, secretly visited the prominent ex-Communist Lillian
Gates, the wife of John Gates, once the editor of the *Daily Worker*. Lillian Gates
quietly arranged for several experienced organizers to join the Metro chapter.
As Cameron remembered, "We got a number of very, very, good people" who
knew "how to plan publicity, write press releases and do all kinds of activities."
Within a few months, the Metro branch was turning out hundreds of leaflets
and pamphlets, sponsoring well-attended workshops on the danger of nuclear
war, and allying itself with other pacifist groups in the area. Two weeks before
the Operation Alert 1960 drill, Sharmat and Smith's group, assisted by the Metro
chapter, had collected pledges to join the protest from almost 300 mothers-
with-children volunteers. Mary Sharmat was an aspiring actress with a sure

sense of costume and dramatic effect. She instructed the women volunteers to be polite to the police and to dress carefully for the protest in their best dress and hose, so no one could suspect them of being "beatniks."[28]

In preparation for May 3, the women passed out thousands of leaflets at subway exits, recruited on playgrounds and at PTA meetings, and distributed material with supportive quotes from mainstream political leaders, famous scientists, notable writers and artists, and religious figures. Their most widely distributed flyer quoted Democratic governor Robert Meyner of New Jersey, who called civil defense "a cruel deception on the American people," and President Eisenhower, who had said: "I think people want peace so much that one of these days governments had better get out of their way and let them have it." The leaflet stressed that the only purpose of civil defense was "to frighten children and to fool the public into thinking there is protection against an H-bomb." Senator Stephen Young warned that "civil defense today is a myth. . . . In the nuclear age there can be no realistic civil defense programs. We must devote ourselves to the utmost to finding a peaceful solution to the world's problems." The literature reassured readers that the protesters were people without common religious or political opinions, representing only themselves, united by only one belief: "PEACE is the only defense against nuclear war." The material spelled out the three forms of protest in which the reader might choose to participate on the day of the drill. If prospective protesters did not want to come to the park, they could write supportive letters to government officials. Just in case anyone had missed the point, the leaflet reassured the hesitant that peaceful dissent was an "American tradition."[29]

Solicited by the Civil Defense Protest Committee, prominent New Yorkers and celebrities like Kay Boyle, Nat Hentoff, Kenneth Clark, Paul Goodman, Dwight McDonald, and Norman Mailer promised to join the 1960 civil disobedience action. Kay Boyle explained that "war is not possible if we all say 'No.'" Mailer promised to sign autographs in the park and vowed he would court arrest because he believed that "politics is like sex. You have to go all the way."[30]

The women's most successful innovation was their reliance on the image of protective motherhood to win public notice and support. They made detailed plans to surround themselves with children and toys during the Operation Alert protest, arranging for trucks to bring the heaviest items to the park before the drill began. Plans were made for single male activists to hold babies too so they could practice civil disobedience alongside the young mothers. All guessed correctly that the police would not want to take parents, complete with children, playpens, trikes, bikes, and assorted childhood paraphernalia, into custody.

On May 3, 1960, President Eisenhower reviewed the troops in Georgia and then broadcast a warning that "civil defense is no joke." For this year's drill, baseball players were forced to leave the field in Yankee Stadium; 2,000 fans from the bleachers huddled under the stands. The New York Stock Exchange floor was cleared; airplanes were grounded; bus traffic was halted; and hundreds of citizens were herded into Grand Central Station and other points downtown. Newspaper photographs showed eerie, deserted streets. All seemed quiet, except at City Hall Park.

The crowd began to gather around noon. More than 1,000 people, about two-thirds women, including about 500 well-groomed mothers and many children, completely filled the small park when the sirens wailed at 2:15 p.m. Sharmat, wearing a large white hat trimmed in lace, described the scene:

> I was not alone, Janice [Smith] was not alone, the two mothers from the Grand Concourse in the Bronx were not alone. Over five hundred friends gathered at City Hall Park. Many men came down. Our skirts gave them courage. We loaned out extra babies to bachelors who had the misfortune to be childless. Dozens of children played in an area designated "Stay Off the Grass." Some of the students brought their musical instruments and softly played folk songs such as "We Shall Overcome" and "We Shall Not be Moved." The sirens sounded. We stood. Mothers with children, fathers with mutual deep concerns, bachelors who had hopes and a borrowed baby, maiden aunts who had no children but were taking care of the rest of us. We stood. There was dead silence through the park.[31]

When the sirens sounded, about 500 people stood firm, refusing to move. A group approximately the same size crossed Broadway when the police ordered them to take cover and stood on the sidewalk but did not take shelter. Hundreds of spectators left the shelters to watch. Meanwhile, the civil defense officer in charge stood on a park bench, waved his arms over the crowd, and pronounced them all under arrest. The crowd responded with cheers and applause. The police made twenty-six token arrests, deliberately singling out men—and women in slacks. The crowd surged up with more cheering and clapping for the accused. Day and Ammon Hennacy, who had never missed a civil defense protest, were not arrested because they were surrounded by protective admirers. Nor were there arrests of any members of the CDPC, all wearing special armbands, nor of any of the celebrities, nor of any of the jubilant band of old pros. Led by the protest organizers, the audience sang "Gandhi is our leader. / We shall not be moved," as well as "America the Beautiful," "Battle Hymn of the Republic," and for a finale, "The Star-Spangled Banner." When the all-clear sounded, hundreds more moved back into the park, to shake hands and to join Hennacy in the singing of "John Brown's Body" in joyful celebration of what they had accomplished. As David McReynolds exulted in the park that day: "This law is dead!"

After the arrests, there was a preplanned march to the police station to urge the freeing of the accused. Fifteen men and eleven women were sentenced to five days in jail. The judge accused them of "disservice to their country" because their arrests were used by communists to illustrate the restrictions on free speech in the United States. He was met with laughter from the uproarious crowd of supporters in the courtroom—some of whom one reporter judged to look suspiciously like "beatniks" with their beards, toreador pants, and flutes. For the next five days, until the protesters were released, a reported 3,000 people picketed outside the Women's House of Detention. The newspapers featured pictures of the picket lines showing finely dressed women wearing white gloves and hats and marching with baby carriages and strollers. One woman pushed her shopping cart around the line before continuing on to the market.[32]

In 1960, hundreds of New York City college and high school students joined the protest against Operation Alert, refusing to take cover during the bomb drill. Smith took the lead in contacting student leaders, who organized their peers. Three hundred City College students, as well as student groups at New York University, Barnard College, Queens College, Hunter College, and Columbia University, refused to take cover. One hundred and fifty Brooklyn College students refused to take cover, and fifty-nine were suspended for four days for their action. About 500 New York high school students protested, another sign of the revival of campus activism. A few arrests were made in nearby New Jersey and in Rockland County.[33]

Any lingering doubts that the old pros might have harbored about the entry of nonpacifists into the peace movement disappeared. Radical Jim Peck judged the 1960 demonstration to be "the biggest civil disobedience peace action [ever] to take place in the United States . . . as phenomenal as the southern sit-ins." Another first was the large number of supportive pieces in the mainstream press, including a denunciation of civil defense in the popular men's magazine *Esquire*. In a letter of reassurance to a concerned CNVA leader, A. J. Muste wrote that radical pacifists could not shape a mass peace movement if they were

> arbitrary and schematic and imply that there can be no effective or justifiable activity except that which calls for immediate complete unilateral disarmament. . . . Undermining civil defense is no small part of understanding the deterrence-mechanism. Listen to the brain trusters of the Rand Corporation and you will realize that they understand this.

McReynolds became a publicist for the tactic of "building a revolution by degrees." The demonstration convinced him that "'discipline' often comes through action and not through long training sessions. . . . It is possible for the demonstrations to be truly a radical protest and yet also be a mass protest. . . . Let us find ways of involving people in our action projects *to whatever degree they are able*, rather than demanding that they come all the way with us or not take part at all."[34]

In the next year, protest against civil defense drills in the New York City schools, supported by the CDPC and scores of women, also became an important extension of the organized opposition to Operation Alert. After the 1960 protest, Mary Sharmat noted: "Civil defense at last became an issue. It was no longer ignored as an unimportant nothing to put up with because it's easier. . . . Voters back home at the polls began to care." *New York Post* columnist Murray Kempton summed it up: "We seem to be approaching a condition of sanity where within a year or so there'll be more people defying than complying with the Civil Defense drill." The Civil Defense Protest Committee at once began to organize for the next federal air raid drill, determined to create an even larger opposition to the Operation Alert of 1961, with Muste, McReynolds, Rustin, Sharmat, and Smith named in September 1960 to plan and lead the next campaign.[35]

●   ●   ●

When Eisenhower became president in 1953, the United States held about 1,200 nuclear warheads. Eight years later, there were more than 30,000. Yet he had successfully resisted the call for yet more weapons and for the creation of an even larger civil defense program. Eisenhower's farewell address has long been remembered for its warnings about the "military-industrial complex," the possible militarization of American society, and the growth of a garrison state. But he had failed to achieve a ban on testing.

Eisenhower understood that a test ban, although highly desirable, should not be sought as a kind of magic solution. He worked to ensure that government officials understood the new reality of American society. His period in office was, he knew, the first moment of a revolutionary change in human development—the creation of weapons that made possible the mass destruction of human societies. John McCone, the director of the CIA, long remembered a meeting with Eisenhower in early 1960, when he found the president so "entirely preoccupied with the horror of nuclear war" that he could not discuss any other subject. At that moment, Ike was focused only on "freeing the people of the world from the dreadful fear that now hangs over them."[36] Eisenhower was reasonably optimistic that the test ban would be a prominent issue for discussion when he and Khrushchev met at the Paris summit talks planned for May 1960. But Khrushchev called it off when an American U-2 spy plane was

FIGURE 3.3. Fallout shelter. This simple basement construction was one of many fallout shelter designs suggested by federal authorities as a way to save your family from nuclear destruction. *National Archives.*

shot down over Russia just weeks before the summit was scheduled to begin. Eisenhower's failure to reach a test ban agreement remained one of his greatest unrealized hopes.

In his final days as president, at a National Security Council meeting three days before Christmas 1960, Ike listened to a discussion about civil defense among a group that included the secretary of state, secretary of defense, attorney general, chair of the Joint Chiefs of Staff, and director of the Central Intelligence Agency. These top officials seriously considered at length such questions as the value of fallout shelters and the proper goods to be stockpiled for use after nuclear attack. Near the end of the meeting, Eisenhower again questioned the validity of making any Oz-like plans about the post-attack economy. He reminded the group that these problems had no real solutions. No one knew in what condition a nuclear attack would leave the country, he said. "Perhaps after a nuclear attack we will all be nomads." He also doubted that a stockpile of goods of any kind, or any transportation to carry it anywhere, would survive a nuclear war. He concluded: "War no longer has any logic whatsoever."[37]

Until his replacement by John Kennedy in 1961, Eisenhower continued to resist the idea that civil defense must be treated as a serious component of nuclear strategy. Congress also had consistently proven its own skepticism and hostility regarding even a barely functioning civil defense, let alone allocating billions for a vast new shelter system. The OCDM request for 1959 was $13.1 mil-lion for shelters; Congress granted $2.5 million. In fiscal year 1960, the request for shelters was a little over $11 million; Congress approved only $5.3 million. Representative Albert Thomas from Texas again led the attack, accusing civil defense officials of devising useless statistics, while Senator Stephen Young de-nounced civil defense in the thermonuclear age as "about as useful as flintlock muskets, tallow dips, mustache cups, or Civil War cannon balls." Young also blasted the civil defense bureaucracy as an "utterly useless organization with many thousands of men and women feeding at the public trough, but rendering no useful service." In his committee and hearings activities in 1959 and 1960, Congressman Holifield again failed to convince the public to accept the cost of building and equipping large public shelters.[38]

Although OCDM director Hoegh announced in 1960 that many enthusias-tic citizens were building shelters, Congressman Holifield quickly exposed that falsehood. His subcommittee announced in March 1960 that, to date, based on "the roughest kind of estimates and guesses" collected from the civil defense organizations in thirty-five states and sixty-six cities, there were only about 1,500 fallout shelters in the country and 356 shelters in cities. The states reported a mere fourteen public buildings modified to provide shelter, and cities reported only nine buildings modified, with two more planned. All of the states and cities reported a combined total of five public school buildings modified. As Holifield pointed out, "civil defense throughout the country as a whole is in a deplorable state."[39] Indeed, at this point, American civil defense had never been anything more than a paper endeavor and a propaganda failure.

The next administration would call for an end to the presumed missile gap between the United States and the Soviet Union. John F. Kennedy would begin the first great civil defense hype of the early 1960s. But the new emphasis on civil defense would quickly create another powerful wave of peace activism. Under Kennedy, government civil defense propaganda reached a new peak, as did the national protest against it.

FOUR

Kennedy's Civil Defense Gap, 1960–1964

President John F. Kennedy's short term in office is remembered in part for his call for a major new commitment to civil defense. In the summer of 1961 he asked for, and quickly received, a large congressional appropriation that amounted to almost 60 percent of the total expenditure for civil defense over the previous decade. Yet the Kennedy civil defense program was short-lived. Announced in May 1961, it was dead by December. Forsaken by Kennedy in late November at the fervent urging of his staff and advisors, the civil defense program was denounced by thousands of intellectuals, scientists, and peace activists and by many mainstream newspapers and journals. In early 1962, Congress stalled approval of further funds, effectively erasing the expanded civil defense program it had supported only months before. By the fall 1962 election, public rejection of Kennedy's drive for civil defense was so pronounced that a spate of anti–civil defense peace candidates won wide support and even defeated regular Democratic candidates in several areas of the country.[1]

Kennedy's warnings of possible nuclear destruction did not reflect his own fears, as some have interpreted his actions. His loud call for civil defense was chiefly in response to the bluster and threat of Nelson A. Rockefeller and, to a lesser degree, Nikita Khrushchev. Public dissent very quickly drowned out the voices of those few who spoke in favor of civil defense. Kennedy shut the whole program down within six months, not because of his concern over the panic of a terrified public seeking protection against nuclear attack, as is often argued. He closed it down because he feared the negative effects upon his nuclear policy created by the pronounced rejection of civil defense by a skeptical and angry public, an opinion also held by many of his senior staff members.

Much has been written about the presumed public fear and hysteria of the early Kennedy years, which supposedly led to a "bomb shelter craze" as Americans scrambled to build underground retreats for their families. However, the public rejection of civil defense propaganda has not been well understood or reported. This is partly because media attention centered on other important issues of this time: the civil rights movement, the Cuban crisis, the presidential assassination. Many later commentators have focused on the pro–civil defense content of *Time* and *Life* magazine articles that appeared in September and October 1961. The readings present a deeply conservative response to the Soviet "threat" and show evidence of radical survivalist attitudes on the part of a few. The insanely wild presentations are indeed immensely quotable. Yet the inaccurate predictions presented in these widely read pieces were recognized at once by millions of Americans to be nothing more than what citizens today would dismiss as simply one more media hype, designed to excite, not inform. Not indicative of popular beliefs, these articles were visible, yet failed, propaganda efforts by Henry Luce's publishing empire. They could not persuade an unbelieving public of the possibility of surviving nuclear war through civil defense measures. No matter how well financed, the Luce propaganda campaign was no match for the much larger published expression of anti–civil defense sentiment and of the public will it reflected. The first years of the 1960s were marked by a hugely popular, reinvigorated commitment to sanity and nuclear peace.[2] And it all began with the antinuclear response to the federal push for civil defense, which first emerged in the mid-1950s and then reached a new peak during Kennedy's term.

•   •   •

Nelson Rockefeller had been truly obsessed with the issue of civil defense for many years before Kennedy called for civil defense as a form of "survival insurance." But Kennedy was actually more interested in his own political survival. The Kennedy civil defense drive, as it developed before the Berlin crisis in the summer of 1961, seems little more than an ill-conceived political effort motivated almost entirely by the need to counter the political appeal of Rockefeller. Elected governor of New York in 1958, Rockefeller was a vocal proponent of fallout shelters and had influenced Eisenhower to commission the work of the Gaither Committee. Kennedy embraced the civil defense cause only to prevent Rockefeller from using the lack of civil defense preparation as a club during Rockefeller's expected attempt to defeat Kennedy in the 1964 presidential election.

Born into awesome wealth, Rockefeller longed for influence in shaping foreign policy. He used his multimillions to achieve that quest for power, helping to shape inter-American affairs under Franklin D. Roosevelt and also working as an advisor to Harry Truman. During the Eisenhower administration, Rockefeller served as special assistant to the president for psychological warfare—a fancy term for propaganda chief. Rockefeller worked closely with the covert-action officials in the CIA and was a good friend of master propagandist C. D. Jackson, his predecessor in the psychological warfare post and a former mainstay of the *Time-Life-Fortune* publishing effort under Henry Luce.[3]

Rockefeller several times brought together well-known groups of academics, policy makers, intelligence agents, and military and nuclear strategists to address foreign policy issues and present their advice to the president. The most influential of these groups, known as the Special Studies Project, released its report in 1957, soon after the Sputnik scare. Prime participants in this effort were C. D. Jackson, Henry Luce, generals and ex-generals, foundation bosses, big businessmen, and a couple of university presidents. The two most forceful intellects in the group were archconservative Edward Teller and Henry Kissinger, who left the Council on Foreign Relations to direct and write the Special Studies Report.

Rockefeller was heavily influenced by both Teller and Kissinger. "Once in a while," Rockefeller stated, "I have encountered an individual of energy, dedication and genius so extraordinary as to mark him indelibly on my memory and leave me eternally in his debt for the services he has rendered mankind. One

FIGURE 4.1. Physicist Edward Teller (1908–2003), a major civil defense enthusiast, was known as the "father of the hydrogen bomb" and believed that properly prepared Americans could survive and prosper after a nuclear war.

Edward Teller Papers, Hoover Institution Archives, Stanford University.

such a person is Henry Kissinger. Another is Dr. Edward Teller."[4] Teller, who
hardly recognized any distinction between nuclear and conventional warfare,
had long been committed to an extensive civil defense. Kissinger's bestselling
Nuclear Weapons and Foreign Policy, published in 1957, argued for limited nuclear war—the use of battlefield nuclear weapons—as the most effective strategy. It is not surprising that the two men so idolized by Nelson Rockefeller not
only supported civil defense, but have both often been suggested as the real-life
model for Stanley Kubrick's Dr. Strangelove, the crazed nuclear strategist in
Kubrick's now-classic 1964 film. Kissinger's and Teller's idea of "winning" a
nuclear war depended on stashing much of the populace underground, but only
for two weeks, before the citizens could emerge and return to their relatively
unchanged and secure world. This optimistic vision of nuclear exchange was
adopted by Rockefeller as well.

As governor of New York in 1960, Rockefeller put forward the most ambitious civil defense plan ever attempted by a state official. It would have required
New York citizens to spend a billion dollars and would have forced owners to
put shelters in every building, while the state would build bomb shelters in the
schools. The civil defense plan failed to address the danger to shelter occupants
from heat, fire, or asphyxiation and gave no consideration to post-attack conditions, such as lack of food and water in a devastated and radiated environment.
Although he failed in 1960 to convince the New York state legislature to adopt
his mandatory shelter system, Rockefeller did construct a fallout shelter in the
governor's mansion and in his apartment building on Fifth Avenue in New York
City. In downtown Albany, Governor Rockefeller directed the building of the
largest bomb shelter in the country, a $4 million underground giant structure
that could supposedly protect 700 preselected key state officials, business figures, and professionals against both blast and radiation. Rockefeller's fixation
on civil defense was so extreme that Jawaharlal Nehru, India's prime minister,
remarked after his visit to New York in 1960: "Governor Rockefeller is a very
strange man. All he wants to talk about is bomb shelters." Nehru added, "Why
does he think I am interested in bomb shelters? He gave me a pamphlet on how
to build my own shelter."[5]

In his first message to the New York state legislature in 1959, Rockefeller
called for a special task force to study the best means of protection from radioactive fallout. Rockefeller made no pretense that a shelter would help anyone
who lived in or near a prime target, as the impact of the hydrogen bomb was
widely enough understood that no government official could still pretend that
a blast shelter would protect anyone living within twenty-five miles of heavily
targeted major cities. The New York Special Task Force report of 1959, according
to Rockefeller, "became the basis on which civil defense planning in our State,
and, in many respects, in the nation has gone forward."[6] It is true, as Rockefeller

often claimed, that the Kennedy civil defense program never got any better than Rockefeller's 1959 special task force report.

Informed opponents always found the Rockefeller and Kennedy civil defense plans remarkably easy to refute. The plans' conclusion that survivors of nuclear war would need to spend no more than two weeks underground before emerging into a livable environment was obvious nonsense. Denial of problems in the postwar environment, but also the government recognition that no shelter could protect anyone in the target area from blast effects, caused many experts and common citizens to refuse to take civil defense seriously in the Kennedy era.[7]

The year 1960 was marked by another major moment in civil defense history: the publication of the best seller *On Thermonuclear War*. Its author, Herman Kahn, then a defense analyst at Rand Corporation, was one of the leading nuclear strategists of the time. The 600-page book sold more than 30,000 copies, despite dozens of intensely critical reviews. Discussing the prospect of a future nuclear war, Kahn described not how to avoid it, but how to prepare for it, fight it, win it, and survive it, thus escaping nuclear blackmail by the Soviets. He argued that if the country spent billions of dollars for city evacuations and for a well-stocked and -equipped, underground national fallout shelter system, then—instead of losing 100–150 million Americans to nuclear attack—*only* a few million citizens, perhaps a mere one-quarter of the population, would die. With an adequate civil defense system, Kahn claimed, a nuclear war could be limited, allowing each side to stop fighting at some point before reaching total elimination of life in a mutual suicide. A "managed" war of this type would presumably allow surviving Americans the opportunity to recover and rebuild.

Herman Kahn is almost forgotten today, except when he, too, is mentioned as the most likely model for Dr. Strangelove. Kahn helped to produce the hydrogen bomb, publicized the use of mine shafts for civil defense, and came up with the idea of the Doomsday Machine featured in Kubrick's classic movie. Short and very fat, about 375 pounds when he died in 1983 at age sixty-one, Kahn was a man of dazzling verbosity, charm, and unquestioned genius. The son of poor immigrants, he spent much of his life in think tanks, first at Rand and then at his own Hudson Institute. As a "policy intellectual," Kahn pondered nuclear issues and the future of the race, wrote hundreds of articles and sixteen books, and made thousands of speeches.

Kahn's willingness to think about the unthinkable— the prosecution of nuclear war—was the real source of his popularity with some policy elites in the early 1960s. During the previous decade, the mutually assured destruction (MAD) version of deterrence policy was dominant among defense analysts. Still, a significant number of strategists, such as Paul Nitze, Henry Kissinger, and Edward Teller, always rejected MAD in favor of the nuclear utilization target selection (NUTS) policy of deterrence. In 1960, Kahn became a leading publicist for the NUTS doctrine of "limited," "managed," "no cities" war. His followers believed that NUTS provided the best way to prevent the total destruction of both sides. The limited-war theory of NUTS was immensely strengthened by the election of Kennedy and the appointment of Robert McNamara as secretary of defense.[8]

On May 9, 1961, Rockefeller's long-anticipated meeting with Kennedy took place at the White House. With him were seven other governors. As chair of the Civil Defense Committee of the Conference of Governors, he badgered the president about civil defense, claiming that a shelter program was needed "to stiffen public willingness to support U.S. use of nuclear weapons if necessary." Kennedy stalled, telling Rockefeller he was not yet ready to provide specifics about the new civil defense program that he knew was so important. In a note given to the president before the meeting, McGeorge Bundy, the national security policy advisor, noted that Rockefeller's New York shelter program had failed "partly because Eisenhower did not back him, but also because Democrats in the big cities said it would do no good."[9] Rockefeller, sensing a good campaign issue in the next presidential election, would continue to hammer Kennedy on civil defense. At the next governors' conference, Rockefeller again pushed through a resolution calling on Kennedy and the Congress to provide fallout protection for all Americans.[10]

Still smarting from his humiliating April 1961 defeat at the Bay of Pigs, Kennedy asked two staff members to investigate civil defense possibilities more fully. White House aides Marc Raskin, a member of the special staff of the National Security Council, and Carl Kaysen, a Harvard professor, were assigned to write a "Modest Proposal for Civil Defense," as Raskin slyly phrased it in his memo to Bundy ten days after the meeting of Rockefeller and Kennedy. Kaysen was unenthusiastic. He concluded that Kennedy should either stop wasting money on civil defense or take it seriously and turn it over to the Department of Defense. Although Raskin wrote the civil defense portion of Kennedy's speech to Congress, he was from the beginning highly critical of any attempt to establish a civil defense program of any consequence. Raskin wrote:

> We have also to decide whether we are building a world which is safe for democracy—or one only finitely safe even for a garrison state. I have great fear for this civil defense program. I do not think that it will decrease the probabilities of war. At best it won't change the odds, although it will utilize resources that can better be spent elsewhere. At its worst it will change our society and reinforce mis-perception and distort awareness of reality more than our senses are distorted already.

Raskin emphasized that he had frequently warned Bundy that civil defense efforts "could kid many people into thinking we could do many things (wrong ones I suspect) that some would be constrained psychologically to do" otherwise. Raskin also feared that if both blast and fallout shelters were built, along with the adoption of NUTS, the combination would create a "dangerous and tragic turn in events for the United States and for the world."[11]

Despite these warnings, on May 25, 1961, Kennedy asked Congress to create a national civil defense system. He admitted that the public had historically been apathetic, indifferent, or skeptical toward civil defense, but that was largely because previous programs had been so "far reaching or unrealistic." His program, however, was not designed to protect against blast, only fallout. It would not protect against assault, but would serve some purpose if war came accidentally or by irrational attack. The middle-class public could buy or build their own shelters, according to the Kennedy plan, while his proposed program would identify communities' fallout shelter capacity in existing structures and provide matching grants and other incentives for building shelters in state and local government buildings. Kennedy warned that this would be expensive, but it was necessary and reasonable.[12]

He also assigned responsibility for the new program to the secretary of defense. This marked the third major reorganization of the ill-fated federal civil defense agency since Truman's establishment of the FCDA in 1950, and Eisenhower's shift to the Office of Civilian and Defense Mobilization (OCDM) in 1958. Kennedy decided to scrap OCDM due to the embarrassment caused by his initial appointment of Louisiana attorney Frank B. Ellis as head of the agency. Ellis, a devoted Catholic, believed that the "revival for survival" that he launched on behalf of civil defense was "the Christian thing to do, the Godlike thing." He was planning a visit to the pope, whom he hoped to persuade to issue a public appeal for the construction of fallout shelters in all church basements. At this point, Kennedy closed the OCDM and transferred the direction of civil defense to attorney Steuart L. Pittman, in the new Office of Civil Defense (OCD) in the Department of Defense.[13]

Cold War tensions rocketed when Kennedy and Khrushchev met in Vienna in June 1961. Khrushchev threatened to block Americans from entry into West Berlin, which lay inside communist-controlled East Germany. The rhetorical bluster and belligerence of U.S. and Soviet leaders escalated to near-hysteria proportions. The escape hatch to the West taken by so many East Germans was a propaganda embarrassment for Soviet officials already angry at Kennedy's vast increase in nuclear and military capabilities. Kennedy contended that the defense of West Berlin was central to the defense of American survival as a nation. Kennedy responded with a defense of American might, with calls for an increased draft, more military buildup, and a call-up of the reserves. Khrushchev erected the Berlin Wall in August and broke the bomb-testing moratorium in effect since 1958 by detonating a number of bombs, including a gigantic fifty-eight-megaton hydrogen bomb, most likely the largest ever exploded.

In a televised national address on July 25, 1961, in response to what was now called the Berlin crisis, JFK made his second and most alarming speech on civil defense. It was nearly a presidential proclamation of a national emergency, with the unmistakable implication that nuclear war might be imminent. A week earlier, Raskin had again warned Bundy about the dangers posed to U.S. security by an American civil defense program, which he believed was foolish, useless against hydrogen bombs, and capable of provoking an attack. Raskin's prophecy of the public's reaction to Kennedy's call for fallout shelters was exactly correct: "Any comprehensive civil defense program will be met in the United States with effective organized opposition led by intellectuals and students. It will be used as a convenient handle to effect [sic] our entire defense scheme."[14]

JFK nevertheless told the public in July that in preparation for thermonuclear war, they should begin "without delay" to build and stock fallout shelters in their homes. Kennedy made a direct appeal to the male head of the family: "In the coming months I hope to let every citizen know what steps he can take without delay to protect his family in case of attack. I know that you will want to do no less."[15] He requested that Congress allocate $207.6 million in civil defense funds to identify and mark fallout spaces and to stock them with food, water, first-aid kits, and other essentials. He asked for expansion of the defense budget to $35 billion. A scant nine days later, the Senate approved the full amount requested for civil defense.

Ohio Democratic senator Stephen Young, supported only by long-time progressives Senator Wayne Morse from Oregon and Senator Ernest Gruening from Alaska, denounced Kennedy's civil defense request. While Morse and Gruening are remembered for being the only two senators in 1964 to oppose Lyndon Johnson's Tonkin Gulf Resolution, less well known is their opposition to civil defense in 1961, on the grounds that it provided no real protection against nuclear war. Senator Young charged that $1 billion had already been wasted on civil defense since 1951, "exclusive of one hundred million dollars worth of surplus government property turned over to civil defense agencies." He blasted the federal civil defense officials as hacks and as defeated officeholders drawing top salaries for whom the job had become a comfortable haven, while they talked "vaguely about survival, plan[ned] alerts to annoy their neighbors, and distribute[d] countless reams of literature." He stressed the utter impossibility of the survival of American society after a full nuclear attack. His contempt for the OCDM was unrelenting:

[Public reaction] to the hopeless shenanigans of the OCDM has changed from an early tolerant amusement . . . to massive indifference, and finally to boiling indignation. . . . In the nuclear age, there can be no realistic civil defense program. We must devote our efforts to the utmost toward building a peaceful solution to the world's problems. It is our only permanent shelter.[16]

Only fifteen days after he first asked for the money, the president signed the bill appropriating $207.6 million. Thus, civil defense funds reached a total of $306.2 million during fiscal 1962. All prior civil defense outlays of the past ten years combined totaled only $532 million. In the midst of the Berlin crisis, with little discussion, Congress simply decided to accept quickly, even if only symbolically, the need for protection of the population.[17]

After Congress so hastily passed the civil defense appropriation, a large number of critics rose in howling protest against the civil defense crusade. The vigilant opposition to civil defense was composed of academics, students, peace groups, scientists, religious organizations, media figures, and government officials. Public debates swept the nation, as experts emerged to denounce the government's program. The protest further educated the public about the effects of nuclear war.

*   *   *

After the 1960 New York City action against Operation Alert, organization of the 1961 protest began at once. The year-long effort of mothers, radical pacifists, and progressives brought a reported 1,800 protesters, including some 80 babies in strollers, to City Hall Park on April 28, 1961, where they refused to take cover. Police made fifty-two random arrests. At least another 1,500 protesters demonstrated to defy Operation Alert throughout the city, with several dozen more arrested. High school SANE chapters throughout the city encouraged students to refuse to take shelter. Significant demonstrations and scores of arrests also occurred in New Jersey, Connecticut, New Hampshire, Pennsylvania, Massachusetts, Illinois, and Minnesota. Hundreds of college students demonstrated at Cornell, Drew, Rutgers, and City College of New York. At Princeton, forty-five faculty and undergraduates refused to take cover. Five hundred students at Columbia University sat on the steps of the library and sang hymns during the drill. The civil defense protest was now a national movement.[18]

The radical pacifists who opposed Operation Alert believed that peace required justice. They sought to transform America's core ideals and public consciousness through nonviolent acts of resistance that would challenge the

FIGURE 4.2. Civil defense protest crowd. Demonstrators, many of them high school and college students, refuse to take cover during civil defense drill, New York City, 1961.
Swarthmore College Peace Collection.

violence of authority and open the way to spiritual growth for the nation. Emerging in nonviolent direct action against Cold War nuclear strategies, specifically against civil defense policy and the production and testing of nuclear weapons, radical pacifism was strengthened by its contact with the first stirring of women's resolve to assume new roles. Through the tactics that young mothers publicized, civil defense protest became a moral issue, rather than a political one. It served as a single cause that thousands could support for a day, with no political tests required for participation.[19] In his *Rules for Radicals*, the famed organizer Saul Alinsky taught that effective protest must go beyond the expectations of the opposed authority and encourage public laughter at that authority. The Smith-Sharmat team with their baby carriages and tricycles did just that. A revitalized radical pacifism, heightened by women's efforts to create a mass protest against nuclear war, converged with political liberalism, the New Left, and the civil rights movement to produce by the early 1960s a significant challenge to the Cold War state. Indeed, the Operation Alert drill of 1961 was the last to be held. In 1962, without explanation, federal officials quietly and permanently canceled the annual federal air raid drills.

•   •   •

The confrontational tactics developed in 1960 would later be used by Women Strike for Peace (WSP), which organized in late 1961—with Mary Sharmat and

Janice Smith among its earliest members. On November 1, 1961, some 50,000 women in sixty U.S. cities calling themselves Women Strike for Peace marched in protest against civil defense and bomb testing. That same month, the Women's Direct Action Project picketed the Soviet mission at the United Nations in New York, also in protest against civil defense plans, and urged the Russians and the Americans to stop testing at once. A group of Chicago women marched for the same cause, and WILPF met with Soviet women who came to Pennsylvania to urge disarmament and an end to testing.[20]

In 1962, WSP dealt a powerful blow to the House Un-American Activities Committee. When fifteen WSP leaders were called in December to testify before the feared committee, women affiliated with WSP brought their babies to the hearing, passed out bouquets to those subpoenaed, and applauded their leaders when they refused to denounce possible communists in their organization. These tactics left the confused congressmen looking foolish, and they were further belittled by the press. Sharmat, Smith, and the assemblies of women inspired by their opposition to civil defense and nuclear testing helped to transform nonviolent direct action, once the province of a small band of radicals, into an effective weapon of ridicule used by angry mothers to discredit the nuclear policies of the militarist state.[21]

Operation Alert presented a classic form of political ritual designed by the state to legitimize authority, ensure mass solidarity, and calm public fears. Its function was to present a controllable, orderly pattern of action in an attempt to reorder the uncontrollable, ambiguous, and dangerous aspects of the situation and to make nuclear confrontation appear manageable. But reality defeated

NOW APPEARING ON WSP's BILLBOARD   designed by Pat Gollin
8236 Santa Monica Blvd., Los Angeles

FIGURE 4.3. "Kiss the Children Goodbye." Women Strike for Peace flyer, 1961.
Swarthmore College Peace Collection.

ritual. Operation Alert failed as political ritual because civil defense protesters shaped a powerful counterconstellation of symbols. Inspired by the tenacity of Dorothy Day and the members of the War Resisters League, the young mothers organized by Smith and Sharmat helped to defeat Operation Alert because they reworked the cultural meanings of motherhood and protection of children. In so doing, they provided protesters with an identity different from that urged by the nation-state, which served to attract others to their side.[22]

●   ●   ●

Operation Alert failed partly because its observance required that the public be given enough information to justify a civil defense program and to ensure widespread public cooperation with civil defense drills. Unlike other knowledge held by the government about nuclear strategies or nuclear weapons systems, the effect of nuclear war on the population could not be kept "secret" or "classified." Given some access to facts about the dangers of blast and fallout, especially after the development of the hydrogen bomb, the public soon realized that the rationale behind civil defense was ludicrous. As experts reacted to the federal denial of reality, political and scientific elites began to disagree in public. The federal pretense of an adequate defense against nuclear bombs could not endure.

The public rejection of civil defense was again strengthened when the *Time-Life* campaign to alert Americans to the need for civil defense fired up in September 1961. *Time*'s "Gun Thy Neighbor" piece angered many readers and led millions of Americans to reach firm opinions about the fuss over shelters and guns. In this famous article, *Time* approved the "toughness" of those farsighted folks who had prepared shelters for their families and who were determined to gun down any unwanted friends or strangers who might try to enter their refuge when the bombs fell. As one Chicago family man put it: "I'm going to mount a machine gun at the [shelter] hatch to keep the neighbors out. . . . If the stupid American public will not do what they have to to save themselves, I'm not going to run the risk of not being able to use the shelter I have taken the trouble to provide for my own family."

A few weeks later, a sternly anxious priest, L. C. McHugh, received wide national attention when he announced in the Jesuit magazine *America* that killing shelterless neighbors was a righteous form of Christian self-defense. *Time*'s selective poll of religious leaders found several who supported McHugh and downplayed the outraged reaction of others, who like the Episcopalian bishop of Washington, D.C., Angus Dun, believed that the highest Christian morality would be to denounce killing one's neighbors, or millions of innocents by nuclear weapons. As one cleric stormed: "I cannot imagine [Jesus Christ] gunning down His neighbors to defend His rights to a hole in the ground."[23]

Meanwhile, civil defense leaders in Nevada and eastern California made plans to defend themselves against fleeing hordes who might descend upon them from Los Angeles when the bombs came down. Some Las Vegas officials considered forming a 5,000-man militia to fight off the big city refugees. A few officials in Riverside County, California, about fifty miles east of Los Angeles, suggested that each survival kit contain a loaded pistol to shoot intruders. *Time* lauded the patriotic courage of the twenty-three vigilante groups in California that had cached water in hillside retreats, along with plenty of ammunition, and trained in guerrilla warfare: "Their aim: to survive, and to fight the Russians if they should attempt to land in the U.S. after a nuclear attack."[24]

Life extended the propaganda campaign with a special issue in September. Its cover showed a handsome young man covered head to toe in a transparent vinyl fallout suit, surrounded by headlines announcing, "You Can Survive Fallout" and "97 Out of 100 People Can Be Saved." In what may be the single most mendacious piece of mindless advice on civil defense ever printed in the mass media, the issue called for Americans to stand ready to fight "for power and for honor," to defend freedom in Berlin, even if that required nuclear war. *Life* presented elaborate construction and decoration plans for various types of shelters. The father was to guard it and store the tools, the mother to stock it with food and water, the son to keep track of flashlights, batteries, and radios, and the daughter to take care of the linens or provide books and games to help "pass the time" underground. A letter printed in the issue, from none other than the president of the United States, gave this advice his highest endorsement. Kennedy wrote: "I urge you to read and consider seriously the contents of this issue of *Life*. . . . in these dangerous days . . . we must prepare for all eventualities."[25]

In October, *Time* also reached new heights of factual misrepresentation of nuclear survival issues. One inaccurate prediction announced that with an hour's warning of a thermonuclear attack and with an effective shelter system, only 25 million would die. The rest would "surely arise from the rubble, fight back, survive, put together a society again, and, ultimately, prosper once more." Many communities were reported "bristling with shelters, bustling with civil defense activities." The town of Glendo, Wyoming, population 296, bought a vast storage shelter and equipped it with food, water, and toilets to serve 1,000 people. Minneapolis was said to be considering a labyrinthine cavern under the city for a shelter and Detroit was thinking of using an empty salt mine. The effect of fallout after a full nuclear attack, *Time* assured its readers, was not a real concern. Emerging from their shelters, "most Americans would not find scorched earth; more than 95 percent of the nation's land would still be green."

Only two days after a thermonuclear attack, many adults could come out of the shelter "for brief periods," although children and young people should wait two weeks, in order "to avoid the hazard of radiation-created mutations in future generations." Focused on the family patriarch, the magazine described how, with his trousers tucked in his boots and sleeves tied at the wrist, the shelter survivor would find the food in his kitchen edible—after careful washing, of course. He could then "hose off his properties," confident that, in the words of President Kennedy, he "would be neither Red nor Dead, but alive and free."[26]

Despite the media crusade, American citizens were not persuaded that shelters were either moral or effective. Questioned by Gallup pollsters in the fall of 1961, a full 93 percent said they had not given any serious thought to protecting themselves from a nuclear attack. By early 1962, 600 recently created companies selling bomb shelters had all gone broke. In late September, the popular national TV program "Twilight Zone" reflected the high level of public skepticism about the necessity or value of bomb shelters. "The Shelter" episode tells of a suburban neighborhood party for a Dr. Stockton that is suddenly broken up by a radio announcement of impending nuclear attack. Stockton takes his family to his shelter and locks the others out. The neighbors have just battered down the door of Stockton's shelter when they learn that the alert was a false alarm. Shamefaced, they realize that their friendly neighborhood relations are forever shattered. The program ends with a sober reminder from the narrator: "Just a simple statement of fact: for civilization to survive, the human race has to remain civilized."[27] Many Americans thought again of President Eisenhower's sober assessment of bomb shelters: "If I were in a very fine shelter," Ike said, "and they [my family] were not there, I would just walk out. I would not want to face that kind of a world."[28]

Even *Time* acknowledged the growing furor caused by the widespread rejection of civil defense. In mid-October, it examined the intellectual debate by asking the question: can Western civilization use nuclear weapons to save itself, or would nuclear war eradicate Western civilization? *Time* used the conservative philosopher Sidney Hook to make the "carefully reasoned moral case" for the use of nuclear bombs, while featuring the ideas of Harvard historian H. Stuart Hughes, then running as a congressional peace candidate, as an example of the "moral confusion the West has suffered in contemplating the Bomb." Hughes pointed out that the ends must justify the means, and no end could justify the extermination of hundreds of millions of human beings, perhaps even the eradication of the entire species, depending on the size of the nuclear explosions. Hook, on the other hand, citing Aristotle as his guide, believed that the West had maintained that some values are more important than life itself and that the man who opts for survival at all costs is morally dead. Adding to *Time*'s reported "moral confusion" of the time, Nelson Rockefeller announced that preparing for nuclear war is really not so different "from the problems our pioneer fathers faced in their log cabins where they never knew when an Indian attack might be launched." Just as our pioneer ancestors pushed westward, despite the dangers, so too would modern Americans work to achieve, through civil defense, "the goal of our Founding Fathers—the ultimate brotherhood of man under the Fatherhood of God."[29]

By November 1961, the questioning of shelter morality, denunciations of both media and government civil defense propaganda, and arguments that civil defense was not only useless but also harmed the cause of peace were clearly the triumphant arguments in the civil defense debate. It was not public apathy nor failure to face unpleasant fears, as the pro–civil defense forces claimed, that determined the negative American response to Kennedy's call for shelters. Rather, growing public recognition of the real effects of nuclear weapons was an early hallmark of the political consciousness that would reshape American society in the early 1960s.

The anti–civil defense crusade exploded in the media, from *Newsweek* to the more liberal *Nation*, in prestigious scientific journals, and among priests, rabbis, and ministers, university professors, and well-known intellectuals, within newly revitalized peace groups, and even among many elected politicians. While the *Nation* blasted the deadly deception of the Luce-funded propaganda, a significant series of stories in *Newsweek* focused on the "shaky premises" of the *Life-Time* treatment of nuclear survival and warned of the dangerous illusion "that shelters make nuclear war thinkable." In one piece, Professor Seymour Melman noted that, to him, "planning a 'good' shelter is like talking about an efficient design for Auschwitz."[30]

Gerard Piel, editor of the prestigious *Scientific American*, charged that the scientists and military men who claimed that substantial number of lives could be saved by shelters were "authors of frauds by computers." Piel was one of dozens of top scientific figures to denounce civil defense in *Science*, the *Bulletin of the Atomic Scientists*, and newspapers and popular journals during the fall of 1961 and the following spring. In early 1962, the Federation of American Scientists, representing more than 2,000 scientists and engineers, issued a public statement protesting the civil defense hype, noting that "few if any people can become 'safe' by building a fallout shelter."[31] Nobel Prize–winner Linus Pauling savaged the scientific validity of the figures presented in the *Life* articles. Seven scientists at the State University of Iowa, headed by James Van Allen, protested a syndicated series of articles by Willard Libby entitled "You Can Survive an Atomic Attack," particularly mocking how Libby's $30 "poor man's bomb shelter" burned down in a brushfire.[32]

One of the most widely noticed protests against civil defense appeared on November 10, 1961, when the *New York Times* published as a full-page advertisement a letter to Kennedy signed by some 200 faculty members, mostly scientists, from major universities in the Boston area, including Boston University, Tufts, Harvard, MIT, and Brandeis, and supported by hundreds more faculty members from the University of Connecticut. The group judged civil defense to be a "cruel deception of the people" and urged its replacement with "a positive program for peace and freedom."[33] Within a few weeks, 450 faculty members from the Midwest and 828 from New York universities had added their signatures. By February 1962, nearly 4,000 signatures had been collected, representing more than forty universities from across the country.

The respected anthropologist Margaret Mead, then sixty years old, welcomed rebellion against civil defense as a hopeful sign of national renewal and moral purpose. Writing in the *New York Times Magazine* in November 1961, she stated her belief that the "fantastic, unrealistic, morally dangerous behavior in which citizenry and government" actually considered, even for a moment, the building and guarding of individual shelters was a necessary step toward human realization in the nuclear age that war was no longer a viable choice. She saw the shelter debate as the beginning of a national moral regeneration—"a mandate for a national effort to invent ways to protect the peoples of the world from a war which might end in the extinction of the human species."[34]

●   ●   ●

Kennedy knew that if Governor Rockefeller's call for shelters failed to win public support in New York, then Kennedy would have little reason to extend his contrived crusade.[35] Rockefeller's plan to make fallout protection mandatory in all new and existing structures in the state was rejected by the legislature in early 1960, a defeat he blamed on the "absence of a well-defined national civil defense policy."[36] The New York state shelter campaign peaked on November 9, 1961, when, spurred by Rockefeller's behind-the-scene maneuvers, his civil defense program was jammed through a special session of the New York legislature so quickly that most of the legislators had not even had time to read the fifty-page bill before voting. They approved a generous $100 million to finance fallout shelter construction in all state buildings and to provide aid to schools, including universities and colleges, private and public, up to $25 per shelter space. Rockefeller was assisted by his friend Edward Teller, who told the state's Defense Council that, without shelters, 140 million Americans would die and the rest would be so helpless they would surrender.[37]

Kennedy had a thirty-four-year-old, first-term New York legislator, Mark Lane, to thank for the final defeat of Governor Rockefeller's drive for civil defense. This neophyte New York politician saved the day for Kennedy by revealing that Joseph Carlino, majority leader of the Assembly and Albany Speaker of the House, hid his financial investment in a company that constructed fallout shelters. The newly elected assemblyman who accused Carlino was one of the very few legislators to vote against Rockefeller's civil defense bill and also had the remarkable distinction of being the only member of the legislature who faced a jail term. Out on bail at the time, he was awaiting trial of his appeal after being sentenced to a four-month term for serving as a Freedom Rider in Jackson, Mississippi. In an ironic historic twist, attorney Mark Lane would later become nationally known as the leading "conspiracy theorist" to write about the assassination of Kennedy.[38]

A few days after the passage of the New York fallout shelter bill in November 1961, Lane received a confidential phone call from a SANE member who told him that Assembly speaker Carlino, who had spearheaded the bill's victory, was also a director of Lancer Industries, whose subsidiary Lancer Survival was the largest manufacturer of fiberglass fallout shelters in the world. The SANE informant told Lane that Lancer's recent brochure predicted that "a strong trend will soon develop" to provide fallout shelters to "the American people" and featured a photo of Speaker Carlino labeled as "director."[39] After the shelter bill passed, Lancer stock immediately jumped almost three points.

Lane's "conflict of interest" and "handsome profit" charges against Speaker Carlino first hit newspapers on November 21, 1961. The *New York Times* featured it in lead editorials on November 24 and December 2.[40] Carlino first denied any financial interest in Lancer Industries, then admitted that his law firm had received a $5,000 fee and that he had been paid $300 for attending directors' meetings. Although Carlino at first claimed to have resigned from Lancer, it was soon revealed that he did so several days after the legislature passed the shelter bill.[41]

The investigation of Carlino by the New York State Assembly was shunted to its Committee on Ethics and Guidance, which apparently had never before spent a dime of its annual appropriation of $5,000 since its establishment in 1954. The *New York Times*'s front-page story reported: "The prospects of the case's ending in a censure vote seems remote. The assembly is strongly in Republican hands, and many of the Democrats also owe political debts of some consequence to Mr. Carlino."[42] Lane produced three affidavits from disgruntled businessmen who had dealt with Lancer. One of them claimed that the Lancer officials had told him that Carlino "was in their pocket" and would come up soon with the shelter bill. In February, the Committee on Ethics and Guidance cleared Speaker Carlino of unethical wrongdoing or betrayal of the public trust, noting that "much distrust and suspicion was unduly generated" in the press.[43] It did recommend further study of a more stringent legislative code of ethics for future legislatures.

In early February, Mark Lane organized an anti–civil defense march in

Albany, an event that was hailed by the *New York Times* as the largest protest demonstration in the New York state capitol since "the rent and discrimination protest of the late nineteen-forties."[44] He brought hundreds of angry protesters from all over the state, most of them middle-class housewives and students. His final attack on civil defense ended Rockefeller's attempt to establish a major civil defense program in New York—or anywhere else.

Refusing to recognize the opposition to his civil defense plans, Rockefeller announced in a speech on April 2, 1962, to the Office of Emergency Planning in New York City his certainty that people were ready for civil defense and would soon achieve it with faith in democracy and God. Less than two weeks later, his speech-writing aides warned that when he next spoke of civil defense, he should be aware that they had known "for a considerable time" that there was

> considerable public opinion ranged against both the Federal and New York State fallout shelter programs. It is also quite evident that the critics of shelters are not merely crackpots, or unilateral disarmers, or any other fringe group. They include men who have thought deeply on the issues involved, and they also include persons of considerable stature.... Some of the most vehement opposition to the shelter program comes from (a) certain scientists, many of whom are highly regarded in the scientific world, (b) liberal writers (the *Nation, New Republic*) and (c) certain conservatives, including most notably Hanson Baldwin and Arthur Krock.[45]

Baldwin was the military editor of the *New York Times* and Krock one of its most respected reporters. Rockefeller knew when he was beaten. His speeches on public protection at once shifted to discussions of the potential of shelters to save lives during severe weather storms. Along with many future presidents, he realized that one way to maintain a place for nuclear civil defense was by tying it to the need for protection against natural, rather than manmade, disasters.

●　●　●

The Kennedy administration had not anticipated the great uprising against civil defense, which began long before Lane's exposure of Carlino. As the battle expanded and quickened, administrative staff like McGeorge Bundy, who had originally backed civil defense, were forced to retreat. In October, Kennedy's science advisor, Jerome Wiesner, wrote Bundy that a fallout shelter for everyone would cost $10–20 billion minimum, and even then would only cover the minority of citizens who were not located in or near target areas. In November, staff member Ted Sorenson reminded Kennedy that one of the most dangerous myths was the claim of *Life* "that 97 percent of the population or anything like it could survive a major nuclear attack if we had a massive shelter program." Sorenson wrote JFK: "Civil Defense is rapidly blossoming into our number one political headache, alienating those who believe we are doing too much or too little, or with too much confusion. What is needed most of all is an all-out effort to get it back into perspective." That month, Jerome Wiesner arranged for the civil defense enthusiast Edward Teller to speak to Kennedy in person about the need for shelters. Wiesner predicted that when Teller began raving to Kennedy about the ever-increasing need to build deeper and deeper shelters as the Russians built bigger and better bombs, the president would be further shocked into realization of the basic nonsense of building fallout shelters.[46]

Over Thanksgiving weekend 1961, Kennedy met with a number of his top advisors at Hyannisport, Massachusetts. The Friday meeting, centered on the civil defense question, reached a decision to lessen public discussion of civil defense and to announce that the federal shelter system would now apply only to community or group, not individual, fallout shelters. This was an answer to the many critics who protested that the previous focus on home shelters left out the poor and all those who did not own their homes. A decision was also made to restrict all future civil defense activity to completing the shelter survey that had been funded in 1961. Eventually, this survey would identify and place shelter signs on buildings providing 46 million shelter spaces and would stock about one-fifth of those. At the urging of McNamara, Kaysen, and Pittman, Kennedy agreed to ask Congress for another $700 million in order to provide federal funds to nonprofit health, educational, and welfare institutions that would construct public fallout shelters big enough to shelter at least fifty people of up to $25 per shelter space. This new effort, to be called the Shelter Incentive Program, was meant to encourage the building of 100 million spaces for a mere $2.2 billion of taxpayer money.

Wiesner glumly noted to those present at the meeting that within five years all fallout shelters would be obsolete due to the development of more-powerful bombs. Steuart Pittman, head of the civil defense agency, remembered how Attorney General Robert Kennedy came in during the

FIGURE 4.4. Fallout sign. In the late 1950s and early 1960s, public shelters across the country were marked with this symbol, which can still be seen today in many older buildings.

National Archives.

meeting, heavily perspiring after touch football. When Arthur Schlesinger discussed the way in which private shelters had seemed designed for the elite, Robert Kennedy said grimly, "There's no problem here—we can just station Father McHugh with a machine gun at every shelter." The president then "speedily decided in favor of the public program," Schlesinger reported.[47]

The Thanksgiving weekend meeting also focused on how to deal with the most extraordinary failure of judgment within the Kennedy civil defense program—the decision to tell the public in August 1961 that President Kennedy would soon issue a personal letter and booklet to every American family instructing them how to design a shelter to survive nuclear war. This mailing was trumpeted as the largest and most widely distributed piece of literature in history since the Bible, with 60 million copies to be printed and mailed to homeowners. Writing of the booklet was assigned to the *Time-Life* book division. Arthur Schlesinger remembered the document:

> In the draft submitted to the White House, it did not make clear that American policy was to avoid a holocaust; and it offered a relatively sanguine picture both of life in the shelter and of the world into which people would emerge after the attack. Moreover, it seemed to be addressed exclusively to the upper middle class—to people owning houses with gardens or basements; there was nothing in it for those who lived in tenements. . . . Moreover, the tract assigned the protection of the population to private enterprise. "The anticipation of a new market for home shelters," it even said, "is helpful and in keeping with the free enterprise way of meeting changing conditions in our lives." Kennedy . . . was dismayed both by the booklet and the public reaction. He remarked ruefully that he wished he had never said the things which had stirred the matter up, and wanted to diminish the excitement as expeditiously as possible.[48]

"It was really a ridiculous episode," Pittman recalled, "and I think it did more than any one thing to queer people on the whole subject." Kennedy asked the famed economist John Kenneth Galbraith to comment on the proposed booklet. Galbraith thought the draft presented a "design for saving Republicans and sacrificing Democrats," for it offered nothing to those who lived in modest apartments or low-cost tenements. "It is absolutely incredible to have a picture of a family with a cabin cruiser saving itself by going out to sea. Very few members of the UAW [United Auto Workers] can go with them." The draft was an "ostentatious form of war preparation" and falsely optimistic about life in the shelters and after the attack. "The latter will be a barren and hideous place with no food, no transportation and full of stinking corpses. Perhaps this can't be said but I don't think the people who wrote this pamphlet quite realize it." Galbraith predicted a "minor disaster" if the booklet were released without major revisions.[49]

At Hyannisport, the draft of the booklet was turned over to one of the lesser civil defense officials to rewrite. The final result was much like the propaganda of Ike's term in office—vague and optimistic. Twenty-five, not sixty, million copies were released in December 1961. It was cut from 100 to 24 pages, signed by Secretary of Defense McNamara, not the president, and placed in post offices for interested citizens to pick up, rather than mailed to every homeowner.

Despite the vast revision, the now aroused and informed citizenry and expert commentators, in scores of articles and newspaper stories, blasted even the new version of the booklet. Although Kennedy now planned to push community rather than individual shelters, the booklet still had seven pages describing family shelters and only two pages on rudimentary group ones. In one suggested structure, a four-foot-diameter pipe was meant to house a family of four for two weeks, along with a supply of food and water. No mention was made of how the inhabitants would eat and drink in the irradiated world or how they would breathe pure air during that two weeks in the pipe or afterward.

In one of the many published critiques of the booklet, Gordon Christiansen, chair of the Chemistry Department at Connecticut College, described the conditions likely to be faced, based upon the information given at the 1959 Holifield committee hearings, which assumed a relatively moderate 1,446-megaton attack on 224 strategic targets throughout the United States. Christiansen pointed out that the area bounded by Washington, D.C., and Portsmouth, New Hampshire, and for about a hundred miles inland, would be covered by such devastating fallout that, even after six months, survivors could only be aboveground for an hour each week, if they survived by spending six months in a fully equipped shelter four feet underground with a truly efficient air-cleaning system and a generator that never failed. Even then, the entire area would have been devastated by firestorms and no living creatures would have survived, with the possible exception of insects.[50]

* * *

Kennedy sent his request to the House Appropriations Committee for $460 million to fund the new Shelter Incentive Program in December 1961. To the dismay of shelter advocates, the committee chair, Clarence Cannon, Democrat from Missouri and a long-time critic of civil defense, assigned the responsibility for civil defense to the Independent Offices Subcommittee under the direction of Texas Democrat Albert Thomas, the most outspoken and long-standing congressional opponent of civil defense. This was viewed as a deliberate move to shatter the civil defense program, and the Kennedy administration sent a clear political message when it did not seriously protest the assignment to Thomas.[51]

Thomas opened the hearings on March 13, 1962. After the case for civil defense was presented by a few of the old faithful, Thomas made the highly unusual move for the time of allowing the testimony of nongovernmental witnesses who opposed civil defense, among them members of SANE, the Quakers and other religious groups, and several academic and scientific organizations.[52] To no one's surprise, the Thomas subcommittee approved only $75 million of the requested $695 million, maintaining only the most basic CD operations. In August, the entire House passed the watered-down civil defense appropriation by a vote of 368–12, again with no serious objection from the White House.[53] The final congressional allocation, with no funds for the Shelter Incentive Program, was $128 million for the OCD in fiscal year 1963.

Articles supporting Christiansen's assessment appeared many times before Kennedy's death. Not even the Cuban Missile Crisis of October 1962 could quicken interest in civil defense.[54] At that time, when McNamara was asked at a news conference about plans to protect the public, he mentioned looking into shelter options, whereupon the reporters hooted with laughter.

Throughout the Kennedy period, American peace activists continued to pay close attention to the Easter marches of tens of thousands of peace demonstrators in Great Britain. American anti–civil defense protesters were greatly inspired by the worldwide publicity given to the British anti–civil defense movement, which was much more militant and successful than that in the United States. Perhaps because the size of Britain made it apparent that most of the population could not survive a nuclear war, the British government's CD program made no serious effort to shelter citizens nor to store food or medical supplies. The government instead set up several secret underground shelters called regional seats of government (RSG) to protect the post-attack elite, mostly military and political officials, who would plan the "recovery" from war in the hope that some organized life might actually be possible after the H-bombs hit. Like the Americans, the British governing elite talked of civil defense in order to silence awkward questions from the public about the national preparation to fight a suicidal war.

British civil defense propaganda was characterized by an even more pronounced form of the cheerful assurance that shaped American CD publications. In 1957, for example, the Home Office booklet entitled *The Hydrogen Bomb* pointed out that it was safer to wash clothes contaminated by fallout in a bucket or tub of warm water than in the electric washing machine, because the whole machine would become contaminated and then have to be destroyed. As late as 1963, another government booklet advised citizens about where to park cars before a hydrogen bomb attack: "Park off the road if possible; otherwise along the curb, but not near crossroads or in narrow streets." One of the most ridiculed of British CD documents urged housewives to take the few minutes before the bombs struck to take down their curtains, soak them in borax, and rehang them, which would thus reflect the thermonuclear radiation away from entry into their homes.

British activists devised a few anti–civil defense strategies which never really caught on in the United States. For example, British disarmament movement members frequently joined the local civil defense volunteer corps in order to upset meetings or to take over the group completely and then refuse to cooperate with government directions. These disruptive activities were often carefully crafted into media events which were immensely entertaining, as well as educational. But the most important anti–civil defense exercise in Great Britain was the 1963 activity of Spies for Peace, which was widely publicized throughout Europe and the United States.

The Spies for Peace, who after lengthy police investigations remain unidentified even today, were apparently a team of eight anarchists and libertarian socialists, two of whom were women. Spies for Peace was associated with the Committee of 100, which was organized in 1960 to persuade the British Campaign for Nuclear Disarmament (CND) to adopt the practice of nonviolent civil disobedience. In 1963, four members of Spies for Peace broke into the RSG near the village of Warren Row, gathering papers and leaving without being detected. A few days later they returned, to copy and photograph documents, some of which revealed that the authorities had no plans to protect the general public but only to counter, with violence if necessary, the presumed panic-stricken and out-of-control masses who would be searching for food, shelter, and medical care after the bombs hit. The RSG papers also showed that only about 5,000 preselected citizens would be allowed into the country's elite shelters. The Spies for Peace duplicated several thousand copies of these papers and mailed them to newspapers and to Conservative and Labour politicians. Thousands more copies were passed out at the 1963 Aldermasten march, including maps showing the locations of fourteen RSGs throughout Britain. In an inspired last act of political malice, the Spies took the debris from their copying operation and placed it in the garbage cans outside the Communist party's *Daily Worker* office.

The government's attempt to deal with the released documents made it look even more ridiculous. First, the prime minister rushed to London from his country home to meet with his advisors. They decided to forbid newspapers from publishing this material and then backed down after Radio Prague received a copy from Spies for Peace and broadcast the whole story. The police did arrest one marcher who was formally charged with "singing the secret" in a musical rendition he had created. But after the famous actress Vanessa Redgrave read the entire document from a podium to about 8,000 of the 1963 Aldermasten marchers, the government gave up any further attempt at prosecution.

Back in the United States, the Spies scored again, this time against the CIA, which reported supposed communist influence on the British peace movement. Former CIA director Allen Dulles told a group of top policy makers that communists dominated the British antinuclear protest, perhaps illustrating the passage of information from the garbage cans of the *Daily Worker* to the agenda of U.S. strategists. Dulles warned that with the Spies for Peace protest, the communist-influenced "'ban the bomb' movement achieved a level of unusual insidiousness." So embarrassing to authorities was the entire set of incidents set off by the Spies for Peace exposé, that by 1968, the British civil defense organization was completely dismantled, not to be resurrected until the 1980s, a process that would be almost exactly duplicated in the United States.[55]

While British authorities were forced to deal with the Spies for Peace in 1963, one of the most humiliating setbacks for American civil defense officials came that year when Oregon publicized the cancellation of its entire civil defense program, on the grounds that it was a worthless, expensive boondoggle and a dangerous provocation for nuclear war.[56]

Portland, Oregon, unlike many other cities, had a splendid civil defense support record. It had been the first city to build and equip an underground center for civil defense during the Korean War. It had carved a $1.6 million civil defense communications center out of the rock of Kelly Butte and had stored biscuits and water for the post-attack hours in 326 buildings meant to hold 500,000 persons. Then, suddenly, on Columbus Day 1962, Portland citizens lost all faith in civil defense. When one of the worst windstorms in Oregon history hit, for days, thousands of telephones were inoperative, downed tree trunks blocked the streets, and millions of dollars of damage occurred. The crucial civil defense officer, who was deer hunting in eastern Oregon, could not be reached, and so no civil defense workers warned people of the storm or did anything to help afterward. In November, Portland voters overwhelmingly rejected a call to provide a special five-year levy of $75,000 for the local civil defense office.[57]

A few months later, on May 23, 1963, Portland became the first American city to dump its entire civil defense program. Stanley Earl, the city commissioner and a former labor union official, led the fight. Earl said that Portland was supposedly to be given two days' notice of an impending "surprise" attack, but could actually expect no more than fifteen to twenty minutes' notice due to the speed of modern missiles. The city council, by a 4–1 vote and against the fierce objections of the mayor, opted to close the Kelly Butte rock cavern, fire all of its civil defense staff, halt the federally financed shelter program, and abandon more than $1 million of already acquired and stored equipment. The city council also boasted that it had saved almost $100,000 a year by turning over future disaster operations to its police and fire department officials. Earl announced his certainty that other cities would soon follow Portland's example and stop spending money on civil defense, when most everyone understood that peace was the only guarantee of survival.

Steuart Pittman, head of the federal Office of Civil Defense, traveled to Portland in June in an unsuccessful attempt to convince the city government to restore the civil defense effort. He was greeted at his hotel by picketers holding signs that read "Pittman Go Home" and "No CD." An exasperated Pittman warned city officials of the grave danger to nuclear strategy posed by democracy: "It is not realistic to look to the public as an index of what to do," he announced. "They will follow, not lead." At this point, Portland citizens generally felt more than justified in their refusal to support the Office of Civil Defense.

During the next week, the Oregon legislature, led by progressive Senator Wayne Morse, also shattered its civil defense program, cutting the annual budget from $410,000 to $56,000 and leaving the pro–civil defense governor, Republican Mark Hatfield, without recourse to a veto. Morse called the CD program "senseless, wasteful and unrealistic." On the same day, Lincoln County on the Oregon coast voted to abolish its local civil defense offices. The action of Portland and Oregon against civil defense planning and operation was widely reported throughout the nation and further ensured the burial of a fallout shelter program in the United States. Officials in Baltimore, Maryland, and Los Angeles, California, made drastic cuts in their civil defense budgets in the summer of 1963, at least partly in response to organized mothers demanding an end to preparation for war, a scenario that would soon become common in cities across the country.[58]

·   ·   ·

Throughout the early 1960s, mothers, Parent-Teacher Associations, and national peace groups across the country protested to their school boards in hundreds of successful local efforts to end the civil defense drills in the public schools. Women Strike for Peace often led this effort, especially on the West Coast. One of the first nationally reported demonstrations against fallout shelters in the schools was in early 1962 when 250 loud and angry members of Women Strike for Peace marched to California governor Edmund G. Brown's office and refused to leave until he came out to hear their demands. The story of the well-dressed matrons raising such a ruckus during the fifteen-minute exchange with the governor was carefully orchestrated by WSP into widespread media coverage. Meanwhile, SWAP, or Seattle Women Act for Peace, also organized against civil defense in the state and in the schools, establishing what would become one of the nation's most powerful antinuclear forces by the early 1980s.[59]

In 1962, the superintendent of schools in Wichita, Kansas, made national news for canceling the drills in the city schools. He simply noted the uselessness of civil defense measures as protection against thermonuclear war. After the government canceled the 1962 Operation Alert exercise, anti–civil defense organizers and protesters in New York City quickly refashioned to become the Citizen's Committee to Abolish School Drills. School drills had already met with unexpected resistance from the students themselves. Dozens of students had been suspended, and one junior high teacher, James Council, was dismissed in 1963 when he refused on grounds of conscience to take part. The fight to restore Council's job brought a bevy of determined supporters into the fray, including two New York state congressmen, the American Civil Liberties Union, Norman Thomas, Erich Fromm, Roger Baldwin, David Riesman, Murray Kempton, Grace Paley, Paul Goodman, James Farmer, Bayard Rustin, Stanley Aronowitz, and the United Federation of Teachers.[60]

In 1963, at the University of California's Berkeley campus, Jackie Goldberg, who would gain renown several years later as one of the major leaders of the free speech movement, organized Campus Women for Peace and successfully closed down the fallout shelters on campus. She and her followers pointed out the impossibility of surviving a nuclear attack and noted that since 87 percent of all the fallout shelters in Berkeley were on campus, it was "a sham and a crime" that "in a world close to the brink of nuclear catastrophe, the University should abdicate its responsibility to turn from hysteria to reason." Goldberg received her political baptism in the civil defense revolt, and she would lead a fierce battle for progressive social change as an activist member of the Los Angeles School Board and of the Los Angeles City Council in the 1990s.[61]

In response to public antinuclear sentiment and activism and to the Cuban Missile Crisis of 1962, when the world seemed to come so close to nuclear holocaust, Kennedy appeared to move from competitive confrontation to a more mature understanding of thermonuclear realities. His American University speech of June 1963, partially written by Norman Cousins, founder and cochair of SANE, displayed a new tone of conciliation. Soon the long-awaited nuclear Test Ban Treaty of 1963, forbidding all but underground test explosions, brought new hope to Americans.

Another important step in the near-elimination of civil defense was House consideration in the fall of 1963 of the OCD request for $346.9 million for fiscal year 1964. Representatives Albert Thomas and Clarence Cannon were clear on the matter. "We haven't changed our minds," Thomas stated. "We're not building any fallout shelters, period." Cannon added: "[Fallout shelters] will never be needed because there will never be another world war. With modern weapons, an international war amounts to international suicide. Most of the people would die and all cities would disintegrate within 3 days after hostilities started."[62] Again, with little protest from the administration, the congressional appropriation for fiscal year 1964 was cut to $111 million, sustaining only the most basic CD operations. By this time, Kennedy was dead. The final possibility of obtaining funds for the Shelter Incentive Plan was permanently destroyed in early 1964 when Senator Henry Jackson, Democrat from Washington and chair of the Senate Armed Services Subcommittee, refused to continue committee hearings on the new civil defense bill. In March, Steuart Pittman resigned from OCD in disgust. Within a few weeks, OCD was downgraded, and the civil defense function of government was reassigned from the office of the secretary of defense to the office of the secretary of the army.

The great Kennedy civil defense hype was over. Since its initial appearance during the Berlin crisis of 1961, Kennedy's civil defense program had presented the spectacle of administration officials facing a cavalcade of opponents, while devising a system that by 1964 had achieved little except political patronage for civil defense officials, theorists, and suppliers, the stocking of a few shelters, and the appearance of the famous yellow-and-black civil defense shelter signs in various cities. Civil defense would not regain its vigor for more than twelve years, when it connected to the strength of the new nuclear strategy called NUTS, which featured civil defense as the centerpiece, the rationale, and the necessary component of its strategic doctrine.

FIVE

MAD, NUTS, and Civil Defense, 1963–1980

In March 1964, Democratic senator Henry Jackson's refusal to hold Senate hearings on the Shelter Incentive Plan effectively ended any federal effort to establish a civil defense program of any consequence. Even the 1966 death of Congressman Albert Thomas, the fierce foe of civil defense appropriations, did not increase congressional support. The existing shelter program continued to fall apart. Shelter surveys became outdated. Stored supplies were stolen or spoiled without replacement. Whereas the *New York Times* carried seventy stories about civil defense in 1963, by 1969 there were only four.[1] By the early 1970s, remaining shelter food stocks were sent as disaster aid to Latin America and the Near East.

After its victory over the issue of civil defense, the antinuclear movement declined in numbers and intensity from the mid-1960s until its renewal in the mid-1970s. The passage of the 1963 Atmospheric Test Ban Treaty was a great victory for the movement and temporarily reduced public concern with nuclear destruction. In addition, many weary activists momentarily retreated, burned-out and exhausted after their long years of struggle. During the 1970s, several important arms control agreements between the United States and the Soviet Union also raised the hopes of those who fought against the use of nuclear weapons. The Strategic Arms Limitation Treaty (SALT) I, signed by the United

States and the Soviet Union in 1972, limited the number of nuclear delivery weapons, although it allowed multiple warheads to be placed on a single missile. The Anti-Ballistic Missile (ABM) Treaty of that year confined each side to only two ABM sites and restricted the number of missiles. More than any other factor, the long campaign to stop the war in Vietnam consumed the energies of activist groups after 1963. The American antinuclear movement coalesced by 1965 into a powerful antiwar movement that combined radical and liberal members of the older peace groups with blacks, veterans, students, and the New Left.

Senator Jackson's 1964 denial of Senate hearings on a new shelter plan was a result of the continuing battle between nuclear strategists. Jackson claimed that Senate deferral was necessary only because the civil defense program was tied to the issue of the antiballistic missile. He argued that neither should be decided without full consideration of the other. At this time, Secretary of Defense Robert McNamara announced his similar view at a news conference: "A fallout shelter program can stand alone and be justified independently of an antiballistic missile system, and we believe should be given priority over such a system. But an anti-ballistic missile system cannot stand alone without a fallout shelter program."[2] It seems most likely that Jackson and McNamara, both of whom were opposed to the development of the ABM and aware of the unpopularity of civil defense, connected the two in order to discredit and defeat the financing of a larger ABM program.

The complex relation of ideas did not end there.[3] The ABM system was a feature of NUTS, the new model of nuclear deterrence under hot debate in the mid-1960s. The fight concerned the effort to replace the older strategy of mutually assured destruction, MAD, with a new vision of nuclear utilization target selection, NUTS. Positions taken on this question were closely tied to one's concept of the nature of the Soviet civil defense system. Thus, for both supporters and opponents of the new NUTS model of nuclear deterrence, and for believers and nonbelievers in the existence of a vast Soviet civil defense system, the central base for action was the same: it was their attitude toward the need for an American civil defense program. When the connectedness of these issues is recognized, the central use of civil defense by both sides, in pursuit of completely different goals, becomes readily understood.

•   •   •

The search for a new deterrence policy to replace MAD began in earnest in the 1950s in think tanks like the Rand Corporation and intensified by the early 1960s with the appointment of Robert McNamara as secretary of defense. McNamara, who served from late 1961 until early 1968, longed to bring nuclear weapons under rational control. When he received his first briefing in February

1961 on the actual battle plan of the U.S. military forces in the event of nuclear war, McNamara, like so many others before him, was stunned by its preposterous level of overkill and its disregard of the effects of fallout.

The American war plan for the conduct of nuclear war—known as the single integrated operational plan, or SIOP—was the central and most secret part of American nuclear policy. Its details shaped by interservice rivalries and determined by a few military leaders, SIOP was essentially a first-strike plan to kill hundreds of millions of people in the Soviet Union, China, and Eastern Europe with 1,400 warheads, followed by 3,500 more within twenty-four hours. This preemptive first-strike plan—with its resultant murderous effect on millions of American allies due to widespread fallout—was planned in response to a supposed Soviet invasion of Western Europe, even if the Soviets did not use nuclear weapons. Horrified, McNamara pushed for the creation of more limited options.

He convinced Kennedy to revise SIOP with a more flexible response to enemy threats, even in the event of nuclear attack. The core principle of this new plan—dubbed nuclear utilization target selection, or NUTS, by its critics—would be to first hit military targets, rather than cities, thus allowing a "limited" nuclear war to be fought. This strategy would also give leaders of both sides the opportunity to reach an agreement to end the conflict before mutual suicide occurred. Targeting military forces but not civilians was a more familiar way of conducting war and, in strategists' eyes, solved the problem of mutual annihilation associated with this new type of warfare. The new doctrine would save the use of war as an option in international conflicts. NUTS was also appealing to national leaders because both sides would agree not to target the enemy elite, safe in their deep underground shelters, for how could a war be "limited" and "negotiated with stages," unless the elites on both sides were saved for conducting those negotiations?

McNamara publicly announced the new strategy of NUTS in his speech at the 1962 commencement ceremony at the University of Michigan. In an earlier speech that year, he had more fully elaborated the new nuclear doctrine:

> Our forces can be used in several different ways. We may have to retaliate with a single massive attack. Or, we may be able to use our retaliatory forces to limit damage to ourselves, and our allies, by knocking out the enemy's bases before he has time to launch his second salvo. We may seek to terminate a war on favorable terms by using our forces as a bargaining weapon—by threatening further attack. In any case our large reserve of protected firepower would give an enemy an incentive to avoid our cities and to stop a war. Our new policy gives us flexibility to choose among several different operational plans.[4]

The sharply hostile response to McNamara's new nuclear doctrine caused him to back away quickly from his idea of limited war. First, the Soviet government's reaction was immediate and furious. The Soviets called McNamara's idea for limiting war "monstrous," naturally assuming that McNamara's plan was simply a strategy to prevent immediate Soviet retaliation against a first strike by the United States. This obvious Soviet conclusion, amazingly, had not been anticipated by McNamara. Second, the American public reacted in much the same way as the Soviet leaders, with anger, suspicion, fear, and revulsion at the concept of actually planning to fight and survive a nuclear war of any kind.

Many American citizens asked an obvious question about NUTS: with only a few minutes to consider their options before the missiles hit, how could the leaders of the targeted country know if the incoming missiles were directed at cities or government sites, or if they were limited in numbers and yields or not? Without such knowledge, the targeted nation would have to instantly respond with a powerful retaliatory attack. In addition, liberal arms-control advocates feared that NUTS would set off a new arms race and even frighten the Soviet Union into a preemptive first strike. Kennedy's civil defense initiative and talk of preparing for nuclear war had already sufficiently horrified the American people about the possibility of a nuclear conflict, and NUTS—the limited war doctrine—made nuclear war seem more thinkable.

Perhaps the most important reason that McNamara dropped his new limited war strategy, however, was to counter the U.S. military's demand for more money in order to vastly expand the number of nuclear weapons. Military leaders argued that if they were required to hit military targets first, they would require more bombs than if they simply aimed for enemy cities, since military targets are more numerous and difficult to destroy than city targets.

By January 1963, McNamara devised a new strategic doctrine—"assured destruction"—designed to limit the military's demand for new weapons. Ever the dispassionate number cruncher, McNamara defined *assured destruction* as the ability to survive a Soviet first strike and to retaliate with enough nuclear power—400 megatons to be exact—to destroy the government, one-half of the industry, and one-fourth of the population in the U.S.S.R. In short, this was a continuation of MAD deterrence policy as the basis of declared U.S. nuclear strategy. This meant the end of any serious attempt to revive civil defense until the mid-1970s since any effort to make Americans less vulnerable to attack could actually lead to destabilization of the balance of terror so aptly described as MAD. Yet despite the nuclear deterrence policies pronounced by respective presidents, the actual war plan of SIOP remained intact throughout, a plan centered upon a massive attack in response to any sign that a Soviet attack was imminent.

Meanwhile, the conventional war version of the "no cities," "limited war" doctrine became U.S. policy in Vietnam. Both General Maxwell Taylor, Kennedy's top military advisor, and Henry Kissinger, a chief presidential advisor for Kennedy, wrote about the need to develop means of fighting communists with conventional weapons. McNamara, who after Kennedy's death served as secretary of defense under Lyndon Johnson, believed in the possibility of using the tactics of limited war for conventional, as well as nuclear, warfare. In Vietnam, he would use force to coerce the enemy, while withholding a larger force that could destroy the enemy population if it did not back down and reach a reasonable settlement. Kennedy and Johnson built up conventional and counterinsurgency forces to deal with this eventuality of limited war. But the stalemate and destruction in Vietnam made it clear that "managed" war was not easily controllable after all.

* * *

Although American civil defense was in full collapse by 1964, its core of tenacious admirers adopted various strategies to revive the program, a goal successfully achieved by the mid-1970s. Prime among these civil defense supporters was renowned physicist Eugene P. Wigner, recipient of the Nobel Prize in physics in 1963. Born in Hungary and educated in Berlin, Wigner came to the United States in 1938 to teach at Princeton University. He worked at the Manhattan Project in Chicago during the war and served briefly as director of civil defense research at the Oak Ridge National Laboratory in 1964–1965.

Wigner was chair of the National Academy of Sciences' 1963 summer study, Project Harbor, on the present and future problems of American civil defense. Nearly seventy scientists, engineers, and statesmen were invited to spend six weeks on Cape Cod, producing a 1,000-page report that recommended an expanded civil defense program to include blast shelters for residents of very large cities. The group included the most important civil defense proponents, such as Edward Teller, Herman Kahn, Willard Libby, Leon Goure, and Chet Holifield. Despite this highly prestigious collection of contributors, the National Academy of Sciences downplayed the findings to the point of near-extinction, most likely due to the current unpopularity of civil defense. The results were publicized in 1965, when the Committee for Nuclear Information (CNI) in St. Louis attacked the report in its magazine, *Science and Society*. This led the *New York Times* to print a long story, the first time any appreciable number of readers had even heard of Project Harbor. A public debate continued for several years, as Wigner replied to the growing critique of his belief in the value of blast shelters. Despite his scientific reputation, Wigner built his civil defense case primarily upon an unwillingness to recognize the likely multimegaton nature of an assault and upon his conviction that the Soviet Union could use its presumed superior civil defense system to blackmail the United States into submission. Even after his retirement from Princeton in 1971, he continued his crusade for blast shelters and the provision of tunnels under every large city, reaching fewer and fewer listeners with every passing year.[5]

Another prominent die-hard supporter of civil defense was the nuclear strategist Herman Kahn, author of the bestseller on how to win and survive a nuclear war. Kahn believed that a massive civil defense system could save millions of lives, even though he admitted the sad but probable loss of at least one-fourth of the American population during a nuclear war. The often furious reaction to Kahn's work embarrassed even the Rand Corporation. When Rand president Frank Collbohm told him not to do any more work on civil defense, Kahn left and in 1961 founded his own think tank, the Hudson Institute. It became the base for the development of "war games" and for the production of more than $2 million in government contracts for the study of civil defense. This led many commentators to note that it seemed particularly appropriate that the Hudson Institute was located on the former site of a private mental hospital. In 1968, the General Accounting Office (GAO), the financial watchdog of Congress, exposed the fantasy nature of Hudson's "research" on civil defense. In a stern reprimand, the GAO cited three Hudson Institute reports on civil defense that cost taxpayers $600,000 but were judged as nothing more than a rehash of old ideas and unsuitable for distribution. Nevertheless, Kahn continued to weave government strategies, including Vietnam plans reportedly adopted in part by Nixon. Kahn turns up again and again in the nuclear strategy debates of the 1970s and was even given an office in the Pentagon in 1970 to plan for wider acceptance of the antiballistic missile (ABM).[6]

Edward Teller also continued his drive for civil defense. After failing to stop the Test Ban Treaty of 1963, he pressed on to support ABMs and to oppose disarmament efforts. Teller persisted in his hope that Americans would someday erect a $50 billion system of underground shelters, which could be buried deeper and deeper every time the Soviets improved the range or magnitude of their nuclear bombs. Teller was certain that the Soviets had built such an effective civil defense system that they would soon be able to launch an attack on the United States without fear of retaliation. By the late 1970s, Teller called for the study and production of high-energy lasers and similar technologies to create revolutionary new weapons with beams traveling at the speed of light that could destroy incoming missiles thousands of miles away. This was Teller's final fantasy vision of the ultimate antiballistic missile defense.[7]

●   ●   ●

The battle over the ABM—a missile built to shoot down an incoming missile —was another strategic element, along with civil defense, that was closely tied to the wider debate over how to fight a limited nuclear war. Proponents of NUTS believed that both civil defense and missile defense were crucial to national survival during the first stages of a limited war, whereas advocates of assured destruction, the new version of MAD, thought ABMs were ineffective and civil defense dangerous because it provoked Soviet suspicions. During Eisenhower's term of office, two distinguished panels of scientists, engineers, and technicians had recommended to the Pentagon and to the president that an ABM program should not be developed, since the Soviets could create effective countermeasures at little cost. Any ABM system can be defeated when the enemy sends over so many dummy warheads that there are not enough defense missiles capable of destroying both the dummy and the real incoming enemy missiles. Soviet decoys would easily cancel the ability of any ABM system to stop all incoming missiles. Moreover, the Soviets could disable the American tracking radars with bombs, or temporarily blind the radar through exploding large bombs at high altitudes, which would black out all American radar systems for several minutes, or even days, during which enemy missiles could reach their targets. Furthermore, the Soviets would surely build ABMs if Americans did, thus creating a wholly new and incredibly expensive arms race. In addition, the inability of civil defense to protect the public during a nuclear war was closely related to ABMs in the public mind. Americans understood that if a high-altitude incoming enemy missile were destroyed before it hit its ground target, the explosion would send fallout showering down on those living below. Also, as McNamara soon realized, no citizens wanted an ABM site near their homes, unless they could be assured of a fully supplied, ventilated, and deeply buried underground civil defense system, costing billions of dollars per year, which the public and Congress were unwilling to approve. Many Americans also knew that the enemy could explode large-yield bombs upwind of the ABM sites, saturating that area with fallout as well. In short, the ABM could be easily countered by any attacker, at very little cost, while the cost of building ABMs was enormous. In 1967, McNamara again noted the obvious: "it is important to understand that none of the systems at the present or foreseeable state of the art would provide an impenetrable shield over the United States."[8]

McNamara had learned the wisdom of connecting the new ABM program to the old failure of civil defense so as to ensure the defeat of both. He also convinced President Lyndon Johnson to stop the building of ABMs, although by this point political pressure was also mounting from the military leaders, weapons makers, and their allies in Congress. McNamara first tried to defeat the ABM by giving its advocates millions of dollars a year for research and development, but not production. Although Johnson could no longer resist the political pressure of the pro-ABM faction and was forced to fund production of the Nike-X missile, McNamara was able to limit ABM production. In the fall of 1967, he announced the development of the ABM system known as Sentinel, restricted to a "thin" defense against China only.[9]

With the advent of Sentinel, the ABM battle rested until the ascent to power of Richard Nixon and his national security advisor, Henry Kissinger. In early 1969, President Nixon ordered a completely new direction for civil defense. His call for a "dual purpose" program provided for peacetime disasters, particularly those caused by weather, as well as for protection against nuclear attack. Dual purpose was characteristic of federal civil defense agencies for years to come, culminating in the establishment of the Federal Emergency Management Agency (FEMA) in 1978. The dual track made the idea of civil defense more acceptable to the American public, while also providing the needed cover to continue covert development of the continuity-of-government system. By 1970, John Davis, Nixon's new director of the Office of Civil Defense—who like so many other CD directors before him, was also a defeated politician, in his case the ex-governor of Idaho—asked Congress for $73.8 million. This was the lowest CD budget request submitted to Congress since 1959 and the sixth consecutive year of request decline.

A 1971 General Accounting Office report questioned whether civil defense should even remain a part of national policy. The study exposed the program as both inadequate and deteriorating: "the nation lacks . . . and will continue to lack, a sufficient number of properly dispersed, adequately equipped fallout shelters . . . to accommodate the population in the event of a nuclear attack."[10] In 1972, the Office of Civil Defense was abolished and replaced by the Defense Civil Preparedness Agency (DCPA). It was no accident that the new name did not contain the words "civil defense." The change of designation was designed to alleviate some of the public scorn of discredited civil defense fiascoes of the past. After 1972, no future civil defense agency had those words in its title, including the current Department of Homeland Security.

Shortly after assuming office, Nixon replaced the Sentinel ABM system with an even more modest program called Safeguard. The 1972 Strategic Arms Limitation Treaty, or SALT I, led to a sharp curtailment of any further ABM effort by either side. In 1974, a treaty revision allowed the United States and the Soviet Union to each maintain only one ABM site, with the American site becoming operational in North Dakota in the fall of 1975. After strong congressional opposition, led by Senator Edward Kennedy, this single Safeguard site was terminated after only four months in operation. The site ultimately cost American taxpayers $21.3 billion before it was completely shut down in 1978.[11]

Through the Johnson and Ford administrations, any call for civil defense was thus considerably weakened by the dominant foreign policy, which continued to rely on MAD to deter the Soviets. MAD supporters approved assured destruction as the best hope for preventing nuclear war, fearing that a more adequate civil defense would nullify the mutual vulnerability to retaliatory attack. Although NUTS was not part of official policy during the Nixon administration, its advocates grew in number and in volume during those years, achieving their greatest prominence among nuclear strategists since the Kennedy years.

The first official statement that outlined NUTS as the preferred "flexible response" method to deter nuclear devastation was what came to be known as the Schlesinger Doctrine. Announced in early 1974 by Nixon's secretary of defense, James Schlesinger, a former Rand nuclear strategist, the new policy was a clear limited war statement:

> If a nuclear clash should occur—and we fervently believe it will not—in order to protect American cities and the cities of our allies, we shall rely into the wartime period upon reserving our "assured destruction" force and persuading, through intrawar deterrence, any potential foe not to attack cities. It is through these means that we hope to prevent massive destruction even in the cataclysmic circumstances of nuclear war.[12]

Although Schlesinger's speech marked the first public declaration of what was touted as a new deterrence policy, Nixon had already made clear his own distrust of MAD in his message to Congress in 1970: "Should a President, in the event of a nuclear attack, be left with the single option of ordering the mass destruction of enemy civilians in the face of the certainty that it would be followed by the mass slaughter of Americans?"[13] Thus did Nixon also join the large number of people vilifying MAD since the 1950s, a group ranging from Left to Right, including nuclear strategists, militarists, peace advocates, and politicians at all levels. As one scholar has so aptly described the contradictory situation:

> The [MAD] policy is denounced for its reliance on the slaughter of millions of civilians as the basis for deterring war, alternatively because of its unprecedented savagery or because of its lack of military credibility. The promise of mutual suicide in the event "deterrence fails," the basic tenet of MAD, is no more comforting to military commanders than to pacifists. At the same time every innovation in nuclear doctrine suggesting the intention to deviate from this posture has met with profound resistance in the American body politic. MAD may be repugnant, but that is its virtue. Anything that suggests that nuclear war might fall short of mutual annihilation . . . suggests sinister and misguided plans to engage in actual nuclear combat. . . . any hint of change from the

doctrine of MAD has been greeted with genuine shock in the American public and the Congress, provoking the grotesque thought that nuclear weapons could be seen as acceptable instruments of politics and war.[14]

Once again, the announcement by a secretary of defense that nuclear war might be waged and even won with a NUTS plan frightened the public and many in Congress. Nixon rushed to deny that any new deterrence doctrine was being considered, but in the midst of the Watergate scandal, few found anything he said credible. Several senators, including Edward Brooke (R-Mass.) and Edmund Muskie (D-Maine), took the lead in questioning Schlesinger carefully before several congressional committee sessions. By 1975, Schlesinger was furiously backpedaling, insisting that the targeting strategies he had proposed "were not as novel as perhaps had been advertised," because these were the same ideas put forward by McNamara in 1962. Nevertheless, the new emphasis upon saving cities revealed their current lack of protection. For some, this served to revitalize the idea of civil defense, giving it the theoretical justification it had long been lacking. During Carter's term, the drive toward NUTS became ever more evident. Plans for civil defense arose once again.

●　●　●

In his inaugural address, President Jimmy Carter, who had served as a nuclear officer in the navy and desperately wanted peace, vowed to work toward "the elimination of all nuclear weapons from this earth." Early on, he also promised to end assistance to dictators. He immediately pardoned 10,000 draft resisters to the Vietnam War, appointed record numbers of women and minorities to federal offices, and took action on several levels to save the environment. He scrapped the B-1 bomber and the neutron bomb and promised a more sane approach to the Cold War. In a nation reeling from the effects of Vietnam, followed by Watergate, Carter came into office with the hope of bold reforms.

Yet Carter's budget showed a 3 percent increase in military spending rather than the $5–7 billion cut he had once promised. He was the first president since 1945 to raise the military budget for three consecutive peacetime years, and he spoke in favor of increasing nuclear forces, including the new MX missile. President Carter left a legacy of precise plans for the prosecution of NUTS, supported by his hawkish national security advisor, Zbigniew Brzezinski. It was also Carter, the defender of peace, who reactivated civil defense, now in the form of evacuation and called "crisis relocation." In 1979, he established the Federal Emergency Management Agency (FEMA), which became known for its corrupt management in the early 1980s and its utter failure to deal with natural disasters in the late 1980s and early 1990s. It is now evident that FEMA spent most of its efforts in the 1980s to save the elite from nuclear destruction, in a newly conceived, covert, and expensive continuity-of-government system.[15]

When Carter took office in 1977, the foreign policy establishment was so fiercely split, as scholar Frances Fitzgerald noted, that future historians may wonder whether the liberals and conservatives even lived on the same planet.[16] Liberals were intent on dealing with the threats and promises posed by global interdependence, environmental problems, and Third World nationalism. At the same time, the Vietnam disaster, the recognition of China, the détente with the Soviet Union, and the general social and cultural changes of the 1960s and 1970s so frightened Cold War ideologues that a strongly conservative national reaction emerged. During the 1970s, conservatives worried about Soviet establishment of nuclear parity, a new situation that the Right wanted to challenge with a military buildup and the formation of a strong civil defense program.

Presiding over this turmoil was the triumvirate called VBB by Washington insiders, a threesome fiercely locked in internal war throughout the Carter regime. "V" stood for Secretary of State Cyrus Vance, the liberal super-WASP who sought détente with Soviet leaders. The two "Bs" were Zbigniew Brzezinski, the super-hawk head of the National Security Council who had fled from Soviet occupation of Poland, and Harold Brown, the technocratic thinker and ex-designer of nuclear weapons, who served as secretary of defense. Carter listened to Vance, Brzezinski, and Brown and tried to please all three at various times. As a result, his foreign policy was stumbling, often contradictory, and frequently indecisive.

*   *   *

One of the most important results of the Left-Right conflict splitting the foreign policy elite in the mid-1970s was the establishment of what came to be known as Team B.[17] Shortly after Nixon's resignation, the new president, Gerald Ford, fired Schlesinger as secretary of defense and put Donald Rumsfeld in his place. In 1976, Ford gave the senior George Bush, then the CIA director, a special assignment to create a group of outsiders to investigate the validity of previous CIA intelligence estimates of Soviet power and intentions. Bush selected a group of hardline conservatives, known as Team B, who believed that earlier CIA studies had underestimated the true Soviet threat and that this lack of knowledge was a major reason for what Team B perceived as insufficient American military power and preparation.[18] Richard Pipes, a right-wing Harvard professor of Russian history, headed Team B, and its members included Paul Nitze, four generals (including Lieutenant General Daniel O. Graham, who had headed the Defense Intelligence Agency), William Van Cleave, professor in international relations at the University of Southern California, whose politics were on the far Right, and Paul D. Wolfowitz, then with the Arms Control and Disarmament Administration. Not surprisingly, Team B found the previous CIA estimates to be inaccurate and misleading.

Team B member General Graham told reporters that one of the major factors influencing their conclusion was their "discovery of a very important [Soviet] civil defense effort . . .very strong and unmistakable evidence that a big effort is on to protect people, industry, and store food." This "strong" Soviet civil defense program had earlier been dismissed by CIA analysts as insignificant.[19] Graham would soon begin work with Edward Teller on the creation of a large American civil defense effort and a space-based missile defense. Defense Secretary Donald Rumsfeld gave his support to Team B and noted his belief that the Soviets had "a tendency toward war fighting . . . rather than for the more modish Western models of deterrence through mutual vulnerability."[20]

Initiation of Team B led in the spring of 1976 to the creation of the privately formed Committee on the Present Danger (CPD), a group of elite foreign policy analysts who pledged to alert the nation to what it viewed as the growing Soviet threat and to call for a U.S. military buildup. The CPD, which counted four of its members among the seven top persons on Team B, believed that the Soviets had no intention of honoring the MAD deterrence strategy and planned to risk nuclear war to conquer the world since they had less regard for life than did Americans. The CPD was devoted to the containment of communism worldwide as the cornerstone of U.S. foreign policy. It sought to weaken the call for détente in this period, to turn away from any arms control effort, and to return to a strong military posture intent on resisting the growing Soviet power.

Hoping to appeal to conservatives in both parties, the CPD waited until the week after the 1976 election of Carter to go public. It announced that the "threat to our nation, to world peace, and to the cause of human freedom is the Soviet drive for dominance based upon an unparalleled military buildup." Soviet leaders were accused of being motivated by one overwhelming goal: the creation "of a world dominated from a single center—Moscow."[21] In many ways, despite his essential animosity to its political ideals, President Carter would reflect the needs and serve the antidétente ideals of the CPD and its Team B.[22]

The CPD was composed of well-known neoconservatives, intensely anticommunist liberals, and traditional right-wingers. It included many persons of significance in politics, trade unions, and strategic policy jobs, among them Paul Nitze, Eugene Rostow, Clare Booth Luce, Lane Kirkland, Dean Rusk, and Richard Pipes. Prime among its earliest leaders were Rostow, Nitze, and Pipes. The attorney Rostow was the former dean of the Yale law school and had served under both Johnson and Nixon as a leading supporter of the Vietnam War.

Paul Nitze perhaps more than any other member shaped the structure and goals of the CPD.[23] Nitze had been instrumental in the signing of SALT I and the passage of the 1972 ABM Treaty. He left the Nixon administration in May 1974, stating his opposition to the events that led up to the Watergate scandal. President Carter, who believed Nitze to be arrogant and obsessive, did not appoint him to any position. Displaced from government leadership, the angry Nitze began to preach a warning that the United States was gravely endangered by the Soviet Union, which, in its drive for world control, had completed an unparalleled military buildup after the Cuban crisis. Central to this estimate of Soviet evil was the CPD belief in a Soviet civil defense system of such strength and effectiveness that during a full nuclear exchange the Soviet Union would suffer only one-tenth the casualties of the United States. More important, the CPD argued, Americans, when confronted by Soviet demands and without adequate civil defense, would have no choice but to give in to Soviet blackmail and allow the Soviets to have their way. As many commentators have noted, Nitze's warnings of a dire Soviet threat were reminiscent of those he raised in his writing of "NSC-68" in 1950 and his support of the 1957 Gaither Report. Once again, in Team B and in the creation of the CPD, Nitze called for a great new civil defense effort to fend off the Soviet menace that threatened destruction of American freedoms.

●　　●　　●

From the mid-1970s through the mid-1980s, the CPD warned of the civil defense gap that put the survival of American society at risk. No one really disagreed with the CPD's message that the United States essentially had no civil defense. Rather, the debate was over the size, quality, and validity of an extensive Soviet program complete with shelters, training, and evacuation plans. The Soviet system was said to protect the great majority of the Soviet population from nuclear destruction and to ensure continued industrial production during wartime. The Soviets did not believe in deterrence or MAD, the CPD argued; the communists cared only about fighting and winning a nuclear war on their way to world domination. The American hardline Right also insisted that the Soviet military buildup, and its collection of very large ballistic missiles, would soon surpass the nuclear power held by the United States. The Soviet Union's commitment to civil defense, CPD members said, was clearly as dangerous as its growing military strength, for its elaborate system would allow it to win and survive a nuclear conflict. Secretary of Defense Donald Rumsfeld, in his 1977 report to Congress, warned: "This [Soviet] civil defense capability . . . could adversely affect our ability to implement the U.S. deterrent strategy. Thus, it could provide the Soviets with both a political and military advantage in the event of a nuclear crisis."[24]

Leon Goure, director of Soviet studies at the University of Miami, was most often cited by those who believed in an effective Soviet civil defense. From the early 1960s to the mid-1980s, Goure wrote dozens of books and government-financed reports for Rand and for the successive U.S. civil defense agencies. Relying almost entirely upon the information printed in Soviet civil defense manuals and broadsides, Goure argued that the Russian civil defense system was greatly expanded after the signing of the ABM Treaty in 1972 and was then moved into the Ministry of Defense, making use of thousands of soldiers to run and monitor its programs. According to the Soviet description of its civil defense system, all citizens received compulsory and extensive training; even schoolchildren were given hours of instruction. The Soviets claimed that their civil defense system included hardened shelters to protect necessary industrial workers, as well as detailed plans to evacuate millions of people from the cities. In the event of nuclear attack, urban dwellers were expected to walk thirty miles, where they would dig trenches, cover them with dirt, and survive the attack. Goure and his supporters, including Edward Teller, Paul Nitze, and other notable CPD members, taught that the Soviet civil defense program made it possible for more than 90 percent of the Soviet population to survive a full nuclear attack, allowing the U.S.S.R. to recover from nuclear war in two to four years and for its leadership to remain relatively intact.[25]

Determining the true nature of Soviet defense was a challenge since, unlike in the United States, no public opposition to civil defense was allowed within the Soviet Union. "Evidence" of the Soviet program was chiefly restricted to communist-approved government sources. Still, most American commentators could agree on a few points. The Soviet civil defense, even if considered more rhetorical than real, was thoroughly militarized, headed by a respected general in the Ministry of Defense. Moreover, the party elite was clearly in charge, using the civil defense program to reinforce a garrison-state mentality and to convince the Soviet public that safety from nuclear war was assured. It was also agreed that the Soviet program focused on protection of work sites and of essential workers, rather than on survival of the suburban home. Believers and nonbelievers in the existence of an effective Soviet civil defense program could also agree upon the existence of substantial protective structures for Soviet political, military, and Communist party leadership. These havens included deep tunnels dug inside a hollowed-out mountain 500 miles southeast of Moscow. A 1978 CIA report estimated that the Soviets spent tens of millions on these hardened shelters, designed to house some 110,000 members of the select Soviet leadership.[26]

The CPD assessment of a powerful Soviet civil defense system met immediate, furious dissent in the United States. Criticism of the CPD's civil-defense-gap doomsday scenario centered on four points. First, reports from travelers to the Soviet Union and from recent émigrés to the West showed a high degree of public skepticism about the value of the program. Many cited the existence of several jokes prominent among the Soviet citizenry. One concerned a worker who asked a party official what to do if the Americans attacked with nuclear bombs. The party man told him that he should wrap himself in a sheet and head slowly for the local cemetery. "Why slowly, Comrade?" the worker asked. "So as not to cause panic," the party leader replied. Another familiar joke reported by Western visitors to the Soviet Union was about the supposed civil defense instruction given to the public about what to do when the nuclear bombs dropped. The advice: "Bend over, put your head between your legs, and kiss your ass goodbye." Western accounts also noted the popular nickname given by Soviet citizens to the civil defense program: *grob*—the word for coffin.[27] Other major doubts about the effectiveness of Soviet evacuation plans revolved around the inadequate transportation system. The country had relatively few automobiles, scarce and poor-quality paved roads, and single-track rail lines. In addition, the frigid winter conditions, as well as limited food, water, and heat sources throughout the country, would vastly complicate digging trench shelters, piling thousands of pounds of protective dirt around factories and machines, and providing housing and food for the millions of refugees from the cities.

Regardless of the efficacy of Soviet civil defense plans, the American lack of civil preparedness was considered a weak link by some. In 1976, the House Armed Services Committee initiated an investigation of the state of American civil defense, holding public hearings on the subject for the first time since 1963. A focus of attention was the state of the Soviet civil defense system in comparison to that of the United States. Here, the press first encountered the ever-quotable CD enthusiast T. K. Jones. Then a manager at Boeing, later a deputy undersecretary of defense under Reagan, Jones told incredulous committee members that if Soviet citizens had twenty-four to forty-eight hours' notice to leave target areas and dig foxholes, 96 percent would survive a massive U.S. nuclear attack on Soviet industrial areas. The committee recommended that the civil defense budget be raised from $71 million to $110 million; Congress gave $82.5 million.[28]

But why did the American hardline Right so push the existence of a superior Soviet civil defense system from the time of the Team B report into the Reagan years? First, they worked to stop any further efforts at arms control and to prevent the signing of any SALT II. They feared that the Soviet Union was reaching nuclear parity with the United States and pushing for war. Second, in order to prepare for a limited nuclear war, it was necessary to build public confidence in a new American civil defense program. This in turn depended on frightening the American public into believing that the Soviet civil defense program would protect 90 percent of Soviet citizens from death in a nuclear exchange, while Americans would be unprotected. Finally, and perhaps most important, even if not stressed publicly, was the effort to strengthen the American continuity-of-government system, in case deterrence failed. All agreed that the Soviet civil defense system concentrated on saving their elites as well. Thus, both the U.S. and the Soviet political and military leaders concentrated on using civil defense for saving themselves, preparing costly elite shelters under the cover of highly secret government agreements.

* * *

By the end of the Vietnam War in 1975, the American antinuclear movement had reemerged to again focus on issues of disarmament and nuclear proliferation. During the 1970s, the movement was at first mainly directed toward nuclear power and highly decentralized in several hundred local groups. Strengthened by the new interest in environmental issues, it confronted the danger of nuclear power plants: the release of radioactivity, the creation of fissionable material for use in nuclear bombs, and the disposal of nuclear waste. Inspired by events in 1975 at Wyhl, Germany, where 20,000 activists stopped the building of a nuclear reactor by occupation of the site for almost a year, thousands of American activists in many local groups around the nation held marches or practiced civil disobedience in protest against the hazards of nuclear power. The Clamshell Alliance, a coalition of environmental groups, in 1977 attempted to block construction of a reactor at Seabrook, New Hampshire, where 24,000 people occupied the site in nonviolent direct action and 1,114 protesters who refused to obey the governor's order to leave were arrested. The Abalone Alliance in California attempted to shut down the Diablo Canyon plant in a series of progressively larger demonstrations; the biggest brought 40,000 in 1979, and in 1981, 1,900 activists were arrested. By the time of the near-meltdown of the reactor at Three Mile Island in early 1979, the antinuclear movement was vigorously expanding into a wider movement against nuclear weapons. In April 1977, Mobilization for Survival was formed, bringing together 280 groups, including 40 national organizations, to call on the government to ban nuclear power, abolish nuclear weapons, and end the spiraling arms race. The Mobilization for Survival was a conscious effort to bring together the supporters of the anti–nuclear bomb testing movement of the late 1950s and early 1960s with those of the anti–Vietnam War movement and of the anti–nuclear power protests of the 1960s and 1970s. It grew rapidly, forming a powerful antinuclear coalition which reached out to form alliances with religious organizations, as the civil rights movement had done so successfully, and with women's and environmental movements as well.

The revival of the antinuclear movement in the late 1970s led the American Friends Service Committee, the Fellowship of Reconciliation, and the Catholic

Conference of 350 bishops to demand disarmament. The Physicians for Social Responsibility, gaining thousands of members in the last years of the 1970s, opposed civil defense as hopelessly naive and ineffective and made clear to all that, in the event of nuclear war and the consequent loss of drugs, doctors, and hospitals, there would be no decent medical care available to the few who survived. Major women's groups, including the National Organization for Women, WILPF, and WSP, also demanded an end to the arms race. The 1980 Women's Pentagon Action brought women's groups together for a day of protest by 2,000 women. They circled the Pentagon, accompanied by drumbeats and moans, and blocked the doors to the building, shouting slogans such as "Take the toys from the boys." The arrest of 150 women excited media attention and inspired hundreds more to join the struggle against the use of nuclear weapons. The American antinuclear movement would reach new heights of power during the 1980s.

* * *

The belief of many on the American Right in the Soviet plans to evacuate their cities in preparation for surviving a nuclear war led proponents of civil defense to reinvigorate the old American evacuation model, which was originally touted in the early 1960s by Herman Kahn.[29] In 1977, Secretary of Defense Harold Brown initiated a departmental study of the wisdom of various civil defense alternatives. He concluded that the option of "crisis relocation" would supposedly increase the survival rate to about 80 percent of the population, all for a mere $2.3 billion.

Pushed by national security advisor Brzezinski, Carter quickly began a major review of nuclear defense policy. Presidential Review Memorandum (PRM) 10 ordered the National Security Council staff, headed by the conservative Harvard professor Samuel Huntington, to prepare a comprehensive analysis of the military, political, and economic balance of Soviet- American power relations and of the role of civil defense in strategic policy. Completed in June 1977, the study concluded that civil defense was crucial to crisis management and American survival and that a crisis relocation system would be the most cost effective and efficient operation mode.[30] Brzezinski influenced Carter to order a new study exercise called Presidential Directive (PD) 18. Signed in August 1977, PD-18 went a long way past reliance on MAD, promising to develop a strong war-fighting ability should deterrence fail.

This in turn was incorporated into a much larger document, finally completed in September 1978, known as PD-41 on civil defense. It illustrated how the new focus on a major Soviet civil defense system meant that the earlier American emphasis on civil defense as humanitarian insurance would be replaced by a concept of civil defense as crisis management.[31] The American version of civil defense, like the Soviet one which it sought to equal, would be based upon an evacuation policy. Under Carter, crisis relocation planning (CRP) became the basis for the revitalized civil defense program and remained the center of the American civil defense system until its final collapse in 1985, after years of public rejection of relocation plans. PD-41 also promised two other significant changes in American civil defense, again based upon the supposed Soviet model. There would be new emphases on targeting Soviet military leaders and their hideaways and on developing new and expensive methods to ensure the survival of the selected American elite, so that they could continue to direct and "win" a protracted nuclear conflict.

Carter always had a special interest in plans designed to protect the "key personnel" of the nation from nuclear attack.[32] During his first year in office, he participated in several command-post exercises designed to ensure the survival of top political leaders. These exercises were so unsuccessful as to be humorous. At one point, the takeoff of the large plane meant to carry the president to safety, where he could then direct the war from the air, was delayed for more than an hour due to an engine malfunction. Another time, the helicopter designated to evacuate the president from the Oval Office before the bombs arrived was almost shot down by the Secret Service when the craft appeared unannounced over the White House. And exercises to test the reliability of the "red phone," over which the president was to determine the need for a nuclear launch, were equally faulty. As one of Carter's top aides remarked, since there were twenty-three people on the phone line and Carter knew none of them, there was no way for him to be sure with whom he was talking. If nothing else, Carter's nuclear drills made clear the need for presidential repair of the continuity-of-government system.[33]

Within a month of the approval of PD-41, Carter had agreed to initiate its recommendations with a five-year program costing $2 billion. Press reports of this decision produced a crescendo of negative criticism. Carter at once denounced the newspaper accounts as "erroneous," amid rumors that the National Security Council had deliberately leaked the $2 billion plan as a "trial balloon." When the ideas of crisis relocation and elite protection in preparation for nuclear war elicited such public opposition, Carter gave up making open attempts to achieve the goals of PD-41 and instead requested $108 million for the civil defense program in 1979. The $100 million that Congress finally voted was, in constant dollars, the lowest amount allotted to civil defense spending since 1951.[34]

Carter established the new civil defense agency in the summer of 1979. The formation of FEMA consolidated five emergency-related programs, which had been separately housed in various federal units. To make preparation for nuclear war less frightening to the public, FEMA was publicized as a group devoted to a dual purpose, the protection of Americans against weather disasters or other national emergencies and against nuclear war. But in fact FEMA contained an enormously expensive secret component, a highly classified and covert plan to provide for the rescue and shelter of top government, industrial, and military leaders during any future nuclear war, thereby assuring the centrality of FEMA to plans for the continuity of government and "national security." The secretary of defense and the National Security Council were now responsible for overseeing FEMA's readiness for nuclear attack.[35] Still, FEMA, just as the twelve federal civil defense agencies that preceded it, would continue to be a target of ridicule and scorn, reaching even higher levels of public and intellectual rejection under subsequent administrations.

From the accumulated furor surrounding PD-41 came the more important commitment to NUTS embodied in PD-59, signed by Carter in the summer of 1980. Some felt that its rapid leak to the press was a campaign tactic to make Carter appear "tough" before the upcoming election against Ronald Reagan. PD-59 was touted as new, especially by the hawks, because it spoke of managed or flexible responses. But it was actually the culmination of a process that had begun in 1974 with the Schlesinger Doctrine's call for protracted, limited war, the essence of the NUTS deterrence concept. Brzezinski openly praised PD-59 as "moving us toward a war-fighting doctrine."[36] PD-59 did contain a new emphasis on the "decapitation" of enemy leaders. Large numbers of targets were chosen to eradicate the underground hideaways of the Soviet war-making elite and all known KGB and Communist party headquarters and regional offices.

The directive downplayed economic and industrial targets in favor of military command, control, and communication sites. But, as critics pointed out, even without cities targeted, millions of urban citizens would die on both sides from the effect of extensive fallout, no matter which direction the wind was blowing.

In the last years of Carter's term, while achieving support for its view of the need to prepare for limited nuclear war, the CPD also continued to lobby fiercely against efforts to establish détente with the Soviet Union. The group pushed its message on television and in print. Carter's arms controllers responded with an ineffective group of speakers sent out to tour the nation in support of the SALT II effort. After the Soviets invaded Afghanistan in 1979, the SALT II Treaty, previously stalled in the Senate, was never submitted for ratification.

*   *   *

While President Ronald Reagan frequently gets the blame for encouraging the NUTS strategy, for establishing a revitalized civil defense system complete with a focus on evacuation, not shelters, and for strengthening a continuity-of-government effort, these plans were initiated and supported by Carter. Still, it was Reagan who built the hothouse for these policies.

Reagan bought the whole CPD doomsday scenario. He even improved on the right-wing fantasy of a highly superior Soviet civil defense system.[37] Reagan also repeated the CPD mantra that the Soviet Union was planning to fight and win a nuclear war, since it had less concern for the loss of human life than did the United States. To ensure American survival, Reagan believed that it was necessary to increase our military spending and to invest in a massive civil defense system, lest the communists blackmail us into submission.

Reagan's version of Soviet preparation for war was heartfelt. The scholar Frances Fitzgerald has succinctly summed up Reagan's understanding of the core of the CPD doomsday warning, with its use of NUTS to fight and win a nuclear war:

> Reagan had gotten the gist of the scenario. He had understood that civil-defense measures were the key to it. He had also grasped the idea that the danger lay in a Soviet capability for nuclear blackmail at some point in the future—and the logical corollary that did not appear in the CPD papers: if the Soviets could use nuclear superiority for geopolitical ends, the U.S. could too.[38]

Reagan began his civil defense hype in the early 1980s. His attempt to strengthen the civil defense program created a massive public protest in the United States and abroad, greatly expanding the size and influence of the American anti-nuclear movement.

SIX

The Fantasy Dies

The Reagan Years

The Reagan civil defense hype commenced in early 1982, when the administration proposed a $4.3 billion civil defense appropriation to Congress. As resistance to civil defense reached new heights, the Reagan administration suffered the roaring refusal of twenty-two states and more than 120 cities to participate in civil defense exercises. Meanwhile, FEMA, mired in tales of corruption and incompetence, threatened Oregon and Washington with the loss of millions of dollars of federal funds if they did not honor the civil defense tests scheduled in their states. As public fear of U.S. plans to fight a limited nuclear war exploded, the peace movement also expanded, creating by the summer of 1982 what was, by far, the single largest protest march in all of American history.

Less than two years later, Reagan brilliantly devised the option that ended his CD hype and cooled down the protest against it. He produced the soothing, illusionary fiction of Star Wars—the largest, most costly, and greatest civil defense fantasy ever conceived.

• • •

FIGURE 6.1. Antinuclear peace march. While more than 100,000 demonstrated in various cities across the nation, almost 800,000 marched in New York City in the antinuclear peace march, June 12, 1982, forming what was then the single largest protest demonstration in American history.
Photo by Steve Cagan.

When Ronald Reagan left office as California governor in 1975, he at once began his campaign for the White House. In 1977, a founding member of the Committee on the Present Danger (CPD), economist Richard V. Allen, joined Reagan's effort. By January 1979, when Reagan joined the CPD as an executive board member, Richard Allen was already writing much of Reagan's foreign policy pronouncements. During his first year as president, Reagan appointed forty-six members of the CPD executive board to top policy posts, including Richard Allen as head of the Office of National Security. By 1984, a full sixty members of the CPD board of directors had been appointed to the Reagan administration.

These positions were not minor ones. They included the secretary of state, the director of the Central Intelligence Agency, the secretary of the navy, an assistant secretary of defense, the U.S. representative to the United Nations, the director of the Arms Control and Disarmament Agency, and a number of the highest officials in the State Department, the White House, the National Security Agency, and the president's Foreign Intelligence Advisory Board. Eugene Rostow, one of the central organizers of the CPD, was made director of arms control and disarmament. Thrilled by the elevation of so many CPD members, Rostow exclaimed in April 1981, that after Reagan's election, "respectable people" could no longer dismiss CPD members as "cranks, crackpots, and lunatics." As the Pulitzer Prize–winning scholar Frances Fitzgerald noted, "In effect the CPD had become the Reagan campaign's brain trust for defense and foreign policy."[1]

•   •   •

As president, Reagan issued the familiar CPD warning: Americans would have to surrender to Soviet demands because the Soviet system could survive a nuclear attack, while the Americans, with no real protection at home, could not. The Soviet threat could best be resisted by building more bombs and constructing more missiles, ships, and planes to deliver the warheads. Central to this position was a demand for a greatly expanded continuity-of-government program, designed to protect the elite, within the civil defense system. For the first two years of the Reagan presidency, these goals were vigorously advanced.

Reagan seemed to recognize earlier than most of his conservative mentors that many Americans now understood that the only type of civil defense that was somewhat adequate would permanently bury the entire society deeply underground. And the vast majority of Americans had rejected this solution that no one could be sure would actually work. In early 1983, Reagan presented the public with a better civil defense fantasy, one that Congress and many Americans would accept, one that promised world peace forever—the seductive dream of a defensive missile shield.

This civil defense illusion had been on Reagan's mind even before his 1980 election. In July 1979, he had been invited to visit the headquarters of the North American Aerospace Defense Command (NORAD) in Cheyenne Mountain, Colorado. A vast underground area had been carved deep into the granite mountain, accessible only through massive steel doors. Inside the command room were a gigantic screen displaying an outline of the United States and hundreds of men and women whose job was to spot through radar any incoming Soviet missiles and alert the president, who would decide if he should order a retaliatory nuclear strike. In an oft-repeated script, visitors would ask the base commander what else could be done if a nuclear missile were discovered to be headed toward an American target. The somber reply was always: "Nothing. Nothing can be done to stop the missile." According to the story Reagan often told, he was incredibly shaken by the Cheyenne Mountain experience, and by the fact that there was nothing that could prevent a Soviet nuclear attack.

Yet this was hardly a new idea to Ronald Reagan. In his failed 1976 campaign for the Republican presidential nomination, Reagan had frequently denounced MAD, describing it as nothing but "two men pointing cocked and loaded pistols at each other's heads," with no defense against mutual suicide, should one man decide to pull the trigger. Reagan later claimed that it was at

Cheyenne Mountain that he began to dream of the protective missile system he would announce to the nation less than three years after his visit to NORAD. Although untrue, it made a dramatic story for the former actor to tell.

No matter what its form—whether evacuation plans, bomb shelters, defensive missiles, or magic beams—a civil defense program for the public and an even more effective one for the political, military, and industrial elite were crucial to the belief of CPD members that it was possible to fight a nuclear war and survive. Ronald Reagan understood this well. *Los Angeles Times* reporter Robert Scheer, who interviewed Reagan over a period of several days during the 1980 presidential campaign, discovered that Reagan's "advocacy of civil defense against nuclear war . . . reached the point of greatest detachment from reality" of any subject they discussed. "Perhaps because he wanted so much to believe that his get-tough stance toward the Soviets really did lessen the risks of global death and destruction, Reagan had come to believe what his advisers had told him: that civil defense can change the deadly implications of the nuclear equation."[2]

The 1980 Republican platform called for sharply increased weapons production and for "a strategic and civil defense which would protect the American people against nuclear war at least as well as the Soviet population is protected." The survival of the leaders who would be directing the protracted nuclear war was central to Reagan's and the CPD's concept of American civil defense. The new vice president and former convener of Team B, George Bush, dubbed this capacity "the survivability of command and control." In the fall of 1981, President Reagan called his new $18 billion program for the continuity of government the most important part of his strategic plan. As later allotments of money would make clear, the Reagan administration's provision for *public* civil defense was little more than a paper plan. A 1982 Library of Congress study revealed that for every dollar being spent per citizen on civil defense, many thousands of dollars were spent to save each selected government official.[3]

      •   •   •

On October 2, 1981, Reagan announced his intention to establish a greatly expanded civil defense program. A few months later, he signed National Security Decision Directive (NSDD) 26, outlining a $4.2 billion program, to be realized over the next seven years. This endeavor, the most ambitious in the nation's civil defense history, was openly proclaimed as a means of achieving three goals. First, it was designed to reduce the possibility that the Soviet Union, supposedly secure behind its efficient civil defense system, might successfully coerce the United States through threat of nuclear attack. Second, to make that nuclear war scenario seem less frightening to the public, Reagan's new emphasis on civil defense also promised to provide an "improved ability to deal with natural disasters and other large-scale domestic emergencies." After the militant civil rights, antiwar, and anti–nuclear reactor protests of the 1960s and 1970s, the possibility of a domestic emergency must have seemed increasingly likely to many in the new administration. And, as always, the public found a promise of civil defense dual use—a focus on preparation for natural disasters rather than for nuclear war—a much less threatening goal for federal emergency management. Also, because many conservative leaders claimed that the Soviet Union was spending huge sums to protect its political and military directors, the third goal of Reagan's civil defense stressed that the United States too would ensure U.S. continuity of government (survival of and communication among the political, military, and industrial leaders) should "deterrence and escalation control fail"—in other words, when nuclear war began.

Continuity of government was very expensive, meaning there would be much less money available to save a portion of the general population from nuclear attack. Yet even a partially adequate underground shelter system for the citizens at large was calculated to cost several hundred billion dollars each year simply to construct, maintain, and equip. The Reagan civil defense program for the public was thus forced to create over the next seven years, not operational systems, but only detailed plans. And even then, these structured schemes were not conceived as plans for shelters, but only plans for evacuation of the public from the expected target areas when war seemed imminent. By the early 1980s, after all of the postwar presidents had tried civil defense attempts at dispersal, evacuation, blast shelters, and fallout shelters, and given up on each of them after public protest, Reagan decided to stick with the evacuation option to which Carter had returned in 1978.[4]

FEMA, the civil defense center created by Carter, provided crisis relocation planning, or CRP, as the media soon named the program. By 1983, the agency claimed to have collected local crisis relocation plans for 1,489 areas out of the 3,135 needed in the nation, admittedly concentrating on areas of lower risk rather than more populated regions. CRPs were designed to protect the people against a total 6,559-megaton attack—the equivalent of about 500,000 Hiroshima-sized bomb blasts occurring simultaneously. By any informed standard, this scale of attack on persons not buried deep in the earth nor supplied with adequate ventilation and food to last many years would mean the quick death of almost all Americans and a good portion of the rest of the world as well. The civil defense bureaucrats neatly avoided this reality by simply neglecting to consider the effects of fallout as part of this scenario.[5]

FEMA planners predicted that about 150 million people, roughly two-thirds of the population, would survive the nuclear assault through evacuation. These survivors, presumably from about 400 "high-risk" areas, would then be moved

to 2,000 safer "host areas," located 50–400 miles away from the expected targets. High-risk areas denoted where nuclear weapons were based or stored, or
where military centers, war industry centers, or cities with populations over
50,000 were found, whereas the safe areas were described as small towns and
rural areas.

CRP was predicated on there being three to five days' advance notice to
complete evacuation before the nuclear attack began. FEMA also predicted that
only about 80 percent of the at-risk population would evacuate, with the other
20 percent being either too old, sick, mentally ill, drug addicted, disabled, or
unwilling to leave. No systematic provision was made for the evacuation of
tens of thousands of persons in asylums, hospitals, old age homes, or prisons.
Those dubbed "political terrorists" would also refuse to evacuate, according
to CRP documents. It was further estimated that about 30 million of the total
evacuees would be "essential workers" who in the post-attack world would be
required to commute back into bombed areas to go to work daily, although how
workplaces would exist in intensely radiated and heavily bombed target areas
was not elaborated. FEMA ordered that all civil defense instructions about
evacuation be made to appear as though they were coming from local authorities, since it would otherwise seem that the process was being managed by the
federal government, and this might antagonize a potential enemy poised to
lob bombs as soon as the evacuation period was over. Understandably, Jerome
Wiesner, the former chief science advisor to President Kennedy, was only one
of many informed skeptics in 1983 who thought the set of crisis relocation assumptions seemed to have been fashioned not by the locals, or the feds, but by
the Keystone Cops.[6]

FEMA planned for evacuation booklets to be given to escaping citizens that
would detail both their exit routes and eventual destinations. Boston's brochure
included a questionnaire to be filled out in duplicate before reaching the host
area. Many CRPs gave precise instructions to evacuees on what to stock in their
cars: stocks, bonds, wills, credit cards, medicine, food, water, money, extra
socks, toys for the children, toilet paper, and sanitary napkins; to be left behind
were guns, illegal drugs, and family pets. In case of breakdown or a traffic jam,
citizens were told to stay in their cars, remain patient and calm, and listen for
instructions. They were reminded to turn over their car keys to the proper authorities when they reached their host sites. Little consideration was given to
how to obtain gasoline or travel over highways that may have been blocked or
closed to serve military goals. Those fleeing high-risk targets on trains, boats,
buses, and airplanes were dependent on drivers and pilots to remain at their
jobs. Schoolchildren would be evacuated safely by conscientious schoolteachers
and bus drivers who could be trusted to forsake their own loved ones in order
to help the thousands of escaping schoolchildren.

In the early 1980s, FEMA hired hundreds of temporary staff, including college students, to mark prospective shelter spaces in a few host areas. The agency estimated that about half of the evacuees would either move in with friends or relatives at the host sites or into already constructed basements and buildings. The other half would construct "expedient shelters," a euphemism for quickly dug trenches covered by a car parked overhead, or by pieces of wood, like doors removed from a nearby building. Each type of covered hole-in-the-ground "fallout" shelter was supposed to hold four people and be covered by four tons of hastily assembled dirt positioned over and around the hole before the nuclear bombs arrived. In a House debate on the wisdom of CRP in the summer of 1981, Representative Edward J. Markey (D-Mass.), a long-time foe of civil defense, detailed how, according to FEMA's car-trench plan, "all that is needed for salvation is four sandbags, 50 feet of strong twine, two long-handled pointed shovels, two bed sheets and two day-laborers (the scheme requires eight hours to dig the car's grave)."[7] Inhabitants of these hastily constructed shelters would simply pile dirt around the area and hide in these holes for two weeks without sufficient air, food, or water. Markey mockingly noted that FEMA admitted that the shoveling of dirt might be very difficult if the ground were frozen, but that the agency promised that the necessary construction equipment would be available if needed. All of this was seriously outlined by FEMA at a time when Soviet missiles were estimated to take less than forty-five minutes to reach targets in the United States.

FEMA-financed studies computed the cost of transporting, feeding, housing, and caring for all of these millions of evacuees to be about $2 billion a day, a very conservative estimate in the opinion of many. This would be quite a strain on the economy, especially considering the substantial cost of repairing the damage caused by hydrogen bombs and perhaps simultaneously fighting a limited nuclear war under the direction of the underground elite saved by the continuity-of-government plan. But the single most criticized element of the official version of FEMA's general CRP was the belief that the evacuees could safely emerge from their shelters about two weeks after the bombs hit. CRP documents do not give serious analysis to post-attack issues, such as the effects of radiation or the difficulty of finding food, water, medical care, and other essentials. Wider problems, such as the presence of rotting corpses, with the consequent spread of epidemic disease, or the varied ecological effects of nuclear war are also not presented. Instead, FEMA produced documents about how to preserve bank records, or how to continue mail delivery after a nuclear holocaust.[8]

The renowned reporter Jack Anderson, along with dozens of other prominent media figures, exposed the bizarre elements in the Reagan civil defense program:

Casualty predictions of only 40 million dead [after nuclear attack] are based on three unrealistic assumptions: that the Soviets would only attack once, that they would somehow fail to hit any nuclear power plants, and that all survivors would have near-perfect fallout protection. . . . to make the government predictions come true, deaths from disease, starvation, mass fires or firestorms are considered insignificant.[9]

In a tongue-in-cheek column in the *Washington Post*, Pulitzer Prize–winning reporter William Raspberry warned readers not to ridicule CRP planners:

Don't laugh. They take this stuff very seriously. Just listen to the instructions the Labor Department gives its employees: "If you are prevented from going to your regular place of employment because of an enemy attack . . . go to the nearest Post Office, ask the Postmaster for a Federal Employee Registration Card, fill it out and return it to him. . . ."

Have you got that? The nukes have hit the fan, we are under attack, the city is burning, and the evacuation routes are clogged. But the guys at the P.O. are just sitting there waiting for you to drop by and fill out your Federal Employee Registration Card, and the folk over at the personnel office are waiting to process it so the faithful in payroll can mail your check.

If the specifics of the civil defense plan seem absurd, so do the basic assumptions—for instance, that we will have a week's warning to get out of town, or that getting out of town would save us from radioactive fallout. . . .

You know what's really funny? The fact that the people who come up with these hilarious plans for what to do in case of nuclear war are the same ones charged with the responsibility for preventing nuclear war. Isn't that a good one? You could die laughing.[10]

Raspberry was not alone in attempting to find words to express horror at the absence of reality so evident in FEMA relocation documents. One sociologist concluded that crisis relocation plans represent "fantasy documents," forms of rhetoric designed to convince audiences that experts can transform incredible uncertainties into manageable risks, solving problems for which there are no solutions. A political scientist writing in 1984 ended his critical study of CRP with a single, plaintive query: "Where are the grownups?"[11]

From the 1960s through the late 1980s, about 2,000 reports and studies concerning civil defense were produced for FEMA and its predecessor civil defense agencies, costing taxpayers hundreds of millions of dollars. Since the early 1970s, approximately 370 of these government-financed documents have addressed the issues of crisis relocation. Again and again, these reports stress that civil defense is moral, wise, and effective. Drawn from a relatively small number of research centers, they were written by many of the same people, who often cross-reference and quote one another to validate their questionable assumptions about the validity of crisis relocation plans.

One of the most startling assumptions often cited by FEMA officials and civil defense proponents is that crisis relocation would allow 80 percent of the population to survive a nuclear attack of more than 6,550 megatons. This fictitious figure was repeated scores of times in speeches, documents, and public statements. The origins and validity of this statistic have been questioned by many scholars and other commentators. In 1981, an official in the office of the undersecretary of defense for policy testified before a Senate committee that the 80 percent figure was really only an "entering assumption" rather than an "analytically derived finding." A member of FEMA's national policy staff confirmed that the number was based solely on the opinions of civil defense managers, contract personnel, and the few academics supportive of CRP. Yet the false survival rate of 80 percent continued to be quoted over and over again.[12]

The most prominent critique of crisis relocation was that it would not save any significant number of lives, not during the nuclear war and certainly not afterward. Only a deeply buried blast shelter system, fully equipped and ventilated to provide all necessities for a period of several years, might save a significant number of lives, and as the public eventually realized, this system was intended only for the use of top military and political figures. A similar system to protect citizens in major cities was estimated by the Federation of Scientists in 1981 to cost more than $100 billion.[13] Such a blast and fallout shelter protection system for the general American public was never considered seriously by the federal government as a solution to the nuclear dilemma.

Crisis relocation planners failed to address a number of Soviet strategies. For example, the Soviet Union could retarget its bombs whenever U.S. relocation began, putting the newly evacuated millions of American citizens at ground zero. The Soviets could threaten war, wait for crisis relocation to empty U.S. cities, then quickly call for peace, wait until the evacuees had returned home, and then threaten war again, starting the process all over. How many times would U.S. citizens be willing to follow government directions for crisis relocation, only to be told to do it all over again? If the first evacuation were judged to be unnecessary, it seemed unlikely that Americans would respond to any second call. Did not CRP thus essentially place the process of crisis evacuation under the control of the enemy? When the Soviets observed the beginning of the American evacuation process, would they not assume that the United States was planning a first strike and thus feel it necessary to attack first? And if the Soviets began civil defense preparation themselves, wouldn't American officials feel the necessity for a first strike?

Writing in 1983, Jerome Wiesner echoed hundreds of other informed critics of civil defense efforts when he pointed out the hopeless inadequacy of CRP:

> Crisis relocation planning is morally wrong; it is strategically wrong; and it is operationally wrong. . . . The studies undertaken by think-tanks for FEMA and its predecessors are the ultimate examples of technical rationality and system analysis gone amuck. . . . CRP is *central* to a war-fighting, first-strike, limited nuclear war—call it what you want—strategy. . . . Without the smokescreen provided by CRP, the administration would have to admit that the vast majority of Americans would be killed in a nuclear exchange. . . . Eisenhower came to this conclusion. Kennedy did as well. Given the facts, these leaders made the only reasonable assessment. In these times of even greater peril, we must demand the same discernment from our own.[14]

Rather than recognizing that nuclear weapons had made war obsolete between nuclear powers, or moving to halt the arms race, the Reagan administration advocated victory in a limited nuclear war and offered civil defense as a means of survival. This choice also allowed the government to continue uninterrupted funding to the military-industrial complex and avoid monetary losses to weapons makers, their employees, and their suppliers.

•   •   •

To direct his new civil defense effort, Reagan initially appointed sixty-one-year-old Louis O. Giuffrida as director of FEMA. Giuffrida—who insisted on being addressed as "General" based on his California National Guard rank—was a self-defined counterterrorism expert. When Reagan was governor of California, Giuffrida had served as head of the newly established California Specialized Training Institute (CSTI). Under Giuffrida's direction, this organization taught thousands the tactics of emergency management and "terrorist control." Some suspected that then-governor Reagan's choice of Giuffrida, made at a time when protests were rocking California universities, was inspired by a paper that Giuffrida wrote while a student at the Army War College. This study outlined a hypothetical situation of widespread domestic violence sparked by African-American militants. The paper laid out a detailed plan to allow military units to control dissent through the detention of blacks in large-scale confinement camps similar to those devised to contain Japanese Americans during World War II.[15]

Upon his appointment, Giuffrida made a number of substantial changes to FEMA, including hiring so many friends from CSTI and the military police to fill high-level agency positions that the *Washington Post* was moved to comment. As director, Giuffrida often spoke casually of nuclear conflict as "nuke-war." In the fall of 1981, he announced: "The other thing this Administration has categorically rejected is the short-war, mutually assured destruction, it'll all be over in 20 minutes so why the hell mess around spending dollars on it. We're trying to inject long-war mentality."[16] He also ordered that henceforth no FEMA official would be allowed to speak directly to congressmen without Giuffrida's prior approval.[17] So dramatic was Giuffrida's impact on FEMA that four years after he took control, the agency lay splintered in incredible disarray, split by internal feuds, investigated by several congressional committees, and ridiculed by the public and media alike. Giuffrida would eventually be forced to resign in disgrace in 1985, accused of mismanagement, financial corruption, and favoritism to selected contractors.

●   ●   ●

During Giuffrida's time at the helm of FEMA, seven states and 120 localities —home to about 90 million people—formally refused to participate in CRP. The vast majority of jurisdictions either ignored or quickly dismissed the CRP documents prepared by civil defense officials and the studies funded through government contracts.

The relocation plan for New York City and for the state of New York was one of the earliest to be attacked by the national press. In FEMA's plan, New York City was scheduled to evacuate 10 percent of its population by air, 13 percent by rail, 2.5 percent by water, 16 percent by bus, and 57 percent by private automobile, all moving toward upstate New York and into Pennsylvania. (To handle possible traffic problems among the millions of panicked citizens leaving the nation's cities by auto, FEMA's overall plan directed citizens leaving the nation's capitol who had auto license plates beginning with odd numbers to wait for those with even numbers to go first in the evacuation.) "Nobody's suggesting you could move New York City in fifteen minutes," General Giuffrida insisted to his critics. "That's stupid. But we could do New York if we had a plan in place; we could do New York in five days, a week."[18]

The plans envisioned moving 11.3 million New Yorkers in three and a half days by sending 75,000 up the Hudson River on Staten Island ferries, 300,000 on subways to rail yards in Hoboken, and 43,000 more from LaGuardia airport on planes. A 1980 FEMA study noted that a half million Hispanic and African-American Bronx citizens moving into rural Ulster County might not be welcome there and "might experience special problems." Certainly one of the biggest problems, not only for residents of the Bronx, but for the entire New York urban area, would be finding a car in which to escape the city. In 1980, the New York Transit Authority was prevented from soliciting bids for equipment to protect operation of the city's subway system from being knocked out by the electromagnetic pulse (EMP) that follows a nuclear explosion. A Brooklyn state senator called it a waste of money, because "the Transit Authority can't keep the trains rolling during an average rush hour," and the plan was dropped the next day. By 1982, the New York City Council, along with many other urban governments, voted overwhelmingly to refuse any and all participation in FEMA's nuclear crisis relocation plans.[19]

On April 3, 1982, a *New York Times* editorial pointed out that most informed persons realized that the CPD-produced descriptions of Soviet civil defense were "a vast exaggeration." Any attempt to upset the balance of fear produced by MAD, or to deny the fact that neither the United States nor the Soviet Union could launch a nuclear attack on the other without suffering unbearable destruction, was incredibly dangerous to human life on earth, the *Times* concluded. To believe that it is feasible to fight a nuclear war and survive, the editorial exclaimed, is an idea that "is not merely irresponsible; it is mad."[20]

In Plattsburg, New York, a population of 44,000 people was directed to locations fifteen to thirty-five miles away from the city's Strategic Air Command base. One of the eight escape routes passed directly in front of the base, and another route was a hopeless bottleneck. Large numbers of residents were to be sent to nearby Dannemora, although the town supervisor there testified to the state legislature that he had been told nothing about the plans. The relocation plan for Plattsburg also relied on the local telephone circuits and radio stations to provide instructions for escaping residents, but like crisis relocation plans nationwide, no provisions were made for after communications were knocked out. Ithaca, New York, was an evacuation site for 280,000 people, but an army nuclear weapons storage center was only thirty miles from the city. The anthropology department chair at Ithaca College warned political evacuees: "Ithaca won't do you much good," with its one hospital and limited housing and space:

> We have lots of trees but no spare tree houses. . . . We have both a conscientious fire chief and a regional disaster planner who have called the relocation plans for the county unrealistic and ridiculous. [Better bring with you] adequate food, water and clothing and toiletries, for several months . . . a refrigerator, your own medicine, doctor and . . . hospital, . . . fire truck[,] . . . tent, shelter and fuel supply. . . . So along with everything else, bring flowers—and pack up your delusions, about the survivability

of a war that will unite upstate and downstate in a great cloud of un-knowing.[21]

The residents of Tucson, Arizona, were slated to head for Nogales, on the Mexican border. Some 542 people were directed to take refuge in the Nogales True Value Hardware Store. When the owner of the store first learned of the plan from an inquiring reporter, he whooped, "Jiminy Christmas!" and noted there were only two toilets in the building. The owner said he would probably just flee south into Mexico in the event of a nuclear warning.[22]

Up north in Minnesota, the Northfield City Council appointed a task force to investigate the city's position as a host area for Minneapolis residents, forty miles away. The committee spent many weeks reading FEMA material and held twenty community discussions. The case of 170 evacuees designated to find refuge in Bob's Shoes was typical: the basement measured about forty feet on each side. After six months of study, the city council unanimously voted not to participate in planning for crisis relocation. It also established a Task Force on Nuclear War Education and Prevention, after community discussions led a majority of the local residents to conclude that the real purpose of CRP was to prepare Americans to fight a nuclear war. That same year, in Grand Forks, North Dakota, the city council joined hundreds of other towns in judging CRP "unrealistic" and solely devoted to promoting "the illusion of protection against nuclear war."[23]

In community after community, large and small, the anti–civil defense protest grew louder and more visible. In Greensboro, North Carolina, a state official removed the Fallout Shelter signs from 170 buildings, on the grounds that they did not offer protection from starvation. Marin County, California, withdrew from civil defense planning because, as one official put it, "there's no way we can evacuate skeletons." In September 1982, about 150 Burlington, Connecticut, citizens, calling their group BOMBS for the Burlington Organization for the Movement of Bodies to Safety, participated in a mock civil defense drill and evacuated to Beckett, Massachusetts, sixty-five miles away. There, they were greeted by members of BLAST, the Beckett League to Assist the Scorched and Terrified. On and on throughout the nation, the people rose to ridicule and denounce crisis relocation planning.[24]

In March 1982, the popular TV program "The MacNeil-Lehrer Report" gave prime coverage to a public meeting where citizens of Boulder, Colorado, rejected CRP. The TV attention all but finished off CRP as a viable govern-ment program. In Boulder, the first public meeting to consider CRP had to be postponed due to insufficient space and moved to a movie theater because more than 1,000 local citizens showed up. "MacNeil-Lehrer" presented excerpts from the speakers who derided CRP as a "treacherous security blanket." The audience was shown cheering for the speaker who proclaimed that "we're not talking here about crisis relocation but about massive casualties, destruction on a scale that no one has ever witnessed, and the possible elimination of the human race." "MacNeil-Lehrer" interviewed one of the county commissioners who had voted unanimously to reject CRP and who had come to see the relocation program as "people in Washington playing games with our lives." She doubted that the "Russian people are taking their civil defense programs any more seriously than the people in Boulder County are taking theirs" and felt that no one could "get in an automobile and drive away from a nuclear war. Now, I don't believe that's true, and I don't believe anyone who tells me that is being very honest with me."[25] Boulder refused to accept CRP, along with hundreds of other locales across the nation, from New York to San Francisco.

Two months after the "MacNeil-Lehrer" broadcast, an episode of "60 Minutes" focused even more closely on the Boulder rejection. The program opened with a discussion of the effects of a twenty-megaton H-bomb. Narrator Ed Bradley then returned to the scenes of angry citizens denouncing FEMA plans in Boulder. Bradley traveled to the little mountain town of Nederland, designated by CRP as the host town to receive Boulder evacuees. The mayor of Nederland, who knew nothing of the host plan, reported that the town had only one three-room motel and one school that might serve as a public shelter. Bradley asked the regional head of FEMA how 3,000 folks were going to make it up the narrow winding road up Boulder Canyon to Nederland, especially with all of the loose large rocks along the sides of the passage. The FEMA local official acknowledged the problem and commented that "if you're a native Coloradan, that's kinda fun to drive up that." The last comment presented by "60 Minutes" was from a grim and tight-mouthed Giuffrida, who conceded that after nuclear war the United States "would be different in many significant ways from the way it is now," but he still insisted, "we're a nation of survivors, always have been."

Washington and Oregon were destined to play major roles in the final destruction of CRP as a federal effort. The first phase of the Washington struggle began in February 1982, when a *Seattle Post-Intelligencer* editorial noted:

> [T]he first and most important defect in nuclear evacuation planning is that it would be another step toward conditioning the nation to an acceptance of nuclear war, and the fragile premise that wholesale evacuation would be a safeguard against instant nuclear death or lingering but equally fatal burns and radiation sickness.

A few months later, a local neurosurgeon, Dr. Richard Rapport, spoke in Seattle and called the CRP plans for nuclear evacuation "rubbish." By July, the

San Juan County commissioners in Washington voted to reject a federal plan to evacuate civilians to the remote San Juan Islands via the Washington state ferry system. More than one hundred people packed the meeting hall and gave standing ovations to the antievacuation speakers, one of whom pointed out that Lopez Island, destined to receive 16,000 evacuees, had one doctor and a two-bed hospital. A San Juan Island commissioner predicted that "the biggest and meanest people with the biggest and meanest guns will be the first people on the boats." A top FEMA official in Washington, D.C., responded that Lopez Island was only a "mini-plan" and needed more work. By March 28, 1983, the county executive of King County in Washington, Randy Revelle, ordered all references to crisis relocation planning for nuclear war be removed from the county's emergency services plan. He announced that CRP was useless and that the only sensible planning should be how to avoid nuclear war.[26]

●   ●   ●

As CRP suffered public embarrassment and defeats, others sought to develop a laser defense system to protect Americans from nuclear attack. This concept called for the use of a few dozen laser beams to be placed into orbit above the earth, to cover every spot on the globe, to be activated when needed, and to be beamed down to destroy any number of incoming enemy missiles before they reached their targets. Yet the public heard little about this dream beam quest for security, which emerged primarily from the work of Edward Teller, fervent cold warrior and long-time convert to civil defense, and of retired army Lieutenant General Daniel O. Graham, once head of the Defense Intelligence Agency. Both were members of CPD, and Graham had served on Team B. A conservative Republican senator from Wyoming, Malcom Wallop, and his New Right staff member Angelo Codevilla were also important propagandists in the effort to sell the president, the Pentagon, and the Congress on the idea of a laser defense.

The campaign for a defensive space-based beam moved slowly. A Senate committee increased the funding for research into orbiting defensive lasers to $68 million in 1979; and the next year the Defense Department was directed to begin a study of space-based defensive laser beams. In early 1981, Edward Teller lobbied in Washington for money to develop an X-ray laser beam, given the code name Excalibur, with an anticipated lethal range of thousands of miles. Yet, by early 1983, the concept of what would come to be known as Star Wars had made no real progress toward significant funding or military or congressional support from any but a few true believers.

The ultraconservative ideology of the CPD members newly installed in the Reagan administration, with their loose talk of fighting and winning a limited nuclear war and their revulsion at détente and arms control, suffered rapid rejection by citizens and lawmakers. By December 1982, Reagan's public approval rating had fallen to 41 percent, the lowest for any postwar president after only two years in office. Moreover, a poll showed that 66 percent of Americans thought he had failed in arms control, and 57 percent thought he might actually involve the nation in a nuclear war. This widespread alarm was in response to a variety of actions and events that formed a frightening pattern. Within two years, the Reagan administration increased the military budget from $142 billion to $222 billion; planned the development of large numbers of missiles, nuclear submarines, cruise missiles, and bombers; urged the expansion of civil defense systems; and sought a hugely expensive increase in the continuity-of-government program.[27] Meanwhile, administration officials, including the secretary of defense, talked openly of the possibility of fighting and winning a nuclear war.

T. K. Jones, the deputy undersecretary of defense for research and engineering, strategic and theater nuclear forces, damaged the administration's credibility considerably with his widely publicized comments on civil defense. Before he came to Washington, Jones had worked for Boeing where he helped to provide the false statistics used to support the CPD claim that the Soviet civil defense system was so efficient that it would protect 90 percent of its people, even during an all-out nuclear war with the United States. In early 1982, his interview with reporter Robert Scheer about Reagan's new civil defense plan ran in the *Los Angeles Times*, creating a startled response among congressional representatives and general readers alike. T. K. Jones told Scheer that people should not fear the effects of nuclear war if they could find, or dig, an empty hole in the ground before the bombs landed. "Dig a hole, cover it with a couple of doors and then throw three feet of dirt on top. It's the dirt that does it," Jones promised. He assured Scheer that Americans could leave the hole in about a week and lead a nearly normal life. In fact, Jones said, "Everybody is going to make it if there are enough shovels to go around."[28]

T. K. Jones was immediately called before several congressional committees to explain his shocking predictions, but three times Jones did not show up to give testimony. The *New York Times* chortled:

> Who is the Thomas K. Jones who is saying those funny things about civil defense? Is he only a character in "Doonesbury"? Did he once write lyrics for Tom Lehrer's darker political ballads? Or is T. K., as he is known to friends, the peace movement's mole inside the Reagan Administration?[29]

Embarrassed CPD regulars and the Pentagon hawks did their best to quiet the furor by keeping Jones away from more public attention. When he finally did appear before the subcommittee of the Senate Foreign Relations Committee, Jones denied he had told Scheer that the United States could fully recover in two to four years from a full nuclear attack in which Russia launched all of its missiles. Jones's denial went sour, however; Scheer had the whole interview on tape.

In July 1982, an effort to reduce funding for civil defense and to prohibit crisis relocation planning was spearheaded by Representatives Edward J. Markey (D-Mass.), Pat Schroeder (D-Colo.), and Ronald Dellums (D-Calif.). Earlier that year, Dellums, a strong progressive and one of the most anti–civil defense members of Congress, became chair of the House Armed Services Committee, which oversaw the civil defense budget. Dellums, described by the journal of the major pro–civil defense organization as "a patrician-looking Black with a masters degree from the University of California at Berkeley in social work," elicited both terror and contempt from civil defense advocates. By late 1983, California became one of the first states to pass a law forbidding the use of state funds for crisis relocation planning as defense against nuclear war. Many more would follow.[30]

By the end of 1982, the Reagan administration's vast weapons buildup and talk by high officials about fighting and winning a nuclear war, all underpinned by equally unpopular concepts of Soviet and American civil defense systems, had thoroughly frightened many political leaders and the public on both sides of the Cold War divide. Nowhere was the fearful rejection of the new militant and threatening tone of American foreign policy more apparent than in Western Europe in the early 1980s. There, a peace movement grew to huge proportions within only a few years.

* * *

The European revolt began in December 1979 when North Atlantic Treaty Organization leaders agreed to place 572 American-developed cruise and Pershing II missiles in five countries: West Germany, Belgium, the United Kingdom, the Netherlands, and Italy. With installation planned for 1983, these intermediate nuclear forces (INF), called cruise missiles, were meant to counteract the threat posed by the very large Soviet SS-20 long-range missiles aimed at Western Europe. The Soviets found the U.S. cruise missiles—small, highly accurate, difficult to detect on radar, and able to reach Moscow from Europe in a few minutes—immensely threatening. The cruise missiles were designed to reassure the Europeans that, if the Soviets threatened Western Europe, the United States would retaliate against the Soviet homeland, but Western Europeans quickly realized that if deterrence failed, the superpowers would surely choose, at least initially, to fight their battle in Europe rather than directly attack each other. The introduction of cruise missiles into Europe ensured that those missile sites would be the first and natural targets if the Soviets ever attacked, leaving Europe a radiated ruin.

When the NATO decision to deploy these missiles was announced in December 1979, 40,000 Belgians gathered at once in protest. This was only the beginning. Never before had there been a European peace movement so large and so rapidly assembled, nor one in which so many citizens of Western Europe came together to support the same issue. Within a year, 2,300 local, national, and international groups had assembled. On Easter 1981, 100,000 peace activists and supporters gathered in Brussels. By autumn, 200,000 marched in London, 250,000 in Bonn, and a half million each in Rome, Paris, and Amsterdam. They were determined and nonviolent, many dressed in skeleton costumes. When Reagan visited Europe in June 1982, he was confronted by even larger demonstrations—a quarter million in London and Rome, another half million in the streets of Bonn and West Berlin—amazingly large numbers for countries with populations less than a quarter of the United States. In 1981, the Greenham Common women's peace camp was created outside the proposed location for the new cruise missiles in Britain, attracting more than 100,000 visitors during the next two years and serving as inspiration for a dozen other women's peace camps throughout the world.

As the time for the deployment of the cruise missiles neared, the peace crowds grew even larger. In October 1983, more than 3 million people demonstrated in Western Europe. On a single day, 1 million protested in West Germany. A rally at the Hague brought out nearly 4 percent of the Dutch population, 550,000 people. A half million marched in Brussels and 300,000 in London. Massive chains of people, including one seventy-two miles long, from Stuttgart to Neu-Ulm, involving almost a million people, dramatized the popular opposition to increased nuclear weapons.[31]

These numbers only represent those who marched in the streets, but the European peace movement of this period was far larger. Neighbors, strangers, colleagues, workers, and professionals met together in thousands of groups, in kitchens, auditoriums, churches, bars, and restaurants, to discuss what had to be done to prevent a nuclear exchange in their countries. Nuclear weapons and nuclear war became subjects for public debate, no longer restricted to military and political experts and never again judged to be government business only.

Within this gargantuan European peace mobilization of the early 1980s, the story of protest in England is particularly important because it strongly influenced and inspired American anti–civil defense activists. Just as in the United States, the British governmental effort to establish a national civil defense program so angered the populace that civil defense itself became the key idea that activated a powerful antinuclear social movement. In early 1980, the British

Home Office published a civil defense pamphlet entitled *Protect and Survive*, which advised citizens, in the event of nuclear war, to hide under tables, paint windows to block the heat of nuclear flash, live in holes protected by old doors and sandbags, and store enough food and water for fourteen days, along with reading material and a can opener. The public responded to this official recommendation with predictable fury. According to one British pacifist, *Protect and Survive* was "the best gift CND (Committee for Nuclear Disarmament) ever had from any government," greatly aiding the revival of CND, England's major peace organization, which had faltered in the mid-1960s, was rebuilding in the 1970s, and exploded in power and numbers in the early 1980s.[32] But the greatest catalyst to anti–civil defense protest in Britain came when an exposure of government plans revealed that the British government anticipated that after nuclear war the small remaining population—left psychologically disturbed, ravaged by epidemics and radiation sickness, and without medical care, food, or water—would need to be ruled by martial law, while looters and dissenters would be placed in concentration camps or, if necessary, executed. As one study of British civil defense noted:

> On the one hand, civil defense planners imagine that the public will do as they are advised: stay at home, prepare a shelter, quietly wrap their dead in plastic bags, listen to the radio, work as directed by the authorities, allow themselves to be turned away from hospital. On the other hand, it is imagined that the same public will panic, evacuate the cities, ignore instructions, challenge the authorities.[33]

At this point, the leading British intellectual and peace activist, E. P. Thompson, responded with a brilliant and contemptuous counterattack on British civil defense, entitled *Protest and Survive*. Thompson's work, read by millions worldwide, rallied protesters and inspired the formation of European Nuclear Disarmament (END), which quickly became the coordinating group for the European peace effort.

Again, just as in the United States, hundreds of local communities in Britain during the 1980s declared themselves to be nuclear-free zones and rejected any participation in civil defense plans. In Bridgend, Wales, the government allotted funds to renovate an underground civil defense bunker, designed to protect one hundred wartime officials and provided with food, air, and decontamination showers. On January 24, 1982, 600 citizens occupied the site, set up a peace camp, and pledged to stay until the building of the bunker was stopped. In early March, concrete mixer machines arrived on the site and poured concrete over about fifty nonviolent protesters—all recorded on national TV. Bombarded by angry letters, calls, and telegrams, local government officials ended bunker construction the next day. After fifty-seven days of siege, the victorious peace protesters planted daffodils on the now-abandoned bunker site, and Wales announced itself to be the first national area to be declared a nuclear-free zone. In July 1982, the British government also conceded, canceling its plans to hold a national civil defense exercise, called Hard Rock, the largest such exercise devised in fifteen years, after a large number of local authorities refused to participate. CND followed the cancellation of Hard Rock by holding a massive exercise of its own—which it called Hard Luck. This campaign featured leading scientists and physicians, who informed local citizens of the actual effects of nuclear attack on the areas in which they lived.[34] After Hard Luck, the British civil defense program for the public was effectively dead.

•   •   •

The American Nuclear Freeze organization, formed in 1980 by Randall Forsberg, a thirty-eight-year-old female defense analyst trained in arms control, emerged at the center of the growing American peace movement in the early 1980s.[35] Forsberg sought to mobilize the middle of the road, moderate middle class with her single-cause appeal to both superpowers for a bilateral freeze on the production, testing, and deployment of nuclear weapons. After Reagan's election, his administration's discussion about the possibility of enduring a limited nuclear war greatly increased support for the grassroots Freeze campaign. In 1981, about 20,000 Freeze activists were organizing in forty-three states and two-thirds of the nation's congressional districts.

Just as in Europe, the American peace movement grew at an extraordinary rate, winning support from millions of citizens. In May 1981, the Massachusetts state legislature endorsed the Freeze, followed by Oregon, Connecticut, New York, Vermont, Maine, Kansas, Iowa, Minnesota, New Jersey, Rhode Island, Michigan, North Dakota, Wisconsin, and California. The Freeze received backing from the National Council of Churches, the American Baptists, the Lutheran Church of America, the Episcopalian House of Bishops, the United Presbyterian Church, the United Methodists, the United Church of Christ, the Unitarians, and evangelist Billy Graham. In a widely discussed bishops' letter of May 1983, the U.S. Catholic church endorsed the Freeze, opposing nuclear weapons as immoral, urging the United States and the Soviet Union to renounce nuclear attacks on civilian populations, and expressing "profound skepticism" that any nuclear war would remain "limited." Another vitally important peace group, the Physicians for Social Responsibility (PSR), with 30,000 members by 1983, pledged support for the Freeze and set out to educate the public on the effects of nuclear war. Even the historically conservative American Medical Association warned citizens in 1981 that there would be no medical help of any consequence available after a nuclear exchange. The Union of Concerned Scientists staged more than 150 teach-ins on nuclear disaster at colleges and universities across the nation in 1981. In Kalamazoo, Michigan, 300 residents collected $10,000 in 1981 to rent seventeen billboards around Washington, D.C., with the words: "Hear Us . . . Nuclear War Hurts Too Much."

In 1982, the antinuclear movement gained additional force with the publication of Jonathan Schell's bestselling *Fate of the Earth*, a powerful warning of approaching nuclear holocaust. In April of that year, more than 1,000 American communities, small and large, participated in Ground Zero Week, when millions of participants learned the precise details of how nuclear war would affect their local areas, their new knowledge magnified by extensive local and national media coverage.

By the end of 1982, the success of the Freeze campaign surpassed all expectations. Public opinion polls showed that 70 percent of Americans supported a bilateral freeze. In the spring, the Freeze resolution failed by only two votes in the U.S. House of Representatives. On June 12, almost 800,000 Americans marched in New York City, making it not only the largest peace march ever held in the United States, but also the largest mass protest demonstration in American history. In the 1982 elections, the Democrats regained control of Congress; and 60 percent of the 30 percent of the American electorate who had a chance to vote on the Freeze approved it. The Freeze passed in nine of the ten states where it was on the ballot and in the District of Columbia.

In less than two years, tens of millions of Americans had registered their fervent opposition to the Reagan administration's discussion of any possibility of preparation for nuclear war. The rejection of crisis relocation plans in all parts of the country was part of a wider current of peace activism in the early 1980s, largely in response to the administration's visions of "limited" and even "winnable" forms of nuclear warfare. Career diplomat and scholar George Kennan perfectly expressed the public mood in the early years of the Reagan administration:

> It is the reflection of a deep uneasiness among our people about the direction in which our present governmental course is leading us. . . . [It] is actually overwhelmingly motivated by nothing other than a deep concern for the security of this country and this civilization in the face of a volume of weaponry capable of putting an end to both.[36]

Another important factor besides the growing peace movement caused Reagan's popularity to plummet in 1982. The quest to find acceptable sites to place MX missiles in order to protect them from attack by large Soviet missiles had begun under Carter and survived into the Reagan years, when it was still no closer to solution. Carter had even seriously considered digging 5,000 miles of trenches in which to randomly shuffle the missiles about, or basing the missiles on flatbed trucks cruising the highways in the western states. In 1982, Pentagon planners, in desperation, came up with one more idea to save the MX program. Called Dense Pack, the plan was to base all one hundred MX missiles very close together on a small strip of land. This would ensure, so the fantasy went, that the Soviet missiles raining down on the MX site would destroy each other as they collided over the MX silos, thus allowing the American MX missiles to survive. Congress and the public found this as unacceptable a concept as the earlier attempts to prepare the MX for use in nuclear war. In December 1982, the House killed the MX once again in a lopsided vote. Reagan was in political trouble, with polls showing that the public felt Reagan was not doing enough for arms control and that more than half of the citizens feared he was moving toward nuclear war. At this crucial moment, Reagan, acting almost alone and without the approval or even knowledge of most of his administrative chiefs, produced a plan "from out of the blue" that saved his party and his presidency.

•   •   •

On March 23, 1983, Reagan startled top administration officials with his unexpected announcement in a TV broadcast of his new plan to end forever the terror of nuclear war, solving the nuclear dilemma for all people for all time. He called on the power of "the scientific community in this country, those who gave us nuclear weapons, to turn their great talents now to the cause of mankind and world peace, to give us the means of rendering these weapons impotent and obsolete." This miracle would be achieved by a missile defense shield, Reagan promised, leaving behind the time-honored American deterrence policy that prevented war only through fear of mutual destruction. "Wouldn't it be better to save lives than to avenge them?" Reagan crooned. He also vowed that the knowledge to be developed by his Strategic Defense Initiative, or SDI—soon to be dubbed Star Wars by a skeptical press—would, when completed, be shared with the Soviet Union and American allies, in order to ensure worldwide nuclear disarmament. A week later, Reagan told reporters, "To look down to an endless future with both of us sitting here with these horrible missiles aimed at each other and the only thing preventing a holocaust is just so long as no one pulls the trigger—this is unthinkable."[37]

Reagan's astonished aides were well aware that SDI technology was nonexistent and that even its feasibility was denied by most defense experts. His staff scrambled to produce vague explanations of the missile defense system that Reagan had described as a goal to be realized through development of a screen which would supposedly destroy all incoming missiles. Democrats instantly ridiculed Star Wars as a Darth Vader hoax. Yet many American citizens responded favorably to their president's welcome recognition of the danger and futility of nuclear weapons. Defense contractors showered politicians with well-placed favors. By 1985, SDI became the largest military research program the United States has ever devised. By 1996, SDI and associated missile defense programs had consumed $51 billion, with additional billions spent to the present day, without any tangible technical success.

Scholars and other commentators have sought to explain the origins of Reagan's call for Star Wars. A variety of explanations were offered at the time, most of them later denied or reshaped by informers. How and why Star Wars appeared, and its historical impact, is the subject of Pulitzer Prize–winner Frances Fitzgerald's deeply researched study, likely to be the last word on this topic and certainly the best to date. After analyzing the different versions of the stories explaining the origins of the Star Wars speech and exploring the various inconsistencies within and among these tales, Fitzgerald concludes that the accounts usually given of the origins of the SDI speech are filled with contradictions and implausibilities. In addition,

> there are pieces of evidence scattered about, particularly in the work of the official [SDI] historian, Donald R. Baucom, and that of the Naval War College historian, Frederick H. Hartmann, that do not fit this story at all. Finally, except in interviews with Baucom, the participants fail to mention a phenomenon of great importance to them at the time. Once this element is introduced, the story begins to make sense—otherwise it is like the score of a piano concerto with the piano part missing. The phenomenon is, of course, the antinuclear movement: the freeze.[38]

Fitzgerald shows that the Star Wars announcement was in response to the severe political crisis Reagan was facing in early 1983. The public clearly had all but lost faith in him, his MX, and his nuclear strategy of preparing for the possibility of limited nuclear war. Above all was the problem presented to him and his team by the extraordinary popularity of the antinuclear movement here and abroad, especially by the success of the Nuclear Freeze movement. His speech erased much of his hawkish public image. Within a year, his approval rating soared, he was about to win the 1984 election in a landslide, and the Nuclear Freeze movement was in decline.

The Freeze movement rapidly lost strength in 1983 and 1984 and dissolved in 1985. It was coopted both by Reagan's new stance as peacemaker and by its nominal friends in the Democratic party. To a lesser degree, it was weakened by the millions of dollars it received from large foundations, which then felt obligated to exert their own moderating influence. In 1983, Freeze leaders supported what they called a "quick freeze," a decision to pull back from their call for stopping production of nuclear weapons, while maintaining their hope that testing and deployment might be ended. In 1983, the House passed a version of the Freeze resolution—a call for a negotiated, verifiable, and mutual freeze with the Soviets—that was so watered down that it was effectively meaningless. Still, Nuclear Freeze and the nonviolent anti–civil defense protests were at the center of the peace movement that permanently established the public right and need to challenge government "experts" and other nuclear "strategists" on all issues concerning nuclear war.

Reagan's intuitively conceived push for Star Wars also permanently altered the terms of the nuclear debate. If successfully realized, his vision of what SDI would accomplish was wonderfully positive, breathtaking in its assurance of peace. Just as peace activists had been doing for years, Reagan attacked deterrence strategy as both insane and immoral and promised to first discover, and then share with all other nations, a system that would make nuclear weapons obsolete, ending nuclear horror forever for all peoples on the planet. On the other hand, the peace movement's opposition to SDI, on the grounds that Star Wars was so far from possible development, placed antinuclear activists in the position of defending the status quo deterrence policy, which they had termed terrifying and wrong and which Reagan had finally denounced and now vowed to destroy with SDI. His Star Wars prospered both as an idea and as a budget line item. The annual research monies quickly created a powerful bureaucratic and corporate constituency that moved to support Reagan's presidency, thus to secure Star Wars' continued existence. That powerful support for a viable missile defense system has continued under George W. Bush, despite the lack of any successful research findings.

.   .   .

The transition to the post–Star Wars era was marked by the collapse of Giuffrida's FEMA on almost every front. The first blow came in February 1984, when allegations of questionable activities by Fred Villella, head of FEMA's National Emergency Training Center (NETC), were made to Senator Al Gore, Jr., then chair of the Subcommittee on Investigations and Oversight of the Committee on Science and Technology. At the instigation of several whistleblowers, the troubles at FEMA set off four separate inquiries: by the subcommittee, the General Accounting Office, the inspector general of FEMA, and the Department of Justice.

The government investigation found that FEMA leaders had prepared a luxurious apartment for their personal use at the NETC site in Emmitsburg, Maryland, spending more than $170,000 on extravagant and unnecessary items.[39] After a lengthy hearing, Giuffrida was exposed for his illegal and preferential methods in assignment of government contracts, unjustified travel abroad for his wife at government expense, and the use of federal funds to pay questionable, undocumented bills, such as seats at a fundraising dinner for a conservative political group. Giuffrida left FEMA in July 1985, denying any connection between his departure and the charges of mismanagement. Senator Gore noted that Giuffrida's departure "marks the end of a disastrous era for FEMA and brings hope for more competent stewardship."[40]

The problems at FEMA were only beginning to surface, however. The crisis relocation plan was buried quietly and with little media notice in early 1985, when FEMA announced it would no longer pursue a relocation policy without a full review of the process. By this time, more than 90 million citizens in twenty states had officially announced their refusal to participate in any nuclear evacuation drills, while most Americans simply ignored the drills. In a statement issued the next year, FEMA admitted that CRP "was contested" and declared 1986 "as a maintenance year while we address the problems of public policy involved in the Civil Defense Program."[41] In fact, relocation has never again emerged in discussions of civil defense tactics.

The major FEMA scandal of the Giuffrida years did not became public until July 1987. The front page of the *Miami Herald* ran a startling article by reporter Alfonso Chardy exposing the details of a secret plan devised under Giuffrida and centered at FEMA from 1982 to 1984. This plan would have taken effect whenever the president signed an order declaring a national emergency in response to "nuclear war, violent and widespread internal dissent, or national opposition to a U.S. military invasion abroad." At that point, martial law would be declared, and the Constitution would be suspended. Military commanders would take over local and state government, protesting civilians would be arrested, and FEMA would assume control of the nation. According to this emergency plan, the full direction of the U.S. government would be taken over at that time by the representative assigned to FEMA by the National Security Council. This designated temporary dictator was none other than Lieutenant Colonel Oliver North.

The *Herald* reported that in August 1984, when then–attorney general William French Smith heard of this secret plan of FEMA, he sent a letter of protest to North's boss, National Security Council advisor Robert McFarlane. French wrote:

> I believe that the role assigned to the Federal Emergency Management
> Agency in the revised Executive Order exceeds its proper function as a
> coordinating agency for emergency preparedness. . . . This department

and others have repeatedly raised serious policy and legal objections to the creation of an "emergency czar" role for FEMA.

In October 1984, a Jack Anderson column also accused FEMA of preparing to suspend the Bill of Rights and establish a totalitarian control system, all in the name of "national security." CIA director William Casey and NSC advisor McFarlane reassigned North to international management of the Contras, from where he would rise to national notice as director of the illegal covert American aid given to the Contra fighters in Nicaragua.[42] The Iran-Contra hearings opened immediately after Chardy's *Herald* article appeared, and North's role in FEMA was raised on the first day. Jack Brooks, the crusty Democratic representative from Texas, asked about North's crisis management function in FEMA and the contingency plan in the event of an emergency that would suspend the Constitution. The chair of the Iran-Contra hearings, Hawaiian senator Daniel Inouye, gaveled Brooks down and insisted on silence, announcing that this issue would no longer be discussed, on the ground that the question concerned important classified matters of supreme secrecy.[43] No more official information was ever heard again regarding North's role in FEMA as the emergency czar.

• • •

With the abandonment of crisis relocation planning, the Reagan administration returned to the idea of bomb shelters, but just for state and local officials. (Protection of federal leaders and important aides was already covertly managed in the continuity-of-government process.) The public was now simply encouraged to rely on "self-help" and federal instructional materials. FEMA drafted a $1.5 billion plan to build 600 bomb shelters for local officials between 1988 and 1992. Eventually, construction of 3,400 shelters was planned although the details of where, why, and at what cost were left vague. According to FEMA, these shelters had a second major purpose: the storage and protection of land records. This meant that ordinary citizens, after nuclear war, "could retain and demonstrate ownership" of property not destroyed by the nuclear attack, as the associate director of FEMA announced on May 9, 1986.[44] In response, the media began to circulate old civil defense jokes—such as the advice to spend fifteen minutes a day in your clothes dryer so as to acclimate yourself for nuclear attack, or to buy stain-resistant fabric in preparation for war since laundry facilities would be unavailable after the bombs hit. Many critics noted that the new plan to protect state and local officials appeared similar to the Soviet civil defense system, which protected its government and communist elites.

Along with the bomb shelter plan, another feature of the new civil defense program was that FEMA now demanded obedience to its orders. Julius W. Becton, the new head of FEMA, drew a line in the sand, insisting in early 1986 that any state government refusing to practice civil defense drills in preparation for nuclear attack would lose its federal funds for other emergencies, such as hurricanes, floods, and earthquakes. Becton said that 1987 would be the year when the agency would again reemphasize preparation for nuclear war.[45] The hostile encounter between FEMA and protesting citizens and officials began when the state of Washington passed a law in 1984 that forbade use of state funds in developing evacuation plans in preparation for nuclear war.[46] The federal government, however, insisted that all states practice national security exercises every five years or lose federal emergency money.

The 1987 civil defense drills proposed by FEMA were code named NUDET for nuclear detonation. The war plan for this exercise was leaked to the media and used by opponents to further ridicule civil defense. FEMA's practice war begins with a twenty-day period of international tension. The U.S. stock market dives, as the army reserves are called to duty, and the Soviets prepare to attack Iran. A neo-Nazi general takes charge in Argentina, while riots rock Mexico and Brazil, and Marxist rebels take over Panama. In Seattle, there is a run on canned groceries, and Boeing closes because people stop going to work. Then comes the shower of bombs, beginning with seven enormous ones high over mid-America, causing an electromagnetic pulse that destroys electronic and telephone equipment throughout the country. Washington, Oregon, and Alaska receive forty-eight nuclear bombs, including one each on the Hanford nuclear reactor and on all of the major cities in Washington; Idaho gets only three. Each bomb is at least ten to twenty times larger than the one that hit Hiroshima. This was the supposed situation for which FEMA's nuclear drill would presumably test the states' ability to evacuate nuclear target areas.

In early 1987, the administrator of emergency management in Oregon said that his agency was keeping "a real low profile" because the majority of Oregonians would object to any participation in civil defense. Alaska residents had voted for a nuclear freeze in August 1986 and for a reduction in the nation's nuclear stockpile. The emergency management director in Alaska said, "If people all of a sudden find out we are having a nuclear attack exercise there will be a backlash." Idaho reluctantly agreed to join the civil defense drill scheduled for March 3–5, when it was told it would lose $860,000 if it did not participate. Oregon, which stood to lose $1.1 million if noncompliant, refused to participate when scheduled for the same time as Idaho. Washington and Alaska were scheduled to have their drills from March 31 to April 2. Washington would lose $1.3 million of federal funds if it did not participate in the federal exercise.[47]

Resistance to FEMA's civil defense drill was widespread in Washington state, among both residents and politicians. State representative Dick Nelson (D-Seattle), chair of the House Energy and Utilities Committee, had helped to write the 1984 law forbidding Washington state to participate in any nuclear drills. He strongly opposed cooperation with FEMA in the mock war drill of 1987. Nelson said that the civil defense drill "encourages people to believe we can survive nuclear war if we make emergency-response plans. It makes no sense." Dr. Rick Rapport, of Seattle's Physicians for Social Responsibility, another important leader in the antinuclear fight, reported that peace groups and their allies in Congress should try to force the federal government to hold a civil defense drill in response to an explosion of the nuclear reactor in Washington state, rather than a nuclear war drill. The spokesman for Washington governor Booth Gardner in January 1987 called the nuclear war test "a federal boondoggle that serves no purpose. . . . We are consistently spending billions and billions of dollars building new weapons instead of trying to fight for peace." Gardner noted the large number of bombs presumed to hit Washington, and added: "our question is, who's left to communicate with anyone at that point?" In late February, Senator Brock Adams (D-Wash.) introduced a bill in Congress to prevent FEMA from taking money away from states that refused to participate in the nuclear evacuation drill.[48]

In the late spring, Oregon stood alongside Washington in its refusal to participate in the drill. Its newly elected activist governor, Neil Goldschmidt, announced in the spring of 1987, "[O]ur citizens do not want to participate in an exercise that may actually threaten world peace by advancing the notion that a nuclear war is survivable." He warned FEMA, "this state is not for sale."[49] Senator William Proxmire, Democrat from Wisconsin and chair of the appropriations subcommittee with jurisdiction over FEMA, also questioned the agency's war drill. But the politician whom FEMA learned to fear was Oregon's senator, Mark Hatfield, a top-ranking Republican on the key Senate Appropriations Committee, an ardent supporter of disarmament, and a prime opponent of nuclear proliferation and testing. "We'll do whatever it takes to get your attention," the popular Hatfield promised. He told FEMA in late March that it had "overstepped its bounds" in attempting to take money from uncooperative states and warned FEMA that it would face cuts in its own budget if it did not reach a compromise with Washington and Oregon soon. Federal funds for civil defense in constant dollars had reached their lowest level since the Federal Civil Defense Act was enacted into law in 1950. FEMA chief Julius Becton at once replied that he was searching for a compromise.[50]

On March 25, a heated four-hour meeting was held before a House subcommittee over the issue of whether or not states should be forced to either participate in FEMA drills or lose federal emergency funds. The General Accounting Office found that there was no nuclear attack condition listed in the law governing FEMA funding. Representative Les Aucoin (D-Oreg.) and another antinuclear progressive, Ron Dellums (D-Calif.), wrote the language for an attachment to the 1988 defense bill that would bar FEMA from withholding grant money from any state that refused to participate in a nuclear drill. Aucoin described their effort as "a kick in the pants for FEMA." By the end of December 1987, the states were nearing victory.

•   •   •

Washington senator Brock Adams's critique of American civil defense in the Reagan years was simple and widely held. He felt that civil defense funds should be spent on saving "the population from more likely, more survivable events than a nuclear war, the survivability of which is unlikely."[51] Adams realized that FEMA was only intent on building a shelter network to protect public officials and that civil defense leaders "want to produce pamphlets for the rest of us which, I assume, will tell us how to 'have a nice day' after a nuclear holocaust." His analysis provides a succinct summary of the history of American civil defense for the public during the 1980s. As the Cold War approached its final moments, civil defense seemed beyond resuscitation. Yet it was destined to rise again to serve its role as protector of the powerful.

Epilogue

From Bush to Bush: Final Gasp to Phoenix Rising

In the mid-1980s, Soviet premier Mikhail Gorbachev repeatedly expressed his knowledge that "the nuclear era requires new thinking from everybody," and "the backbone of the new way of thinking is the recognition of the priority of human values, or, to be more precise, of humankind's survival."[1] Beginning in Ronald Reagan's term, Gorbachev began to announce his support for openness, freedom, and decentralization; proposed massive cuts in Soviet weapons; and called for the mutual destruction by the superpowers of all nuclear weapons. After decades of preparation for a nuclear showdown between the United States and the Soviet Union, the Cold War was coming to a close.

Reagan and his successor, George H. W. Bush, worked with Gorbachev to limit the American and Soviet nuclear arsenals. The Intermediate-Range Nuclear Forces (INF) Treaty, signed in December 1987, eliminated an entire class of nuclear weapons—ground-launched ballistic and cruise missiles with a range from 500 to 1,000 kilometers—and allowed inspections on both sides to verify compliance. By the summer of 1991, the Strategic Arms Reduction Treaty (START I) was in place, requiring the United States and the Soviet Union to cut their strategic nuclear weapons to 6,000 warheads apiece. The signing ceremony was described by Gorbachev as "a moment of glory for the new thinking and the foreign policy stemming from it," while Bush said of the ceremony, "For me this was more than ritual; it offered hope to young people all over the world that idealism was not dead."[2]

Bush's 1992 State of the Union Message to Congress was clear: "America won the Cold War." His speech also focused on civil defense, treating seriously one of its most ridiculed propaganda creations—duck and cover—as symbolic of American victory:

> Tomorrow our children will go to school and study history and how plants grow. And they won't have, as my children did, air raid drills in which they crawl under their desks and cover their heads in case of nuclear war. My grandchildren don't have to do that, and have the bad dreams that children once had in decades past. The threat is still there. But the long, drawn-out dread is over.

START II, signed by Bush and Boris Yeltsin in January 1993, cut the number of strategic warheads in each nation to between 3,000 and 3,500 and eliminated all multiple-warhead intercontinental ballistic missiles.[3]

Despite these achievements, the arms control and disarmament process slowed considerably during Bill Clinton's presidential term, although federal funding and attention to ensuring the continuity of government continued. Yet, after the colossal failure of Reagan's crisis relocation system, followed by Bush's State of the Union announcement of the end of duck and cover, the concept of civil defense for the public did seem to have finally died. All that was needed was an appropriate monument and grave. In 1999, President Clinton signed the bill to construct the National Civil Defense/Emergency Management Monument, a fifteen-ton granite stone topped with an American eagle, at the old Federal Emergency Management Agency training site at Emmitsburg, Maryland.[4] But only a few years later, public civil defense would emerge again, like the mythical phoenix.

●   ●   ●

In the fall of 1989, FEMA's concentration on saving the top leadership from nuclear destruction, coupled with its pretense that it was now dual purpose, intent on protecting the public against both nuclear and natural disasters, created a public relations disaster for the agency. In September, Hurricane Hugo struck the U.S. Virgin Islands, Puerto Rico, and the Carolinas with flood tides and 135-mile-per-hour winds, killing fifty-one people. FEMA's inadequate response received national attention, as homeless citizens waited in line for hours and sometimes days in an effort to obtain the proper papers or to speak with the few FEMA officials on hand. For days after the storm, basic rescue equipment, such as portable power generators, outdoor toilets, or mobile phones, and even food and water, was not provided, while downed trees and power poles remained untouched where they fell. Criticism of FEMA reached new crescendos in the national press. Critics focused on two major reasons for the failure of FEMA to respond appropriately to this natural disaster. Its major concern had always been defense against nuclear attack, and its top leaders were largely untrained, political appointees. Senator Ernest F. Hollings (D-S.C.) publicly and repeatedly dismissed FEMA officials as "the sorriest bunch of bureaucratic jackasses I've ever encountered in my life." The noted *Chicago Tribune* columnist Mike Royko happened to be in Charleston when the storm hit. "Too Bad Hugo Didn't Flatten FEMA" was the memorable title of his frequently reprinted national column. In South Carolina, when a radio station asked for suggestions for horrifying Halloween costumes, callers replied that they were dressing up as FEMA officials.

One month after Hugo, the Loma Prieta 7.1 earthquake struck the San Francisco Bay Area, killing 59 and injuring 3,000 more. In the ravaged Marina district, 100,000 citizens were without power for many hours. FEMA again failed to respond properly, while the agency's top medical coordinator went on vacation the day after the disaster, with the permission of his supervisor. A California congressman roared that "FEMA could screw up a two-car parade," a comment much reported in the national press.[5] Within two months, FEMA had gone from a little-known acronym to a nationally known symbol for bureaucratic nightmare.

The bad publicity continued. Leo Bosner, a forty-four-year-old FEMA program analyst with ten years' experience, was dispatched to San Francisco a few days after the Loma Prieta earthquake to help provide assistance to the thousands whose homes had been destroyed. Within hours, he was recalled to FEMA headquarters in Washington, D.C., and told that he had been taken off the Loma Prieta job because he had a reputation as a "troublemaker." For several years, Bosner had publicly criticized the agency for its relative lack of attention to natural disasters like earthquakes. In May 1989, he had also filed charges accusing FEMA officials of questionable procurement practices, illegal copying of computer software, and alcohol abuse. His case was prepared with the assistance of the Office of Special Counsel, which protects federal whistleblowers. After Bosner reported his recall from San Francisco to Congresswoman Barbara Boxer (D-Calif.) and was interviewed by a number of media sources, including journalist Jack Anderson, FEMA suspended him without pay and assigned a psychiatrist to collect evidence of his supposed mental disorder. Again,

Bosner got welcome national publicity from Boxer and eventually won his case by exposing FEMA's efforts to retaliate and intimidate.[6]

Despite FEMA's publicized failures of 1989, the use of political appointees to fill the agency's leadership positions continued in the Bush administration, with much of the interim direction of FEMA's disaster response handled by a Reagan/Bush ex-campaign manager. Within months of John Sununu becoming the new chief of staff for President Bush, Sununu's next-door neighbor and former aide, Wallace B. Stickney, won the $129,500-a-year job as director of FEMA. Under Stickney, FEMA scandals continued to spread upward. As the *Portland Oregonian* pointed out in late May 1992: "You've got to hand it to the folks at the Federal Emergency Management Agency. When they run short of disasters to respond to, they create one. Like the public-relations and privacy-rights disaster the FEMA folks have been trying to get under control over the last week."[7]

Another round of the FEMA follies began when a thirty-two-year-old management analyst was first refused a security clearance because he was gay and then ordered by FEMA to produce a list of gays in the agency. The analyst then reported to Representative John Conyers's House Government Operations Committee that a FEMA deputy director was misusing government vehicles and drivers. When the story hit the headlines, Representative Barney Frank (D-Mass.) called the FEMA top brass to a committee hearing. Frank canceled the hearing only when Stickney removed the deputy director and destroyed the list. This set off the final clash between the Reagan/Bush political appointees and the long-term civil servants in FEMA. "Troublemaker" Leo Bosner, then head of the recently organized employees' union, publicly exposed Stickney's effort to strengthen the secret continuity-of-government component of FEMA, despite the congressional and public outcry demanding that the agency pay more attention to actual natural disasters. Bosner told reporters that "these political hacks," as he called the political appointees, were highly paid and incompetent managers who "have managed to screw the place up and embarrass us."

Senator Barbara Mikulski (D-Md.), chair of the appropriations committee that determined FEMA's budget, called for a complete overhaul of the agency. The committee report called FEMA a "political dumping ground" and led the House to slash FEMA's 1993 budget, strip executives of chauffeur-driven cars, and sharply reduce the number of the agency's headquarters staff. Mikulski's report noted that FEMA was a "turkey farm, if you will, where large numbers of positions exist that can be conveniently and quietly filled" to pay off political debts and that FEMA leaders under President George Bush had greatly increased the amount of consultant funds, wasting much of the money on frivolous or politically motivated projects. Media sources stressed that the number of FEMA patronage appointments was ten times higher than the national average in all government agencies. "The old FEMA is still functioning under a Cold War framework," Mikulski said, "under which more money goes into preparing for nuclear war than for the [natural] disasters ordinary Americans in our communities are going to face."[8]

It seemed impossible that FEMA's reputation could sink lower. But the bumbling response of the agency when Hurricane Andrew struck southern Florida in August 1992 brought the biggest blow yet to its public image. The class IV hurricane, with gusts of 170 miles an hour, did damage totaling $20 billion and killed twenty-two people. In the last stages of a presidential election campaign, with Bush sagging in the polls, the devastation in Florida remained basically untreated by emergency management at every level. Six days after the hurricane struck, the furious Dade County director of emergency preparedness exploded at a press conference: "We need food. We need water. We need people. For God's sake, where are they?" Only then did President Bush send in the military and name Transportation Secretary Andrew Card to supervise the federal relief effort, bypassing FEMA leaders in the process.[9]

At this point, the exposé of FEMA's pretense of providing defense against either bombs or storms was fully apparent, as was the public rejection and ridicule aimed at this latest version of the long string of discredited federal civil defense agencies. The 1992 investigation of the House Committee on Government Operations, headed by John Conyers (D-Mich.), noted the fantasy of civil defense through the years and provided a full summary of FEMA's sins:

> FEMA has become a political dumping ground for hacks and hangers-on. . . . FEMA's troubles began in the early 1980s, when then-Director Louis Giufrida [sic], a protege of Reagan advisor Edwin Meese, was embarrassed into resigning after his deputies were caught furnishing a FEMA training facility with luxury accommodations for their personal pleasures. Their wackier ideas—working with Oliver North at the National Security Council—include plans for FEMA to take over the government in the event of national emergency, round up "subversives" and place them in military camps, and to essentially suspend Constitutional safeguards. More recently, a Government Operations Committee Investigation has revealed that FEMA officials have abused their positions. . . . The result is an agency unable to provide the basic services it is charged with when needed, and a lack of credibility to such a degree that FEMA may never regain the public's confidence.[10]

To complete the exposure of American civil defense, FEMA's continuity-of-government programs, operational since 1982, were once more exposed to public scrutiny, this time by reporters Larry Lipman and Pulitzer Prize–winner Elliot Jaspin at the Cox News Service's Washington bureau. Lipman and Jaspin conducted a six-month computer-assisted investigation to analyze information taken from government mainframe computers. In February 1993, they released their discovery that FEMA had spent most of its money during the previous eleven years on a covert $1.3 billion effort to protect selected government elites, who would remain alive after a nuclear war began. Even many top FEMA officials did not know about the program. Only twenty members of Congress were informed of this effort, although one-third of FEMA's employees worked in the top-secret project.

Originally set up by Oliver North, the covert program had grown to Dr. Strangelovian proportions since 1982. Devised as a means to keep the government functioning during a nuclear attack and to protect the line of succession beyond the president and vice president, the plan provided for equipment, support facilities, and personnel to transport the elite, if needed, and to provide secure communications for government leaders in a nuclear war. The major continuity-of-government program during these years rested on a fleet of 300 vehicles in five mobile units based in Bothell, Washington; Thomasville, Georgia; Denver, Colorado; Denton, Texas; and Maynard, Massachusetts. Each of these mobile units could power a three-story airport terminal, suck diesel fuel from whatever service stations survived the nuclear blast, and send classified messages anywhere in the world. FEMA also maintained close communication with a number of deeply buried fallout shelters in the country, which were designed to shelter government leaders and other "vital" persons presumed to be necessary to the functioning of the radiated remains of American society.

Journalists Lipman and Jaspin detected the FEMA reality: "For every dollar spent on responding to natural disasters, almost 12 had been spent on plans to keep the government running during a nuclear war." Between 1982 and 1991, FEMA spent a total of $2.9 billion on national security programs and only $243 million on natural disasters, such as hurricanes, earthquakes, and floods. National security funds made up 78 percent of FEMA's budget, while spending for responses to natural disasters accounted for 6.6 percent. Of FEMA's 2,700 employees, 940 worked for the mobile response units and the agency's seven bomb shelters, while 300 employees worked in FEMA's natural disaster assistance office.

Lipman and Jaspin were careful to connect the failure of FEMA to deal successfully with natural disasters to the emphasis placed on national security. They pointed out, for example, that when Hurricane Andrew shredded southern Florida, the city manager of Homestead, Florida, begged FEMA for some hand-held radios, since the hurricane-ravaged town had only one working phone. In response to Andrew's devastation in Florida, FEMA sent in trucks and vans capable of sending radio messages to military aircraft halfway around the world, but could not get more than thirty-six telephone lines operating in Homestead and could not provide even one hand-held radio.[11]

The widely printed Lipman and Jaspin exposé created nationwide fury, as scores of newspapers and thousands of readers protested the stupidity of rushing politicians into underground areas under mountains, for when they emerged, they would be the leaders of nothing but ruins. Most citizens wanted the government to focus on real disasters—both natural and fiscal—rather than on roving bomb shelters for the top few. The need for nuclear war preparation seemed especially ridiculous as the Soviet Union dissolved and the Cold War "ended."

Several days after the Cox exposé appeared, FEMA issued a four-paragraph response admitting that it had spent $11.9 billion since 1982. However, it also said that $1.3 billion had been spent on "government preparedness," while the other 89 percent, some $10.6 billion, had gone toward "domestic preparedness, mitigation, response and recovery." Harassed by skeptical and snickering reporters to clarify the vague statement, the FEMA spokesman fumed, "That's the way it came down. What more can I say?"[12]

Yet another FEMA leader's career ended in embarrassment when Wallace Stickney resigned in January 1993, soon after he sheepishly admitted in a press conference that he did not personally own the bag of emergency supplies, such as canned food, bottled water, a first-aid kit, flashlights, and a battery-operated radio, that FEMA urged everyone to have on hand. Stickney also discovered that, despite his position as FEMA director, he was not to be included in the group to be whisked away to safety when the bombs fell, but rather would be left along with the general public to be "cindered," in the parlance of the covert planners.[13]

*   *   *

In April 1993, President Clinton appointed James Lee Witt as FEMA director, the first person to hold this position who had experience in emergency management, having served as the state director of disaster relief in Arkansas under Governor Clinton. Clad in his usual ostrich-skin cowboy boots, Witt quickly reorganized the agency, hiring qualified persons, cutting political appointments, reducing internal regulations by 50 percent, vastly improving employee morale, and winning high praise from most observers for FEMA's new efficiency and competence. From midwestern floods to the Oklahoma City bombing, Witt responded to disasters with expert speed, winning the respect of many Republican politicians.[14]

In the fall of 1993, Director Witt reportedly rid FEMA of most, but not all, of its continuity-of-government program, apparently turning over its civil defense functions to Pentagon planners and the National Security Agency. During the senior Bush's term as president, the three giant underground shelters for the fleeing elite had at last been recognized as most likely known to Soviet target planners and hence as vulnerable to a massive attack. This perception led to the building of a group of deeply buried small bunkers scattered across the nation. But in the summer of 1994, the federal government announced the end of the Doomsday Project, the eleven-year-old, $8 billion effort to save the government elite to carry on war through and after a nuclear holocaust.[15] By the 1990s, public expression of the idea of a government leadership prosecuting nuclear war for several months, while almost all Americans lay vaporized, roasted, or radiated, was not easily tolerated by the press or public.

It was during the Clinton years that many Americans first learned about the single integrated operational plan, or SIOP. This military plan for the conduct of nuclear war was easily the most intensely guarded nuclear secret in existence, with its own level of government secrecy classification for the most extremely sensitive information, shrouded in impenetrable security, hidden from Congress, and rarely understood even by the presidents. SIOP had long determined the nuclear targeting strategy of the United States. Since 1945, while dozens of nuclear strategists had debated the merits of various deterrence plans, from MAD to NUTS, and presidents had rhetorically supported a variety of these strategies, there remained one amazing truth: the military planners in charge of nuclear targeting consistently devised and maintained only one simple targeting plan, which promised vast overkill and multiple hydrogen bombs aimed at thousands of targets.

A brief history of U.S. nuclear targeting reveals that, from 1945 to 1960, U.S. nuclear war planning was chaotic, uncoordinated among the services, and marked by the duplication of targets and interservice rivalries. In late 1960, Eisenhower first learned the intricacies of the targeting plans and, horrified at the number of targets and enormous overkill, he approved the first SIOP. As the Joint Chiefs of Staff interpreted the new plan, it remained simple: launch on warning or within fifteen minutes if the president could be found, and fire all that the United States has at preselected targets. When war began, the United States would release all of its strategic weapons against China and Russia. Estimated immediate fatalities were 360–525 million people. Beginning with Kennedy, targeting plans became a subject of debate among the strategist insiders. But despite the rhetoric, the SIOP targeting plans remained essentially the same through the Kennedy and Johnson years. In 1970, Henry Kissinger, Nixon's new national security advisor, sought more options than just an all-out attack posture, with his proclaimed purpose of lessening escalation toward the final suicidal exchange between the superpowers. Carter, Reagan, and Bush maintained this rhetoric, while ignoring the complex reality: the actual targeting plans had basically not changed since the early 1950s.[16]

Not until the Clinton years did the SIOP become a subject of limited public discussion, partly through the protest efforts of a high-level military officer. General George Lee Butler, who became the last commander in chief of the Strategic Air Command in 1991, was personally responsible for pushing the button, upon the president's order, to initiate the nuclear war when deterrence failed. General Butler was dazed and appalled after he undertook a month-long effort to examine the more than a million-page SIOP national war plan, containing 12,000-plus targets. He discovered that scores of multimegaton bombs were directed at Moscow, for example, which, if fired, would have left nothing but a mammoth hole hundreds of miles wide and deep and killed everyone tens of thousands of miles downwind. He also found that massive hydrogen bombs, often in duplicate numbers, were intended for small bridges and insignificant factories throughout the Soviet Union. Butler realized that, given this million-page complexity, no president since Truman had ever been given any real option other than the release of a huge number of nuclear weapons at horrendous levels of overkill. Butler was successful in cutting the number of targets by 75 percent, but could achieve little more. In the mid-1990s, after his retirement, Butler joined a number of high-ranking ex-military officials who called for the abolition of nuclear weapons and began an extensive speaking schedule to warn others of the danger of nuclear holocaust.[17]

In 1997, long after the end of the Cold War, Clinton provided new guidelines for targeting. Today, the number of targets is probably close to 2,500. Even after a series of arms control agreements, the United States still maintains at least 5,300 operational nuclear warheads in the U.S. stockpile and at least another 5,000 in the reserve stockpile. These bombs are apparently aimed at Russia, China, and several other countries, most likely Iraq, Iran, North Korea, Libya, and Syria.

When George W. Bush became president, he stated his peaceful desire to cut the number of nuclear weapons, but after the attacks of September 11, 2001, he changed his plans. He announced that the United States would no longer honor the 1972 ABM Treaty and would begin research on a "missile defense system" with the same as-yet-unrealized goals as Reagan's Star Wars. In the spring of 2002, a leaked secret Pentagon report revealed that Bush had directed the military to prepare a contingency plan to use nuclear weapons against seven countries and to build new nuclear weapons—the so-called mini-nukes—and tactical nuclear weapons for use on the battlefield.

On hearing this news, a defense analyst from the conservative Heritage Foundation calmly explained that the United States needed a credible deterrent against "regimes involved in international terrorism and development of weapons of mass destruction" and defended Bush's plans as "the right way to develop a nuclear posture for a post–Cold War World." The president of the Council for a Livable World, however, simply remarked, "Dr. Strangelove is clearly still alive."[18]

Clearly, the nuclear dilemma remains unsolved, fifty years after the creation of the hydrogen bomb. There are now at least eight nations, and surely more to come, developing nuclear weapons. In an interview in 1998, General George Lee Butler spoke for hundreds of millions of people worldwide:

> [I]t is simply wrong, morally speaking, for any mortal to be invested with the authority to call into question the survival of the planet. That is an untenable allocation of authority, and yet it has become the central feature of the nuclear age. Nuclear weapons are irrational devices. They were rationalized and accepted as a desperate measure in the face of cir-cumstances that were unimaginable. Now as the world evolves rapidly, I think that the vast majority of people on the face of this earth will en-dorse the proposition that such weapons have no place among us. There is no security to be found in nuclear weapons. It's a fool's game.[19]

Equally clear is the fact that nuclear civil defense for the public is not pos-sible to achieve. As this study has shown, political and military leaders in the United States and the Soviet Union, while establishing ways to save themselves, cannot admit to the public that if nuclear war begins, the masses are doomed. From the beginning of the nuclear age, the authorities have lied, attempting to sell the public a series of fallacies about how to save their families from nuclear destruction. This, in turn, has created a public display of expert disagreement with the false solutions proposed by state leadership.

Thus the sequence began. The experts denounced the propaganda. The fan-tasy was exposed. The people revolted. And social conflict threatened elite con-trols. As this debate grew in size and intensity, the declared nuclear strategies of MAD and NUTS were so threatened that the government leadership was forced to close down the public civil defense option by the 1990s.

We know now that many national leaders, from Eisenhower to Gorbachev, privately decided never to unleash a nuclear exchange. But it was the public rejection of civil defense and, with it, the massive public recognition, here and abroad, that nuclear war is suicidal, that ended the Cold War nuclear confron-tation.

• • •

When the United States was threatened with attacks on domestic soil, the federal government reverted to its old, familiar civil defense plans. After the attacks of September 11, 2001, the leaders once again headed for their "undisclosed locations" in bunkers underground, while Americans were advised to cover their windows and arm themselves with water, food, and flashlights. Again, we are assured that nuclear weapons, along with the new Star Wars, now called "missile defense," will serve to protect us from the evil ones. We are told that we will receive or be able to purchase anthrax or radiation pills to guard us from germ warfare and from possible attacks on underprotected nuclear reactors. Again, the authorities tell us that we must stand firm, be brave Americans, and not worry. Again, the dissenting experts recoil with disbelieving horror, to once more point out the known realities of the effect of nuclear bombs, or the hundreds of miles of radiation resulting from an attack on a nuclear reactor, or the terrifying, known facts and implications of germ warfare.

FEMA had returned to the way of previous administrations when George W. Bush restored political appointments to FEMA and named his long-time campaign manager, Joe Allbaugh, as director of the agency. In June 2001, Allbaugh commandeered for his own use FEMA's customized military version of a Boeing 747, a version of the supposedly discontinued Doomsday Plane that was meant for exclusive use of the president and his staff to direct a nuclear war from the air. Allbaugh flew the command plane on a routine business trip from Washington, D.C., to San Juan, Puerto Rico. This caused civil servants at FEMA to reveal to the press that the plane trip, with all of its complex communications systems, had cost taxpayers a total of $340,000, or $23,542 an hour. Allbaugh, who resigned from FEMA in March 2003, now heads a consulting firm, New Bridge Strategies, which was created to help clients "evaluate and take advantage of business opportunities in the Middle East following the conclusion of the U.S.-led war in Iraq."[20]

Other recollections of the civil defense of times past are evoked by the Bush administration's post–9/11 actions, such as the memory of the National Security Agency representative to FEMA in 1984, Colonel Oliver North, who was then slated (before the attorney general forced an end to the plan) to direct the nation under martial law whenever Reagan activated the national order. This plan had included input from John Poindexter, who became national security advisor in 1985. Poindexter and North then headed the illegal Iran-Contra project to sell arms for hostages in the Middle East and transfer the profits to the covert effort to overthrow the Nicaraguan government, both actions prohibited by Congress. Poindexter was later convicted of seven felony charges, including lying to Congress and destruction of evidence, but was freed in 1991 after being granted immunity for his testimony during the Iran-Contra hearings. In February 2002, President Bush placed the sixty-six-year-old Poindexter in charge of the Total Information Awareness (TIA) office, within the Pentagon's Defense Advanced Research Projects Agency, to advance homeland security and fight terrorists. Under Poindexter's control, the TIA moved to create the most Orwellian agency ever envisioned within the United States. The agency began the collection of information on Americans ranging from medical records, credit cards, and e-mails, to travel plans, library selections, Web sites visited, and bank accounts. After twenty months in office, Poindexter was forced to resign in August 2003, when the press exposed his establishment of a futures market within TIA, which allowed investors to profit by correctly predicting the timing of future terrorist attacks, assassinations, or regime changes.[21] This led the House and Senate to terminate the TIA program in September 2003, although many of its projects were transferred to other government agencies.

•   •   •

Post–9/11 civil defense has a new name, the Department of Homeland Security, whose creation marked the largest and most significant government transformation in more than fifty years, combining FEMA and twenty-one other federal agencies into one unit with more than 180,000 employees. This huge, unwieldy organization, with a $37 billion first-year budget, marries entrenched bureaucracies which struggle with one another as they pursue the yet-unrealized hope of someday becoming an effective and collaborative whole. The department promises to protect Americans from manmade and even natural disasters through four massive programs: border and transportation security; emergency preparedness and response; chemical, biological, radiological, and nuclear countermeasures; and information analysis and infrastructure protection.

FIGURE E.1. Eagle with duct tape. One of many comic responses to Homeland Security's 2003 advice to citizens to seal their windows with duct tape in the event of a nuclear attack.

Courtesy Peter S. Weber.

During a Homeland Security–initiated "high" alert in February 2003, Tom Ridge, the first director of Homeland Security, advised the public to buy duct tape and plastic sheeting to seal their doors and windows against terrorist attack. This announcement sent many frightened Americans out to strip the shelves of duct tape and led the Democrats to attack the administration for providing false information and inadequate funding for the defense effort at home. The duct tape announcement also created an enormous wave of jokes, from Jay Leno's talk show to hundreds of political cartoons, to dozens of Web sites, which are still devoted to humorous ridicule of the use of duct tape as protection against biological, chemical, and nuclear weapons.

Although in the weeks after his announcement, Ridge did his best to quell citizen anxiety and put a stop to the comedic response, he failed because public recall of pre–9/11 civil defense history remained strong. Ducking under school desks, tilting your hat brim to shield your face from radiation, building home bomb shelters to survive multimegaton attacks, and evacuation from cities to unprepared sites—all of the ludicrous civil defense advice of the past resurfaced during the discussion of duct tape.[22] The duct tape event led Homeland Security to lessen public knowledge about government intelligence concerning impending terrorist actions, more in line with past civil defense history. However, critical analysis of the function of civil defense did change after 2003. Now, the government is accused of deliberately creating a "fear vote" to keep Republicans in power, or creating the new multibillion-dollar security market of equipment and personnel which enriches certain corporate supporters of the administration. But current critics of American civil defense, like critics from before 9/11, all seem to agree on one thing: civil defense for the public is notoriously inadequate at every level.

Homeland Security significantly differs from previous nuclear civil defense programs in the increased and unparalleled power it awards to intelligence and law enforcement agencies. The 362-page Patriot Act, rushed through Congress with few dissenting votes in October 2001, made it possible both to search premises and to make secret arrests without warrants or judicial review; to hold prisoners without access to lawyers, family, or friends indefinitely; and to confer sentences without allowing the offenders access to their accusers. The Patriot Act also gave the FBI and other intelligence agencies new powers of surveillance and the right to spy on the activities and thoughts of American citizens and immigrants alike.

A large grassroots resistance movement against the Patriot Act emerged at once. At first, individual experts expressed grave concern with the dangers that sections of the act posed to civil liberties and the right to legal dissent. This opposition was followed by several important legal actions filed by large organizations intent on the protection of constitutional rights. Just as with the public resistance in the early 1980s to Reagan's crisis relocation plans, the stand against the Patriot Act quickly expanded into local actions across the nation. By May 2005, more than 382 cities and counties in forty-seven states, including Baltimore, Philadelphia, Denver, Detroit, Los Angeles, New York City, and Chicago, representing more than 61.5 million people had approved formal local or state resolutions against portions of the Patriot Act, while hundreds of local and state protests across the country were organizing to do the same. Seven states have formally voted to oppose sections of the act: Alaska, Colorado, Hawaii, Idaho, Maine, Montana, and Vermont.

* * *

In February 2002, the hands of the famous Doomsday Clock, the symbol of nuclear danger, were moved from nine to seven minutes before midnight, an ominous reevaluation that returned the hands to the same setting at which the clock debuted in 1947. Also in 1947, Albert Einstein, as he so often did, once again said it best:

> Through the release of atomic energy, our generation has brought into the world the most revolutionary force since prehistoric man's discovery of fire. This basic power of the universe cannot be fitted into the outmoded concept of narrow nationalisms. For there is no secret and there is no defense, there is no possibility of control except through the aroused understanding and acceptance of the peoples of the world. We scientists recognize our inescapable responsibility to carry to our fellow citizens an understanding of the simple facts of atomic energy and its implication for society. In this lies our only security and our only hope—we believe that an informed citizenry will act for life and not for death.[23]

And now, in addition to the nuclear threat, there are the very real dangers of biological and chemical weapons of mass destruction. Seven minutes to midnight. And ticking.

We must begin again. The history of American civil defense strengthens our understanding of government propaganda and provides inspirational lessons in the effectiveness of massive popular power. The people's fight continues.

Notes

INTRODUCTION

1. Robert Jervis, *The Meaning of the Nuclear Revolution: Statecraft and the Prospect of Armageddon* (Ithaca, N.Y.: Cornell University Press, 1989); and Jervis, *The Illogic of American Nuclear Strategy* (Ithaca, N.Y.: Cornell University Press, 1984); Lawrence Freedman, *The Evolution of U.S. Nuclear Strategy*, 2d ed. (New York: St. Martin's, 1989); Eric Mlyn, *The State, Society, and Limited Nuclear War* (Albany: State University of New York Press, 1995); Scott Sagan, *Moving Targets: Nuclear Strategy and National Security* (Princeton, N.J.: Princeton University Press, 1989); Spurgeon Keeny and Wolfgang Panofsky, "From MAD to NUTS," *Foreign Affairs* 59 (Winter 1981–82): 287–304.

2. Edward Rhodes, *Power and Madness: The Logic of Nuclear Coercion* (New York: Columbia University Press, 1989); Charles S. Glaser, *Nuclear Arguments: Understanding the Strategic Nuclear Arms and Arms Control Debates*, ed. Lynn Eden and Steven E. Miller (Ithaca, N.Y.: Cornell University Press, 1989).

3. Herman Kahn, *On Thermonuclear War* (Princeton, N.J.: Princeton University Press, 1960).

4. Jonathan Schell, *The Gift of Time: The Case for Abolishing Nuclear Weapons Now* (New York: Holt, 1998), 10.

5. James Stegenga, "Nuclearism and Democracy," *Journal of American Culture* 11 (Spring 1988): 93.

6. Stansfield Turner, *Caging the Nuclear Genie: An American Challenge for Global Security* (Boulder, Colo.: Westview, 1997), 9.

7. Stephen I. Schwartz, ed., *Atomic Audit: The Costs and Consequences of U.S. Nuclear Weapons since 1940* (Washington, D.C.: Brookings Institution Press, 1998), 3. The size of a trillion dollars is difficult to grasp; one trillion is equivalent to a million million.

8. Stewart L. Udall, *The Myths of August: A Personal Exploration of Our Tragic Cold War Affair with the Atom* (New York: Pantheon, 1994), 345.

9. Richard Gid Powers, "Introduction, " in Daniel Patrick Moynihan, *Secrecy: The American Experience* (New Haven, Conn.: Yale University Press, 1998), 2. Also see Glenn T. Seaborg, "Secrecy Runs Amok," *Science* 264 (June 3, 1994): 1410; Athan G. Theoharis, ed., *A Culture of Secrecy: The Government versus the People's Right to Know* (Lawrence: University Press of Kansas, 1998).

10. Wes D. Gehring, *American Dark Comedy: Beyond Satire* (Westport, Conn.: Greenwood, 1996), 4. Also see Walter Kerr, *Tragedy and Comedy* (New York: Da Capo, 1985).

PROLOGUE

1. Richard Rhodes, *Dark Sun* (New York: Simon and Schuster, 1995), 499–512, 523–24; Richard L. Miller, *Under the Cloud: The Decades of Nuclear Testing* (New York: Free Press, 1986), 107–19.

2. Robert Oppenheimer, "Atomic Weapons and American Policy," *Foreign Affairs* 31 (July 1953): 529.

3. Albert Einstein, telegram to *NYT*, May 24, 1946, in *Oxford Dictionary of Quotations* (New York: Oxford University Press, 1992), 268.

4. Quoted in Stewart L. Udall, *The Myths of August: A Personal Exploration of Our Tragic Cold War Affair with the Atom* (New York: Pantheon, 1994), 301–8. Sakharov's complete text in *NYT*, July 28, 1968. Also see Andrei Sakharov, *Memoirs* (New York: Knopf, 1990).

5. Discussion of the effects of a hydrogen bomb is drawn from several major sources, especially Office of Technology Assessment, U.S. Congress, *The Effects of Nuclear War* (Washington, D.C.: U.S. Government Printing Office, 1979). Also see Samuel Glasstone and Philip J. Dolan, eds., *The Effects of Nuclear Weapons* (Washington, D.C.: U.S. Department of Defense and Energy, Research and Development Administration, 1977); *The Nuclear Almanac: Confronting the Atom in War and Peace*, compiled and edited by faculty members at the Massachusetts Institute of Technology (Reading, Mass.: Addison-Wesley, 1984), esp. part 2; Arthur M. Katz, *Life after Nuclear War* (Cambridge, Mass.: Ballinger, 1982); Robert Ehrlich, *Waging Nuclear Peace: The Technology and Politics of Nuclear Weapons* (Albany: State University of New York Press, 1985); Nicholas Wade, *A World beyond Healing: The Prologue and Aftermath of Nuclear War* (New York: Norton, 1987); Stephen I. Schwartz, ed., *Atomic Audit: The Costs and Consequences of U.S. Nuclear Weapons since 1940* (Washington, D.C.: Brookings Institution Press, 1998); Stansfield Turner, *Caging the Nuclear Genie: An American Challenge for Global Secu-*

rity (Boulder, Colo.: Westview, 1997), 125–49. Also see William Daugherty, Barbara Levi, and Frank von Hippel, "The Consequences of 'Limited' Nuclear Attacks on the United States," *International Security* 10, no. 4 (Spring 1986): 19. A must exercise for students of this subject is found on www.pbs.org/wgbh/amex/bomb/sfeature/mapablast .htm.

6. Information Bulletin, Office of Civil and Defense Mobilization, February 28, 1961, Katherine Graham Howard Papers, Dwight D. Eisenhower Presidential Library, Abilene, Kansas. This is a reprint of an October 1960 article in *National Fire Protection Association International Magazine.*

7. Robert Scheer, *With Enough Shovels: Reagan, Bush and Nuclear War* (New York: Random House, 1982), 16–17.

8. C. M. Haaland, C. V. Chester, and E. P. Wigner, *Survival of the Relocated Population of the U.S. after a Nuclear Attack*, Report ORNL-5041, Defense Civil Preparedness Agency (Springfield, Va.: National Technical Information Service, 1976), 20–21.

9. Jeannie Peterson, ed., *The Aftermath: The Human and Ecological Consequences of Nuclear War* (New York: Pantheon, 1983); Ruth Adams and Susan Cullen, eds., *The Final Epidemic: Physicians and Scientists on Nuclear War* (Chicago: Educational Foundation for Nuclear Science, 1981).

10. Kosta Tsipis, *Arsenal: Understanding Weapons in the Nuclear Age* (New York: Simon and Schuster, 1983), 101.

CHAPTER 1

1. James J. Wadsworth, *The Silver Spoon: An Autobiography* (Geneva, N.Y.: Humphrey, 1980); Council of National Defense cited in Thomas J. Kerr, *Civil Defense in the U.S.: Bandaid for a Holocaust?* (Boulder, Colo.: Westview, 1983), 13. Susan Zeiger, "She Didn't Raise Her Boy to Be a Slacker: Motherhood, Conscription, and the Culture of the First World War," *Feminist Studies* 22 (Spring 1996): 7–39, discusses the government propaganda focused on maternal representations. Histories of civil defense development include Kerr, *Civil Defense in the U.S.*; B. Wayne Blanchard, *American Civil Defense 1945–1975: The Evolution of Programs and Policies* (Washington, D.C.: FEMA, 1980); Lawrence J. Vale, *The Limits of Civil Defense in the USA, Switzerland, Britain, and the Soviet Union: The Evolution of Policies since 1945* (New York: Macmillan, 1987); Guy Oakes, *The Imaginary War: Civil Defense and American Cold War Culture* (New York: Oxford University Press, 1994), which centers on the 1950s, as do Laura McEnaney, *Civil Defense Begins at Home: Militarization Meets Everyday Life in the Fifties* (Princeton, N.J.: Princeton University Press, 2000); and Elaine May, *Homeward Bound: American Families in the Cold War Era* (New York: Basic, 1988). Also see Andrew D. Grossman, *Neither Dead Nor Red: Civilian Defense and American Political Development during the Early Cold War* (New York: Routledge, 2001); Kenneth Rose, *One Nation Underground: The Fallout Shelter in American Culture* (New York: New York University Press, 2001); Paul Boyer, *By the Bomb's Early Light: American Thought and Culture at the Dawn of*

the Atomic Age (New York: Pantheon, 1985); relevant chapters in Allan M. Winkler, *Life under a Cloud: American Anxiety about the Atom* (New York: Oxford University Press, 1993); Tom Vanderbilt, *Survival City: Adventure among the Ruins of Atomic America* (New York: Princeton Architectural Press, 2002); and Margot A. Henriksen, *Dr. Strangelove's America: Society and Culture in the Atomic Age* (Berkeley: University of California Press, 1997). Also see the studies of civil defense in the 1980s by journalists Edward Zuckerman, *The Day after World War III* (New York: Viking, 1984), and Robert Scheer, *With Enough Shovels: Reagan, Bush and Nuclear War* (New York: Random House, 1982).

2. Thomas Kessner, *Fiorello H. LaGuardia and the Making of Modern New York* (New York: McGraw-Hill, 1989), 492. Also see Melvyn Douglas and Tom Arthur, *See You at the Movies: The Autobiography of Melvyn Douglas* (New York: University Press of America, 1986); Doris Kearns Goodwin, *No Ordinary Time: Franklin and Eleanor Roosevelt: The Home Front in World War II* (New York: Simon and Schuster, 1994); Gregg Mitchell, *Tricky Dick and the Pink Lady: Richard Nixon vs. Helen Gahagan Douglas: Sexual Politics and the Red Scare, 1950* (New York: Random House, 1998).

3. Cited in Richard Polenberg, *War and Society: The United States, 1941–45* (Philadelphia: Lippincott, 1972), 187.

4. Michael Sherry, *The Rise of American Airpower: The Creation of Armageddon* (New Haven, Conn.: Yale University Press, 1987); Ronald Schaffer, *Wings of Judgment: American Bombing in World War II* (New York: Oxford University Press, 1985); David Irving, *The Destruction of Dresden* (New York: Ballantine, 1973); Stewart L. Udall, *The Myths of August: A Personal Exploration of Our Tragic Cold War Affair with the Atom* (New York: Pantheon, 1994), 49–83; and McGeorge Bundy, *Danger and Survival: Choices about the Bomb in the First Fifty Years* (New York: Random House, 1988), 63–68.

5. On Cold War and nuclear doublespeak, see William Lutz, *The New Doublespeak: Why No One Knows What Anyone's Saying Anymore* (New York: HarperCollins, 1996); Stephen Hillgartner, Richard C. Bell, and Rory O'Connor, *Nukespeak: Nuclear Language, Visions, and Mindset* (San Francisco: Sierra Club, 1982); Blanchard, *American Civil Defense*, 26–48.

6. Philip Funigiello, "Managing Armageddon: The Truman Administration, Atomic War, and the National Security Council," *Journal of Policy History* 2, no. 4 (1990): 403–24; Kennedy cited in Kerr, *Civil Defense in the U.S.*, 25. I will sometimes use "CD" to denote "civil defense."

7. U.S. Congress, Joint Committee on Atomic Energy, Hearings, "Civil Defense against Atomic Attack," 81st Cong., 2d sess., 1950.

8. Ibid., 103, 108. Also see Richard G. Hewlett and Francis Duncan, *Atomic Shield, 1947–1952*, vol. 2 of *A History of the United States Atomic Energy Commission* (University Park: Pennsylvania State University Press, 1969); Richard G. Hewlett and Jack M. Holl, *Atoms for Peace and War, 1953–1961: Eisenhower and the Atomic Energy Commission*, vol. 3 of *A History of the United States Atomic Energy Commission* (Berkeley: University of California Press, 1989); Barton C. Hacker, *Elements of Controversy: The Atomic Energy Commission and Radiation Safety in Nuclear Weapons Testing, 1947–1974* (Berkeley: University of California Press, 1994). These large general histories of the AEC are less

critical of AEC policies than most scholarship on this subject. See the review by Gregg Herken of Hacker, *Elements of Controversy*, in *Journal of American History* 82 (September 1995): 820–21.

9. Quoted in Udall, *Myths of August*, 131.

10. "For Your Information," FCDA, Education Series, no. 280, February 20, 1956, Katherine Graham Howard Papers, Dwight D. Eisenhower Library, Abilene, Kansas, hereafter cited as KGH, DDEL. A presentation of Cold War culture, including civil defense propaganda, is available in visual and audio form on www.conelrad.com.

11. "Newsletter," January 1955, KGH, DDEL.

12. May, *Homeward Bound*; Gillian Brown, "Nuclear Domesticity: Sequence and Survival," in *Arms and the Woman: War Gender, and Literary Representation*, ed. Helen M. Cooper, Adrienne Auslander Munich, and Susan Merrill Squier (Chapel Hill: University of North Carolina Press, 1989), 285; Susan S. Northcutt, "Women and the Bomb: Domestication of the Atomic Bomb in the United States," *International Social Science Review* 74, nos. 3–4 (1999): 129–39. Also see Frances Ferguson, "The Nuclear Sublime," *Diacritics* 13 (Summer 1984): 4–10. For 1960s use of motherhood by civil defense protesters, see Dee Garrison, "'Our Skirts Gave Us Courage': The Civil Defense Protest Movement in New York City, 1955–61," in *Not June Cleaver: Women and Gender in Postwar America, 1945–1960*, ed. Joanne Meyerowitz (Philadelphia: Temple University Press, 1994), 221–29. Also see Klaus Theweleit, *Male Fantasies: Women, Floods, Bodies, History* (Minneapolis: University of Minnesota Press, 1987).

13. *Newsletter: By, For, and About Women in Civil Defense*, no. 16, KGH, DDEL; May, *Homeward Bound*, 103–7.

14. Oakes, *Imaginary War*, 132–40; Katherine Howard, *With My Shoes Off* (New York: Vantage, 1977).

15. Oakes, *Imaginary War*, 137; Howard, *With My Shoes Off*, 248–60.

16. Howard, *With My Shoes Off*, 274–76. Jean Fuller, who replaced Howard at the FCDA in 1954, proudly reported that her presence at a nuclear test showed that women could do anything men could. See Jean Wood Fuller, Regional Oral History Office, University of California, Berkeley; Jean Wood Fuller Papers, Schlesinger Library, Radcliffe College, Cambridge, Massachusetts.

17. Public Affairs, "For Your Information," July 9, 1954; *FCDA News* 1, no. 6 (August 12, 1954), KGH, DDEL.

18. JCAE, Hearings, "Civil Defense against Atomic Attack," 138(A). Teller testimony in 88th Cong., 1st sess., House, Hearings before Subcommittee 3 of Committee on Armed Services, Hearings, "Civil Defense—Fallout Shelter Program," part 2, vol. 2, 4912. Edward Hebert from Louisiana, chair of the subcommittee, told Teller: "The last time I was exposed to your talent, [was] the day, the very memorable day in history at Eniwetok when you gave birth to the H-bomb" (4935). Many scholars of nuclear warfare have been struck with the image of male generative forces—the male ability to give birth—that is so prominent in descriptions of the bomb and of nuclear energy that it cannot go unnoticed. The initial coded message reporting the 1945 Trinity test as the birth of a boy, Teller's announcement of the first successful fusion test as "It's a boy," and the naming of the Hiroshima bomb as "Little Boy" are often-cited examples of this

phenomenon. See a discussion of sexual symbolism in Spencer E. Weart, *Nuclear Fears: A History of Images* (Cambridge, Mass.: Harvard University Press, 1988); and Brian Easlea, *Fathering the Unthinkable: Masculinity, Scientists and the Nuclear Arms Race* (London: Pluto, 1983).

19. McEnaney, *Civil Defense Begins at Home*; and Grossman, *Neither Dead Nor Red*, discuss civil defense propaganda and associated race and class issues.

20. Congressman Cannon served from 1923 to 1964. Representative Thomas, a liberal southern Democrat, served from 1937 to 1966. Kerr, *Civil Defense in the U.S.*, and Blanchard, *American Civil Defense*, discuss congressional civil defense actions.

21. The total appropriation was $75 million for 1952 and $43 million for 1953.

22. Boyer, *By the Bomb's Early Light*, 313–34. Also see McEnaney, *Civil Defense Begins at Home*, for media cooperation in FCDA campaigns, 35–38.

23. Oakes, *Imaginary War*, 173–74, n.50.

24. Ibid., 54.

25. Boyer, *By the Bomb's Early Light*, 323–24.

26. Richard M. Fried, *The Russians Are Coming! The Russians Are Coming! Pageantry and Patriotism in Cold-War America* (New York: Oxford University Press, 1998), shows how the Alert America campaign used the earlier version of the popular Freedom Train as a model. The Freedom Train, run by the American Heritage Foundation, is a prime example of the patriotic ritualism common to this early Cold War period. In addition, only a year after its formation, the FCDA boasted that it had distributed more than 50 million copies of civil defense booklets of various types, as well as 26,000 copies of administrative guides. See "Civil Defense News," *BAS* 7 (October 1950): 315.

27. Elizabeth Walker Mechling and Jay Mechling, "The Campaign for Civil Defense and the Struggle to Naturalize the Bomb," *Western Journal of Speech Communication* 55 (Spring 1991): 105–33. Also see Oakes, *Imaginary War*; and Rose, *One Nation Underground*, for examples of media support of civil defense in the early 1950s.

28. Boyer, *By the Bomb's Early Light*, 325–30; Henriksen, *Dr. Strangelove's America*, 96; *JAMA* cited in Paul Boyer, "The American Medical Profession and the Threat of Nuclear War," in Boyer, *Fallout: A Historian Reflects on America's Half-Century Encounter with Nuclear Weapons* (Columbus: Ohio State University Press, 1998), 64. It should also be remembered that beginning in the late 1950s and early 1960s, many medical professionals took the lead in awakening the public to radioactive fallout. In the late 1970s and early 1980s, the medical profession played a leading role in antinuclear activism. By the mid-1980s, members of Physicians for Social Responsibility were telling audiences all over the country that for a physician to listen to pro–civil defense propaganda without publicly refuting it was in itself an immoral act.

29. Boyer, *Fallout*, 71–81.

30. JoAnne Brown, "'A Is for Atom, B Is for Bomb': Civil Defense in American Public Education, 1948–1963," *Journal of American History* 75 (June 1988): 68–90.

31. Michael J. Carey, "The Schools and Civil Defense: The Fifties Revisited," *Teachers College Record* 84 (Fall 1982): 116.

32. Brown, "A Is for Atom," 81–83. My colleague historian David Oshinsky grew up

in New York City and has kept his childhood tag as a memento of those long ago and terrifying school civil defense exercises.

33. "Waiting for September," *Time*, August 14, 1950, 8, cited in Mechling and Mechling, "Campaign for Civil Defense," 105.

34. Bert the Turtle is the central character in the classic film documentary on civil defense, *The Atomic Cafe*, released in 1985. The film created a powerful black comedy from the 1950s government-released films concerning civil defense and bomb tests and from television commercials.

35. Weart, *Nuclear Fears*, 133–34. Also see Phyllis La Farge, *The Strangelove Legacy: Children, Parents, and Teachers in the Nuclear Age* (New York: Harper and Row, 1987); Benina Gould, Susan Moon, and Judith Van Hoorn, eds., *Growing Up Scared? The Psychological Effect of the Nuclear Threat on Children* (Berkeley, Calif.: Open, 1986); Michael Carey, "Psychological Fallout," *BAS* 38 (January 1982): 20–24; Milton Schwebel, "Effects of the Nuclear War Threat on Children and Teenagers: Implications for Professionals," *American Journal of Orthopsychiatry* 52 (October 1982): 606–18.

36. Todd Gitlin, *The Sixties: Years of Hope, Days of Rage* (New York: Bantam, 1987), 22–23.

37. Joan Baez, *And a Voice to Sing with: A Memoir* (New York: Summit, 1987), 42.

38. Jackie Goldberg, interview, 1995, Berkeley, California. A teacher for years, she was a well-known progressive member of the Los Angeles City Council and was elected to the state legislature in 2002; Weart, *Nuclear Fears*, 340; Carey, "The Schools and Civil Defense," 116.

39. Brown, "A Is for Atom," 90; Carey, "The Schools and Civil Defense," 122.

40. Oakes, *Imaginary War*, 47–61; Guy Oakes and Andrew Grossman, "Managing Nuclear Terror: The Genesis of American Civil Defense Strategy," *International Journal of Politics, Culture and Society* 5 (1992): 361; Grossman, *Neither Dead Nor Red*.

41. Cited in Carey, "The Schools and Civil Defense," 123.

42. Lawrence S. Wittner, *One World or None: A History of the World Nuclear Disarmament Movement through 1953* (Stanford, Calif.: Stanford University Press, 1993), 55–80.

43. *BAS* editors make decisions to move the clock hands. In 1969, and again in 1972, the Doomsday Clock hands retreated to ten, and then twelve minutes, in celebration of major arms control treaties. The hands stood at seven minutes before midnight in 1968 and 1980, at ten minutes in 1969, and at nine minutes in 1974. The Doomsday Clock was set at three minutes before midnight in 1984, when both superpowers spoke of the possibility of "limited war." Seven years later, the clock was set at its safest position yet, seventeen minutes before midnight, when an arms reduction agreement was signed. In 1995, a public hearing was held for the first time to determine a new setting; the hands were then set at fourteen minutes before midnight in recognition of the worldwide failure to secure fissionable material. In 1998, the hands were moved to nine minutes before midnight. In February 2002, the clock was reset to seven minutes before midnight, the same setting at which it had begun fifty-five years before.

44. Bernard T. Feld, "A Warning—Not a Prophecy," *BAS* 38 (June–July 1982): 2. See

special issue of *BAS* on *Project East River*, in September 1953. The full *Report of the Project East River* is in Record Group 304, National Security Resources Board Correspondence, Box 99, National Archives.

45. Cited in Oakes and Grossman, "Managing Nuclear Terror," 385; Oakes, *Imaginary War*, 47–51.

46. Fred Kaplan, *The Wizards of Armageddon* (New York: Simon and Schuster, 1983).

47. Irving L. Janis, "Psychological Problems of A-Bomb Defense," *BAS* 6 (August–September 1950): 257. One must remember, of course, that this was written before the 1954 Bravo hydrogen-bomb explosion, the blast that alerted the world to the nature of hydrogen weapons. Also see Oakes, *Imaginary War*, 56, 69–71; Boyer, *By the Bomb's Early Light*, 331–33.

48. Dr. Strangelove has become a classic American figure symbolizing the mad nuclear strategist leading us to destruction, based on Stanley Kubrick's 1964 movie of the same name.

49. Janis, "Psychological Problems of A-Bomb Defense"; also see his book, copyrighted by the Rand Corporation, *Air War and Emotional Stress: Psychological Studies of Bombing and Civil Defense* (New York: McGraw-Hill, 1951).

50. Janis, in later years, wrote extensively about the dangers of "group-think," a term to describe the decline of mental efficiency, reality testing, and moral judgment that can develop within a group of decision makers, who are also likely to recommend irrational and dehumanizing actions directed against those not members of the group. Group-think, as he described it, shares obvious characteristics with Rand-sanctioned teachings on civil defense in the 1950s. See Janis, *Groupthink: Psychological Studies of Policy Decisions and Fiascoes* (Boston: Houghton Mifflin, 1982), a revised and larger edition of a 1972 discussion of group-think. In the 1970s, Janis came to the conclusion that social scientists should give top priority to research problems that have some hope, no matter how faint, of providing guidelines for preventing nuclear war. He then redirected his own research to "concentrate on problems of crisis management in international conflicts." He especially sought to eliminate the conditions producing group-think—collective rationalizations in line with shared illusions, unquestioned beliefs in the group's inherent morality, and stereotyped views of the enemy as evil and stupid. See Janis, "International Crisis Management in the Nuclear Age," in *Psychology and the Prevention of Nuclear War: A Book of Readings*, ed. Ralph K. White (New Haven, Conn.: Yale University Press, 1986), 381–96; and Janis, *Crucial Decisions: Leadership in Policymaking and Crisis Management* (New York: Free Press, 1989).

51. Janis, *Air War and Emotional Stress*, 199–203, 233–57.

52. David Alan Rosenberg, "American Atomic Strategy and the Hydrogen Bomb Decision," *Journal of American History* 66 (June 1979): 62–87.

53. Stanley A. Blumberg and Louis G. Panos, *Edward Teller: Giant of the Golden Age of Physics* (New York: Scribner's, 1990); Edward Teller, with Judith L. Shoolery, *Memoirs: A Twentieth Century Journal in Science and Politics* (Cambridge, Mass.: Perseus, 2001); Alan Lightman, "Megaton Man," review of Teller's memoirs, in *New York Review of Books*, May 23, 2002.

54. Jonathan M. Weisgall, *Operation Crossroads: The Atomic Tests at Bikini Atoll* (Annapolis, Md.: Naval Institute Press, 1994), 306–7. See review by Paul Boyer of Gregg Herken, *The Winning Weapon: The Atomic Bomb in the Cold War* (New York: Knopf, 1980), in *Reviews in American History* 9 (1982): 448–53; and Harold L. Nieburg, *Nuclear Secrecy and Foreign Policy* (Washington, D.C.: Public Affairs Press, 1964). On building the bomb, see Richard Rhodes, *Dark Sun: The Making of the Hydrogen Bomb* (New York: Simon and Schuster, 1995); Thomas J. Cochran, Robert S. Norris, and Oleg A. Bukharin, *Making the Russian Bomb: From Stalin to Yeltsin* (Boulder, Colo.: Westview, 1995).

55. Cited in Lawrence Freedman, *The Evolution of Nuclear Strategy*, rev. ed. (London: Macmillan, 1983), 68. Also see Herbert York, *The Advisors: Oppenheimer, Teller and the Super Bomb* (San Francisco: Freeman, 1976); Richard Sylves, *The Nuclear Oracles: A Political History of the General Advisory Committee of the Atomic Energy Commission, 1947–1977* (Ames: Iowa State University Press, 1987).

56. Cited in Norman Moss, *Men Who Play God: The Story of the H-Bomb and How the World Came to Live with It* (New York: Harper and Row, 1968), 39.

57. Lawrence S. Wittner, *One World or None: A History of the World Nuclear Disarmament Movement through 1953* (Stanford, Calif.: Stanford University Press, 1993), 259.

58. Ernest R. May, ed., *American Cold War Strategy: Interpreting NSC 68* (Boston: St. Martin's, 1993); David Alan Rosenberg, "The Origins of Overkill: Nuclear Weapons and American Strategy, 1945–1960," *International Security* 7 (Spring 1983): 3–71; Robert S. Norris and William M. Arkin, "Nuclear Notebook: Estimated Nuclear Stockpile, 1945–1993," *BAS* 49 (December 1993), 57.

59. Gregg Herkin, *Brotherhood of the Bomb: The Tangled Lives and Loyalties of Robert Oppenheimer, Ernest Lawrence, and Edward Teller* (New York: Holt, 2002); Nuel Pharr Davis, *Lawrence and Oppenheimer* (New York: Simon and Schuster, 1968).

60. Weisgall, *Operation Crossroads*, 303–97. Also see Philip Fradken, *Fallout: An American Nuclear Tragedy* (Tucson: University of Arizona Press, 1989).

61. Richard Pfau, *No Sacrifice Too Great: The Life of Lewis L. Strauss* (Charlottesville: University Press of Virginia, 1984); Richard Allan Baker, "A Slap at the 'Hidden-Hand Presidency': The Senate and the Lewis Strauss Affair," *Congress and the Presidency* 14 (Spring 1987): 1–16.

62. Cited in Moss, *Men Who Play God*, 98.

CHAPTER 2

1. Richard L. Miller, *Under the Cloud: The Decades of Nuclear Testing* (New York: Free Press, 1986), 58–59, 90–91. The United States' nuclear bomb tests from 1945 to 1962 released the equivalent of 137 kilotons of explosive power. The Soviet Union, by testing several enormous bombs in the early 1960s, released 402,000 kilotons, thus accounting for three-quarters of the combined 585,000 kilotons. The two superpowers alone subjected the people of the world to the fallout equivalent of 40,000 Hiroshima bombs during this seventeen-year period. Jay M. Gould and Benjamin A. Goldman with Kate

Millpointer, *Deadly Deceit: Low-Level Radiation, High-Level Cover-up* (New York: Four Walls Eight Windows, 1990), 96.

2. Harold L. Rosenberg, *Atomic Soldiers: American Victims of Nuclear Experiments* (Boston: Beacon, 1980). The AEC cover-up of the true effects of nuclear explosion was the "most long-lived program of public deception in U.S. history," in the words of Stewart L. Udall, a congressman in the 1950s and the secretary of the interior under Presidents Kennedy and Johnson. See his *The Myths of August: A Personal Exploration of Our Tragic Cold War Affair with the Atom* (New York: Pantheon, 1994), 229. For other exposures of the historical record of AEC dishonesty, see Philip L. Fradkin, *Fallout: An American Nuclear Tragedy* (Tucson: University of Arizona Press, 1989); Howard Ball, *Justice Downwind: America's Atomic Testing Program in the 1950s* (New York: Oxford University Press, 1986); Carole Gallagher, *American Ground Zero: The Secret Nuclear War* (Cambridge, Mass.: MIT Press, 1993); A. Constandina Titus, *Bombs in the Backyard: Atomic Testing and American Politics* (Reno: University of Nevada Press, 1986). In the early 1990s, Americans learned about the nuclear medical and radiation experiments performed by the AEC without the consent or knowledge of the victims.

3. Richard Pfau, *No Sacrifice Too Great: The Life of Lewis L. Strauss* (Charlottesville: University Press of Virginia, 1984), 190.

4. Cited in Richard Rhodes, *Dark Sun: The Making of the Hydrogen Bomb* (New York: Simon and Schuster, 1995), 583–84.

5. Campbell Craig, *Destroying the Village: Eisenhower and Thermonuclear War* (New York: Columbia University Press, 1998), introductory page, 56, 41–53. Also see Richard Immerman, "Confessions of an Eisenhower Revisionist: An Agonizing Reappraisal," *Diplomatic History* 3 (Summer 1990): 319–42; John Lewis Gaddis, *We Now Know: Rethinking Cold War History* (New York: Oxford University Press, 1997), 232.

6. House Committee on Appropriations, Hearings on the Supplemental Appropriations Bill, 83d Cong., 1st sess., 1953, part 1, 220–21.

7. U.S. Congress, Senate, Committee on Armed Services, Subcommittee on Civil Defense, *Interim Report on Civil Defense*, 84th Cong., 1st sess., July 1955, 118–19, 121, 124; U.S. Congress, House, Committee on Government Operations, Subcommittee on Military Operations, *Civil Defense for National Survival*, House Report no. 2946, 84th Cong., 2d sess., part 4, May 1956, 1313.

8. Address, National Women's Advisory Committee, October 26, 1954, Central Files, Box 196, DDEL.

9. Cited in Blanchard, *American Civil Defense*, 117.

10. Cited in Thomas J. Kerr, *Civil Defense in the U.S.: Bandaid for a Holocaust?* (Boulder, Colo.: Westview, 1983), 81–82.

11. Blanchard, *American Civil Defense*, 113, 128.

12. The power of that propaganda is demonstrated by how, in 1954, the crew and cast of the movie *The Conqueror* [*sic*], on location near St. George, Utah, took 60 tons of the radiated canyon dirt back to Hollywood in order to finish filming in the studio. Twenty-six years later, 91 of the 220 cast and crew members had come down with cancer, a startling morbidity rate. Over half of these 91 cancer victims were dead by 1980. Among them were John Wayne, Dick Powell, and Susan Hayward. A scientist in the

Defense Nuclear Agency in 1980 reportedly moaned, "Please, God, don't let us have killed John Wayne." See Gerald H. Clarfield and William M. Wiecek, *Nuclear America: Military and Civilian Nuclear Power in the United States, 1940–1980* (New York: Harper and Row, 1984), 206–9.

13. Ralph E. Lapp, "Civil Defense Faces New Peril," *BAS* 10 (November 1954): 349–51; "Radioactive Fallout," *BAS* 10 (February 1955): 45–51. Also see Lapp, *The New Force: The Story of Atoms and People* (New York: Harper and Row, 1953), and *Atoms and People* (New York: Harper and Row, 1956).

14. Lawrence S. Wittner, *Resisting the Bomb: A History of the World Nuclear Disarmament Movement, 1954–1970* (Stanford, Calif.: Stanford University Press, 1997), 137.

15. William Lanouette with Bela Szilard, *Genius in the Shadows: A Biography of Leo Szilard: The Man behind the Bomb* (New York: Scribner's, 1992), 460.

16. Quoted in Robert Divine, *Blowing on the Wind: The Nuclear Test Debate, 1954–1960* (New York: Oxford University Press, 1978), 33–56, 59, 57.

17. Strauss cited in Miller, *Under the Cloud*, 230; Willard Libby, "The Facts about A-Bomb Fallout," *U.S. News and World Report*, March 25, 1955, 21–26; Harvey Wasserman and Norman Solomon, *Killing Our Own: The Disaster of America's Experiment with Atomic Radiation* (New York: Delacorte, 1982), 77, 92.

18. This led to the beginning of the famed annual Pugwash conferences that brought together scientists from many countries, including the United States and the Soviet Union, to discuss nuclear events in the interest of peace. The publicity given to Pugwash each year posed another formidable challenge to the arms race. See "The Russell-Einstein Manifesto," reprinted in J. Roblat, *Scientists in the Quest for Peace: A History of the Pugwash Conferences* (Cambridge, Mass.: MIT Press, 1972); Wittner, *Resisting the Bomb*, 6–7. Also see William Epstein and Lucy Webster, eds., *We Can Avert a Nuclear War* (Cambridge, Mass.: Oelgeschlager, Gunn and Hain, 1983), commemorating the twenty-fifth anniversary of the first Pugwash.

19. George W. Beadle, "Liquidating Unpopular Opinion," *Science*, October 28, 1955, 813.

20. Wasserman and Solomon, *Killing Our Own*, 213.

21. *Civil Defense for National Survival: Hearings before a Subcommittee of the Committee on Government Operations*, House of Representatives, 84th Cong., 2d sess., 7 parts (Washington, D.C.: U.S. Government Printing Office, 1956). Hereafter cited as *Civil Defense for National Survival*. Also see discussion of the hearings in Blanchard, *American Civil Defense*; and Kerr, *Civil Defense in the U.S.*

22. *Civil Defense for National Survival*, 1314. In my taped interview with Chet Holifield at his California home in 1989, when he was eighty-six, he told me that prior to our conversation he had never told anyone but his wife that his real purpose in holding these hearings and calling for a nationwide system of fallout shelters was not to support fallout shelters, but rather to make clear to the public that civil defense was an utterly unrealistic and futile preparation for nuclear war. If this is so, it was not recognized then or later. I suspect that by the 1970s and 1980s, Holifield had come to realize the actual power of nuclear bombs and wished to "correct" his placement in history as a fervent supporter of fallout shelters. Also see Richard Wayne Dyke, *Mr. Atomic Energy: Con-*

gressman Chet Holifield and Atomic Energy Affairs, 1945–1974 (New York: Greenwood, 1989); interview with Chet Holifield, conducted by Enid Douglass, April 25 and May 7, 1975, in Graduate School Library, Claremont College, California; Oral Histories, Chet Holifield interview, 1975, JFKL.

23. Quoted in Blanchard, *American Civil Defense*, 151.

24. *Civil Defense for National Survival*, 3:670; 4:1431–32, 1226. Also see Central Files, Unofficial Files, Box 656, DDEL.

25. *Civil Defense for National Survival*, Part 3, 2847; statement of Mrs. Alexander Stewart also cited in Blanchard, *American Civil Defense*, 186 n.155.

26. Mary Simpson, "A Long Hard Look at Civil Defense: A Review of the Holifield Committee Hearings," *BAS* 12 (November 1956): 346.

27. Ibid.

28. James W. Deer, "The Unavoidable International Shelter Race," *BAS* (February 1957): 66–67.

29. *Civil Defense for National Survival*, Part 4, 1227–28.

30. Gayle Greene, *The Woman Who Knew Too Much: Alice Stewart and the Secrets of Radiation* (Ann Arbor: University of Michigan Press, 1999), is a revealing case study that describes how the nuclear establishment worked to discredit information that threatened its propaganda goals. Only after a very long fight did Stewart's discoveries about radiation successfully challenge international safety standards.

31. William Cuyler Sullivan, *Nuclear Democracy: A History of the Greater St. Louis Citizen's Committee for Nuclear Information, 1957–67* (St. Louis, Mo.: Washington University, 1982), 8.

32. Alan Smith, "Democracy and the Politics of Information: The St. Louis Committee for Nuclear Information," (St. Louis Missouri Historical Society) *Gateway Heritage* (Summer 1966): 5.

33. Sullivan, *Nuclear Democracy*, 8; Smith, "Democracy and the Politics of Information," 2–14; interviews of Alexander Pond, 2002, 2003. I have also profited from reading an unpublished research paper by Jennie Brier, in possession of the author.

34. Harriet Hyman Alonso, *Peace as a Women's Issue: A History of the U.S. Movement for World Peace and Women's Rights* (Syracuse, N.Y.: Syracuse University Press, 1993); Lawrence S. Wittner, *Rebels against War: The American Peace Movement, 1933–1983* (Philadelphia: Temple University Press, 1984).

35. Scott H. Bennett, "Radical Pacifism and the General Strike against War: Jessie Wallace Hugnan, the Founding of the War Resisters League, and the Socialist Origins of Secular Radical Pacifism in America," *Peace and Change* (July 2001): 352–73; Scott H. Bennett, *Radical Pacifism: The War Resisters League and Gandhian Non-Violence in America, 1915–1963* (Syracuse, N.Y.: Syracuse University Press, 2003); Nancy L. Roberts, *Dorothy Day and the Catholic Worker* (Albany: State University of New York Press, 1984); Mel Piehl, *Breaking Bread: The Catholic Worker and the Origin of Catholic Radicalism in America* (Philadelphia: Temple University Press, 1982); William D. Miller, *A Harsh and Dreadful Love: Dorothy Day and the Catholic Worker Movement* (New York: Liveright, 1973); Patrick Coy, *A Revolution of the Heart: Essays on the Catholic Worker* (Philadelphia: Temple University Press, 1988); William J. Thorn, Philip Runkel, and Su-

san Mountin, eds., *Dorothy Day and the Catholic Worker Movement: Centenary Essays* (Milwaukee, Wis.: Marquette University, 2001). The *Catholic Worker* sold for a penny a copy and still had a circulation of about 65,000 in the mid-1950s, despite its opposition to the war in Korea. Also see Ammon Hennacy, *The Book of Ammon: The Autobiography of a Unique American Rebel* (Salt Lake City, Utah: Ammon Hennacy Publications, 1970); Nat Hentoff, *Peace Agitator: The Story of A. J. Muste* (New York: Macmillan, 1963); Jo Ann Robinson, *Abraham Went Out: A Biography of A. J. Muste* (Philadelphia: Temple University Press, 1981).

36. Dan Wakefield, *New York in the Fifties* (New York: Houghton Mifflin/Seymour Lawrence, 1992), 80.

37. Bayard Rustin was a central figure in the Fellowship of Reconciliation and the War Resisters League. In 1956, he was one of the first Gandhian intellectuals to arrive in Montgomery and Birmingham and advise Martin Luther King, Jr., on the use of Gandhian nonviolence. Rustin was also instrumental in the organization of the Southern Christian Leadership Conference and was the major organizer of the 1963 March on Washington. See Jervis Anderson, *Bayard Rustin: Troubles I've Seen: A Biography* (New York: HarperCollins, 1997); Daniel Levine, *Bayard Rustin and the Civil Rights Movement* (New Brunswick, N.J.: Rutgers University Press, 2000); John D'Emilio, *Lost Prophet: The Life and Times of Bayard Rustin* (New York: Free Press, 2003). Bennett, *Radical Pacifism*, also explores the Gandhian theme. Jim Peck, a leader in the War Resisters League and active in the anti–civil defense movement, won national renown as a Freedom Rider in 1961. James Peck, *Underdogs vs. Upperdogs* (New York: AMP&R, 1980).

38. Among the many studies of political ritual and antiritual, I found most helpful Victor Turner, *Dramas, Fields, and Metaphors: Symbolic Action in Human Society* (Ithaca, N.Y.: Cornell University Press, 1974); and David I. Kertzer, *Ritual, Politics, and Power* (New Haven, Conn.: Yale University Press, 1988).

39. Guy Oakes, *The Imaginary War: Civil Defense and American Cold War Culture* (New York: Oxford University Press, 1994), 84–105.

40. "Peoria Ignores Alert," *NYT*, June 16, 1955, 16.

41. Stephen I. Schwartz, ed., *Atomic Audit: The Costs and Consequences of U.S. Nuclear Weapons since 1940* (Washington, D.C.: Brookings Institution Press, 1998), 207–16. Also see Ted Gup, "Doomsday Hideaway," *Time*, December 9, 1991, 26–29; "The Doomsday Blueprints," *Time*, August 10, 1992, 26–41; "How the Federal Emergency Management Agency Learned to Stop Worrying about Civilians and Love the Bomb," *Mother Jones*, January 1, 1994; and "The Doomsday Plan," the cover story of *Time*, August 10, 1992, 32–39. Also see Michael Schuman, "The Under Sanctum," *Philadelphia Inquirer*, December 2, 2001, 1, 14; Bill Gifford, "Bunker? What Bunker?" *NYT Magazine*, December 3, 2000, 132–33; N. J. McCamley, *Cold War Secret Nuclear Bunkers: The Passive Defense of the Western World during the Cold War* (Barnsley, U.K.: Cooper, 2002). Spending on nuclear-related command posts and systems such as these for the select political, military, and industrial elites in the period since the early 1950s has varied immensely over the years, from underground retreats, to escapes via boats or airplanes. The cost through 1995 totals somewhere over 25 billion tax dollars, and the results are often as

bizarre as the efforts devised to "protect" the general public from nuclear attack. What is one to make, for example, of the carefully organized federal effort in the 1950s to be ready to save the 2,080-pound Liberty Bell from nuclear meltdown, or the art treasures from Washington museums, or the copy of the Declaration of Independence, all at a time when the citizens at large were to be left unassisted, on their own, destined to fry or vaporize or be radiated to death, tens of millions of them at a time?

42. Ann Whitman File, NSC Series, Box 5, 182d meeting of the National Security Council, January 28, 1954. For other discussions centered around the continuity of government as tested during the Operation Alert rituals, see meetings of the National Security Council, March 3, 1955, Box 6; June 9, 1955, Box 7; and September 25, 1958, all in Ann Whitman File, NSC Series; DDE's Papers as President, 1953–61, Cabinet Series, Cabinet Paper, Privileged, June 18, 1955, DDEL.

43. "Operation Alert," August 10, 1954, KGH, DDEL.

44. Wittner, *Rebels against War*, 227.

45. Robert Ellsberg, "An Unusual History from the FBI," *Catholic Worker*, May–June 1979, presents a synopsis of FBI files on the Catholic Worker movement. Also see R. Allen Smith, "Mass Society and the Bomb: The Discourse of Pacifism in the 1950s," *Peace and Change* (October 1993): 347–72. On the memorable Catholic anarchist Ammon Hennacy, see Murray Kempton column "Amon [*sic*] and the Wolf," *New York Post*, March 1, 1968; Ammon Hennacy Papers, Marquette University, Milwaukee, Wisconsin.

46. Miller, *Under the Cloud*, 215.

47. *FCDA Newsletter: By, For, and About Women in Civil Defense*, November 5, 1955, KGH, DDEL; also see Jean Fuller Papers; Miller, *Under the Cloud*, 232–39.

48. Cited in Miller, *Under the Cloud*, 236.

49. See Oakes, *Imaginary War*.

50. For clippings and documents on the 1955 arrests, see W6.3, Box 1, Dorothy Day Catholic Worker Collection, Marquette University Archives, hereafter cited as DDCW. Included is a letter from Eleanor Roosevelt to Day, April 21, 1959, in which Roosevelt chides Day for her opposition to Operation Alert and concludes: "I cannot see why you go to such extremes to avoid complying with the law"; Boxes l, 2, CDGA, Civil Defense Protest Committee, Swarthmore College Peace Collection, hereafter cited as SCPC; interview with Tom Cornell by Deane Mowrer, June 3, 1968, W9, Box 1, DDCW. Also see Ammon Hennacy, "Civil Disobedience," *Catholic Worker*, July–August 1955, 3, 7; appeal for support of Orlie Pell in Bess Cameron to Dear WILPF member, June 17, 1955, Box 22, Folder 2, WILPF Papers, Smith College, hereafter cited as SCWILPF; Provisional Defense Committee, "What Happened on June 15?" Box 8, WRL Papers, SCPC; Jim Peck, "28 Arrested in Civil Defense Demonstration," *WRL News*, July–August 1955; Orlie Pell Papers, Archives, Alexander Library, Rutgers University, New Brunswick, New Jersey.

51. Attorneys for the civil defense protesters argued that because the air raid drill was not a real attack, there was no clear and present danger and thus the defendants' rights of free speech and religion had been violated. The attorneys also pointed out that substantial numbers of civilians other than those arrested had been exempted from participation in the air raid drill. *WRL News*, March–April 1960. The 1955 and 1956 ar-

rests were appealed on behalf of the civil defense protesters. In January 1961, the U.S. Supreme Court rejected the case without a hearing, although Justice William O. Douglass voted in favor of hearing the case. Also see Judith Malina, *The Enormous Despair* (New York: Random House, 1972), and *The Diaries of Judith Malina, 1947–57* (New York: Grove, 1984); FBI Files on WRL, Box 1, Marquette University Archives; CDG-A, Civil Defense Protest Committee, SCPC.

52. "Report of Operation Alert 1955," January 4, 1956, KGH, DDEL.

53. DDEP, Cabinet Series, Box 5, Minutes, June 17, 1955, DDEL.

54. Murray Kempton column, *New York Post*, November 23, 1955.

55. Robert Ellsberg, "An Unusual History from the FBI." On the 1955 arrests, also see Jim Peck, "The Civil Defense Trial," *WRL News*, November–December 1955, 1, 4; and additional citations from the Fellowship of Reconciliation Papers, Smith College, and from FBI files on WRL, Marquette University Archives.

56. "Briefing for Operation Alert," 1956, White House Office, Office of the Special Assistant for National Security Affairs, Records, 1952–61, NSC Series, Subject Subseries, Box 6, DDEL.

57. "General Instructions for Operation Alert, 1956," Distributed Cabinet Meeting, July 3, 1956, Ann Whitman File, Cabinet Series, Box 7, DDEL.

58. Proposal read to Cabinet by Dr. Fleming, and Minutes of Cabinet Meeting, July 13, 1956, Ann Whitman File, Cabinet Series, Box 7, DDEL.

59. July–August and September–October issues of *WRL News* have descriptions and pictures of the 1956 arrests.

60. Oakes, *Imaginary War*, 150–51; Notes on the Expanded Cabinet Meeting, July 25, 1956, Cabinet Series; Operation Alert 1956, July 24, 1956; and Cabinet Meeting, July 26, 1956, all in Ann Whitman File, Cabinet Series, Box 7, DDEL.

CHAPTER 3

1. Teller cited in Fred Kaplan, *The Wizards of Armageddon* (New York: Simon and Schuster, 1983), 135; Johnson cited in Michael Sherry, *In the Shadow of War: The United States since the 1930s* (New Haven, Conn.: Yale University Press, 1995), 214; James K. Killian, *Sputnik, Scientists, and Eisenhower: A Memoir of the First Special Assistant to the President for Science and Technology* (Cambridge, Mass.: MIT Press, 1977); Robert Divine, *The Sputnik Challenge* (New York: Oxford University Press, 1993).

2. Cited in B. Wayne Blanchard, *American Civil Defense, 1945–1975: The Evolution of Programs and Policies* (Washington, D.C.: FEMA, 1980), 194.

3. Ibid., 202.

4. Strobe Talbott, *Master of the Game: Paul Nitze and the Nuclear Peace* (New York: Knopf, 1988), 14; Paul H. Nitze, *From Hiroshima to Glasnost: At the Center of Decision: A Memoir* (New York: Grove Weidenfeld, 1989). Nitze began his campaign in the late 1940s for a strong civil defense program when he built a well-stocked, large bomb shelter on his 1,900-acre estate in Maryland. Not until 1960 did he acknowledge that Americans had consistently refused to support a nationwide civil defense program.

5. See Kaplan, *Wizards of Armageddon*; Morton Halperin, "The Gaither Committee and the Policy Process," *World Politics* 13 (April 1961): 360–84; and the partial text of the Gaither Report in Morton Halperin, *National Security Policy-Making* (Lexington, Mass.: Lexington, 1975), 71–111. Also see Gregg Herkin, *Counsels of War* (New York: Knopf, 1985); Herkin, *Cardinal Choices: Presidential Science Advising from the Atomic Bomb to SDI* (New York: Oxford University Press, 1992); Peter Roman, *Eisenhower and the Missile Gap* (Ithaca, N.Y.: Cornell University Press, 1995); David L. Snead, *The Gaither Committee, Eisenhower, and the Cold War* (Columbus: Ohio State University Press, 1999); Robert R. Bowie and Richard H. Immerman, *Waging Peace: How Eisenhower Shaped an Enduring Cold War Strategy* (New York: Oxford University Press, 1998).

6. Kerr, *Civil Defense in the U.S.*, 108.

7. Halperin, "The Gaither Committee."

8. Herkin, *Counsels of War*, 116. Also see discussion of the Gaither Report in Ronald E. Powaski, *March to Armageddon: The United States and the Nuclear Arms Race, 1939 to the Present* (New York: Oxford University Press, 1987); McGeorge Bundy, *Danger and Survival: Choices about the Bomb in the First Fifty Years* (New York: Random House, 1988); Herbert F. York, *Making Weapons, Talking Peace: A Physicist's Odyssey from Hiroshima to Geneva* (New York: Basic, 1987). York and Jerome Weisner, later science advisor to President Kennedy, both report that their experience helping to produce the Gaither Report was a turning point in their lives. It was then they realized that nuclear war could destroy life on earth.

9. Lawrence S. Wittner, *Resisting the Bomb: A History of the World Nuclear Disarmament Movement, 1954–1970* (Stanford, Calif.: Stanford University Press, 1997), 12–15, 29–34.

10. Ibid., 37–38, 39, 138–40. Also see Thomas Hager, *Force of Nature: The Life of Linus Pauling* (New York: Simon and Schuster, 1995). In 1963, months after the final signing of the Test Ban Treaty by the Americans and the Soviets, Pauling won the Nobel Peace Prize. No one in history had ever before received two unshared Nobel prizes. For more startling evidence of unjustified attacks in support of anticommunist hysteria, see the story of FBI harassment of the socialist, pacifist, antiracist Albert Einstein in Fred Jerome, *The Einstein File: J. Edgar Hoover's Secret War against the World's Most Famous Scientist* (New York: St. Martin's, 2002).

11. Wittner, *Resisting the Bomb*, 58, 369–70; Cabinet Agenda for December 11, 1959, Box 15, Cabinet Series, DDEL.

12. W. C. Sullivan, *Nuclear Democracy: A History of the Greater St. Louis Citizen's Committee for Nuclear Information, 1957–67* (St. Louis, Mo.: Washington University, 1982), 28. Also see Mead, "Are Shelters the Answer?" *NYT Magazine*, November 26, 1961, 123–25.

13. Lawrence Scott Papers, Box 1, SCPC. Scott remained an active pacifist, picketing the White House, sponsoring marches, and opposing bomb testing, the Vietnam War, and chemical and biological warfare. In 1964 and 1965, he worked in Mississippi with a Friends group that rebuilt more than thirty African-American churches that had been burned. In the early 1970s, he founded a Friends rural community in Arizona. Scott died in 1986.

14. Milton S. Katz, *Ban the Bomb: A History of SANE, the Committee for a Sane Nuclear Policy, 1957–85* (New York: Greenwood, 1986); Neil Katz, "Radical Pacifism and the Contemporary American Peace Movement: The Committee for Non-Violent Action, 1957–67," Ph.D. diss., University of Maryland, 1974.

15. Operation Alert, Cabinet Paper, January 25 and 28, 1957, Cabinet Series; "Assumptions, Operational Guidance and Time Phasing for Operation Alert 1957: To Heads of Executive Departments and Agencies," February 6, 1957, Cabinet Series; Minutes of Cabinet Meeting, July 12, 1957; Expanded Cabinet Meeting, July 19, 1957, Cabinet Series, all in Ann Whitman Files, Cabinet Series, Box 8.

16. *Newsletter: By, For, and About Women in Civil Defense*, November 25, 1957, KGH, DDEL.

17. Quoted in Malina, *The Diaries of Judith Malina, 1947–1957* (New York: Grove, 1984), 443. Press coverage of the 1957 protest was limited. Day published letters from jail in the *Catholic Worker* and *Liberation*, the radical pacifist journal established in 1956. The *Nation* and *Commonweal* supported the action. For clippings, see W6.3, Box 1, DDCW.

18. See Dorothy Day's detailed and moving description of her imprisonment for refusing to take cover during Operation Alert in Robert Ellsberg, ed., *By Little and by Little: The Selected Writings of Dorothy Day* (New York: Knopf, 1983).

19. Richard K. S. Taylor, *Against the Bomb: The British Peace Movement, 1958–1965* (Oxford: Clarendon, 1988); Christopher Driver, *The Disarmers: A Study in Protest* (London: Hodder and Stoughton, 1964); John Minnion and Philip Bolsover, eds., *The CND Story: The First 25 Years of CND in the Words of the People Involved* (London: Allison and Busby, 1983).

20. Cabinet Meetings, June 6, 1958, Ann Whitman File, Cabinet Series, Box 11; Continuous Activation: High Point, September 2, 1958, White House Office, Office of the State Secretary, Subject Series, Alphabetical Subseries, Box 12; Cabinet Discussion, October 1958; National Security Council Series, Briefing Notes, Subseries, Box 8; Discussion, National Security Council Meeting, March 27, 1958, Box 10, all in DDEL. Guy Oakes, in *Imaginary War*, notes that the federal debriefings on Operation Alert show that the listeners soon learned there could be no protection against nuclear war, yet did not admit this to the public for fear of jeopardizing their deterrent strategy.

21. Cited in Blanchard, *American Civil Defense*, 220.

22. Wittner, *Resisting the Bomb*, 55–56; Charles Chatfield, *The American Peace Movement: Ideals and Activism* (New York: Twayne, 1992), 100–116; Larry Scott, "A Desperate Appeal to American Pacifists," Box 1, Lawrence Scott Papers, SCPC.

23. More than twenty-five years later, several peace groups, including Physicians for Social Responsibility, Nuclear Freeze, and Ground Zero, used the same technique just as successfully to educate citizens about the effects of a nuclear bomb on their own communities.

24. W. K. Wyant, Jr., "50,000 Baby Teeth," *Nation*, June 13, 1959, 535–37.

25. Author's interviews with Mary Sharmat and Janice Smith, 1990, 1991; Sharmat statement in possession of author. On 1959 protest, see *WRL News*, May–June 1959; Deane Mowrer, "Prison Revisited," *Catholic Worker*, June 1959, 3, 6; Larry Scott, "A

Desperate Appeal to American Pacifists," Spring 1959, Box 1, Scott Papers, SCPC; Correspondence, January–June 1959, Series 1, Box 3, David McReynolds Papers, SCPC. *WRL News*, January–February 1991, is a special issue honoring McReynolds.

26. Interview with Smith. See reports of her arrest in *New York Post*, April 17, 1959. Her husband, Jack Smith, was later a journalist with the radical newspaper the *Guardian*.

27. Interviews with Sharmat and Smith conducted by author, 1991; "Civil Defense Protest Day" and "Call to Sanity," Box 22, Civil Defense Protest Committee, SCPC; documents and clippings in Box 6, SANE Papers, SCPC; Box 22, Series VI, Committee for Non-Violent Action, SCPC.

28. FBI files on WRL, Boxes 8 and 14, and FBI files on WILPF, Boxes 3 and 4, in Marquette University Archives; interview with Bess Cameron conducted by B. Parnes, December 30, 1987, in possession of author. The sudden revival of Metro is very evident in SCWILPF. On Sharmat, see Beverly Gary, "A Navy Officer's Daughter Leads Protest on Civil Defense," *New York Post*, December 11, 1969, 38.

29. Sharmat statement in Box 22, Civil Defense Protest Committee, SCPC, WRL, Box 8.

30. Descriptions of 1960 protest in Robert Stein and Carolyn Connors, "Civil Defense Protests in New York," *New University Thought*, Spring 1961, 81–93, Boxes 6 and 33, SANE Papers, SCPC; documents and clippings in W6.3, Box 1, DDCW; Box 22, Civil Defense Protest Committee, SCPC, includes names of those arrested and letter from Sharmat to Dear Friend, Box 8, WRL Papers, SCPC.

31. Sharmat statement, in possession of author.

32. Box 6, SANE Papers, SCPC; Lincoln Adair, "Public Demonstration and Civil Disobedience," American Friends Service Committee, W6.3, Box 1, DDCW.

33. Sharmat statement.

34. Jim Peck, "Biggest Civil Disobedience Action," *WRL News*, May–June 1960, p. 1; Dan Wakefield, "Good-by[e] New York: New York Prepares for Annihilation," *Esquire*, August 1960, 79–85; Muste to Bradford Lyttle, May 16, 1960, DG17, Box 8, SCPC; McReynolds, "Revolution by Degrees," *Peace News*, June 24, 1960; McReynolds to Muste, DiGia, Peck, Box 8, WRL Papers, SCPC. Scott seems less sure of the new tactic in Scott to Albert Bigelow, July 12, 1960, Lawrence Scott Papers, SCPC.

35. Murray Kempton, "Laughter in the Park," *New York Post*, cited in Maurice Isserman, *If I Had a Hammer: The Death of the Old Left and the Birth of the New Left* (New York: Basic, 1987), 147; Box 2, CDPC Papers, SCPC; Box 8, WRLP, SCPC, for other material regarding the drill.

36. Cited in Wittner, *Resisting the Bomb*, 401–2.

37. Memorandum, December 22, 1960, NSC Series, Box 13, Ann Whitman File, DDEL. Also see Accomplishments of the Office of Civil and Defense Mobilization, 1953–60, Central Files, Official File, Box 322, DDEL.

38. Young in *Congressional Record* (105–11), July 30, 1959, 14705, 14708–9; Kerr, *Civil Defense in the U.S.*, 114. Richard Wayne Dyke, *Mr. Atomic Energy: Congressman Chet Holifield and Atomic Energy Affairs, 1945–1974* (Westport, Conn.: Greenwood, 1989), 183–219; Gene Levine and John Modell, "American Public Opinion and the Fall-out

Shelter Issue," *Public Opinion Quarterly* 2 (Summer 1965): 270–79. Also see Francis X. Gannon and Richard W. Dyke, *Chet Holifield: Master Legislator and Nuclear Statesman* (Lanham, Md.: University Press of America, 1996).

39. Quoted in Kerr, *Civil Defense in the U.S.*, 114.

CHAPTER 4

1. Sanford Gottlieb, "Campaigning for Peace," *BAS* 18 (November 1962): 38–39. Among the candidates were Harvard history professor H. Stuart Hughes, who was chair of SANE, 1967–1970; Quaker professor of law Harrop Freeman from Cornell; and Sidney Lens, an independent from Chicago. Lawrence S. Wittner, *Resisting the Bomb: A History of the World Nuclear Disarmament Movement* (Stanford, Calif.: Stanford University Press, 1997), 263.

2. Margot A. Henriksen, *Dr. Strangelove's America: Society and Culture in the Atomic Age* (Berkeley: University of California Press, 1997), 212.

3. Blanche Wiesen Cook, "First Comes the Lie: C. D. Jackson and Political Warfare," *Radical History Review* 31 (1984): 42–70. Jackson was the chief organizer of America's psychological warfare effort during World War I, and between 1937 and 1949 he served as general manager of *Life*, as vice president at Time, Inc., and as publisher of *Fortune*. Also see Robert E. Herzstein, *Henry R. Luce: A Political Portrait of the Man Who Created the American Century* (New York: Scribner's, 1994); and James L. Baughman, *Henry R. Luce and the Rise of American News Media* (Boston, Mass.: Twayne, 1987).

4. Cary Reich, *The Life of Nelson A. Rockefeller: Worlds to Conquer, 1908–1958* (Garden City, N.Y.: Doubleday, 1996), 656.

5. Michael Kramer and Sam Roberts, *I Never Wanted to Be Vice-President of Anything! An Investigative Biography of Nelson Rockefeller* (New York: Basic, 1976), 219; Peter Collier and David Horowitz, *The Rockefellers: An American Dynasty* (New York: Holt, Rinehart and Winston, 1976), n. 344. Also see Ralph Lapp, "Rockefeller's Civil Defense Program," *BAS* 16 (April 1960): 134–36; Joseph Persico, *The Imperial Rockefeller: A Biography of Nelson A. Rockefeller* (New York: Simon and Schuster, 1982).

6. Public Papers of Governor Rockefeller, 1962, 796, New York State Library, Albany, henceforth cited as PPGR.

7. Lapp, "Rockefeller's Civil Defense Program," 134–36. Only after civil defense and Rockefeller's civil defense program in New York had been wholly rejected by the public did Rockefeller admit in a press conference, in June 1963, that he had a report to be "released shortly" that talked about post-attack protection, which Rockefeller finally admitted was the reason that the public had rejected the fallout shelter hype. Governor's Press Conference, June 4, 1963, Press, Box 6, Nelson A. Rockefeller Archive Center, Sleepy Hollow, New York, hereafter cited as NAR.

8. Herman Kahn, *On Thermonuclear War* (Princeton, N.J.: Princeton University Press, 1960), *Thinking about the Unthinkable* (New York: Horizon, 1962), and *On Escalation: Metaphors and Scenarios* (New York: Praeger, 1965); Jeffrey D. Porro, "The Policy War: Brodie vs. Kahn," *BAS* 38 (June–July 1982): 16–19. Kahn originally conceived the

Doomsday Machine, his version of a perfect deterrent to nuclear war. He envisioned a massive computer connected to stockpiles of hydrogen bombs. When the country is attacked, it goes off, and there is no way anyone can stop it from exploding the entire stockpile of hydrogen bombs, which would then kill billions of people around the world with radiation fallout. In the movie *Dr. Strangelove*, the Soviet Union had put in place such a Doomsday Machine, but failed to tell the world it was there.

9. Spencer R. Weart, "History of American Attitudes to Civil Defense," in *Civil Defense: A Choice of Disasters*, ed. John Dowling and Evans M. Harrell (New York: American Institute of Physics, 1987), 21. Memorandum to the President from McGeorge Bundy, President's Office Files, May 9, 1961, Box 85, John F. Kennedy Library, hereafter cited as JFKL.

10. Also see Nelson Rockefeller, "Purpose and Policy," *Foreign Affairs* 38 (1960): 370–90; Elizabeth Walker Mechling and Jay Mechling, "The Campaign for Civil Defense and the Struggle to Naturalize the Bomb," *Western Journal of Speech Communication* 55 (Spring 1991): 105–33. For a full discussion of Rockefeller's efforts to advance his civil defense plans, see PPGR, 1961, 75, 157–63, 622–23, 1058–65, 1142–43, 1312–15.

11. Kaysen quoted in Theodore Sorenson, *Kennedy* (New York: Harper and Row, 1965), 613–14; Marc Raskin to McGeorge Bundy, Memo, May 19, 1961, National Security Files, Box 295, Folder 3, JFKL. Raskin later compared national security advisor McGeorge Bundy to a Paris prostitute, who served the needs of every class, from murderers and thieves to judges and priests. Like others in the national security culture, Raskin wrote, Bundy was "limited to thought, language, and options that outsiders would have immediately concluded were narrow and even absurd." In fact, a large number of the public and of the intellectual class outside government did quickly reach this exact conclusion about the civil defense program pushed by President Kennedy. Marcus G. Raskin, *Essays of a Citizen: From National Security State to Democracy* (Armonk, N.Y.: Sharpe, 1991), 101, 59–62. Raskin was the cofounder of the progressive think tank the Institute for Policy Studies.

12. Summary of Kennedy remarks on May 25, 1961, in PPGR, 1961, 1065–66. Also Wayne Blanchard, *American Civil Defense, 1945–75* (Washington, D.C.: FEMA, 1980), 277–79.

13. Blanchard, *American Civil Defense*, 304, 272–74; Thomas Kerr, *Civil Defense in the U.S.: Bandaid for a Holocaust?* (Boulder, Colo.: Westview, 1983), 116–17; oral history of E. McDermott, JFKL. Also see interview with Adam Yarmolinsky, November 28, 1964, Daniel Ellsberg, interviewer, in Oral History, JFKL.

14. Marcus Raskin to McGeorge Bundy, July 7, 1961, National Security Files, Box 295, JFKL.

15. John F. Kennedy, "The Berlin Crisis," *Vital Speeches of the Day* 27 (August 15, 1961): 644.

16. Stephen M. Young, "Civil Defense: Billion Dollar Boondoggle," *Progressive* 24 (December 1960): 18–20. Blanchard, *American Civil Defense*, 275, notes that Young attacked civil defense eight times in the Senate in 1961. The Tonkin Gulf Resolution, based on LBJ's deliberate use of faulty information, was used to justify later military action in Southeast Asia. It was repealed by Congress in 1970.

17. Stanley Newman, "Civil Defense and the Congress: Quiet Reversal," *BAS* 18 (No-

vember 1962): 33–37. Because civil defense responsibilities were shifted by Kennedy to the Department of Defense, a different set of appropriations subcommittees were involved; this conveniently shut out the influence of Representative Thomas, who could always be counted on to oppose monies for civil defense.

18. Clippings, documents, and lists of arrested persons from the 1961 protest are in CNVA, Box 22, SCPC; W6.3, Box 1, DDCW; Box 22, Folder 3, 7, SCWILPF. Also see SANE Papers, Series 1, Boxes 6 and 13, SCPC; McReynolds to Muste, Rustin, DiGia, Gilmore, "Memo on Civil Defense Protest Committee," is especially interesting for its discussion of the anti-CD strategies and constituencies, WRL Papers, Box 8, SCPC. Jim Peck was brutally beaten in a civil rights Freedom Ride in Birmingham, Alabama, in May 1961. A key "proof" of Peck's association with communists offered by Alabama authorities was his membership on the Civil Defense Protest Committee, erroneously cited by the Alabama attorney general as the Civil Defense Protection Committee, *WRL News*, July–August 1961. See JFK Folders, 1961, 1962, Library, FEMA, Washington, D.C., for correspondence and discussion of the possible enlargement of the civil defense program and of the proposed civil defense booklet. Janice Smith reports that even before the cancellation of the planned 1962 Operation Alert, the New York City police had made a special plea to city civil defense officials to end the exercise. Smith statement, in possession of author. For a full description of the 1961 anti–civil defense efforts, see Scott Bennett, *Radical Pacifism: The War Resisters League and Gandhian Nonviolence in America, 1915–1963* (Syracuse, N.Y.: Syracuse University Press, 2003), 214–16. Also see Carl Dreher, "Hazards of Civil Defense," *Nation*, June 10, 1961, 495.

19. After the defeat of Operation Alert, Janice Smith and Mary Sharmat returned to political anonymity. Although they continued their activism through the 1960s, they blended into the tens of thousands who marched in the antiwar, civil rights, and feminist movements of that decade. In the 1970s, they jointly owned and operated the Ladies Hobby Shop in Manhattan. Aside from selling yarn and craft supplies, the Hobby Shop was a meeting place for women in the city. Mary Sharmat returned to the theater and performing arts in the late 1970s and performed in plays in New York and around the country. Before her death in 2004, Sharmat was very active with the Manhattan Plaza AIDS project. Janice Smith, now Janice Harrison, is a textile designer. She has written three craft books, sold real estate, and taught textile design.

20. The wide activity of women in peace marches is discussed in Amy Swerdlow, *Women Strike for Peace: Traditional Motherhood and Radical Politics in the 1960s* (Chicago: University of Chicago Press, 1993). Both Dagmar Wilson, the chief organizer of WSP, and Mary Sharmat are featured in Marjorie Hunter and Walter H. Waggoner, "Women's Peace Campaign Gaining Support," *NYT*, November 22, 1961, 4.

21. Amy Swerdlow, "Ladies' Day at the Capitol: Women Strike for Peace versus HUAC," *Feminist Studies* 8 (Fall 1982): 493–520; Saul Alinsky, *Rules for Radicals: A Practical Primer for Realistic Radicals* (New York: Vintage, 1972); David Garrow, *The Montgomery Bus Boycott and the Women Who Started It: The Memoir of Ann Gibson Robinson* (Knoxville: University of Tennessee Press, 1987). Radical pacifists Bayard Rustin, Jim Peck, and Dorothy Day served as the political link between the early civil rights and peace movements. Because Dorothy Day and other radical pacifists were vocal op-

ponents of communist dictatorships, the American Right and federal intelligence agencies found it difficult to discredit their ideas and actions. As opponents of the hysterical anticommunism embodied in McCarthyism, radical pacifists also refused to expel any communist supporters in their ranks. This was unlike the liberals in SANE, which suffered a damaging split after its McCarthy-like internal purge of suspected communist members in 1960.

22. Social movement theorist Antonio Gramsci describes the mode of cultural struggle between competing interests as a battle to determine the dominant symbolic paradigm, the fight for ideological hegemony. Gramsci notes that if consumer capitalism is to function smoothly, the state must obtain the cooperation and allegiance of the labor force through the construction of consent. Hegemonic control is established through educational and religious institutions, popular media, and other forms of cultural instruction. In the contest for power in the modern nuclear state, cultural symbolism becomes an important terrain of struggle; the transformation of consciousness becomes part of the revolutionary process. Such issues as community and the construction of identity become salient political forces.

23. "Gun Thy Neighbor," *Time*, August 18, 1961, 58; L. C. McHugh, "Ethics at the Shelter Door," *America* (September 30, 1961): 824–26; "Shelter Morality," *Commonweal* 27 (October 1961): 109; Bruce Watson, "We Couldn't Run, So We Hoped We Could Hide," *Smithsonian* (April 1994): 47–58; Norman Cousins, "Shelters, Survival, and Common Sense," *Saturday Review* (October 21, October 28, and November 4, 1961). Also see *God and the H-Bomb*, ed. Donald Keys (New York: Bellmeadows, 1961); Mechling and Mechling, "Campaign for Civil Defense," 122–26; and "Incivility in Civil Defense," *Christian Century*, Editorial, August 23, 1961, 995, which warned, "Citizens have a right to insist that the civil defense program be built on truth as to what can and what cannot be accomplished. . . . Civil defense as a device for influencing opinion in favor of policies leading to war must be disavowed and out-lawed."

24. *Time*, September 29, 1961, 14.

25. *Life*, September 15, 1961, 95.

26. *Time*, October 20, 1961, 21–25.

27. Kenneth D. Rose, *One Nation Underground: The Fallout Shelter in American Culture* (New York: New York University Press, 2001), 191; Henriksen, *Dr. Strangelove's America*, 214.

28. Ike quoted in Walter Karp, "When Bunkers Last in Backyards Bloomed," *American Heritage*, February–March 1980, 92.

29. "Aristotle & the Bomb: Red, Dead, or Heroic?" *Time*, October 13, 1961, 29; Nelson Rockefeller, "Civil Defense in a Nuclear War," April 2, 1962, 1962, 1226, PPGR.

30. See *Newsweek*, August 7, 1961, 48, and November 6, 1961, 19–23.

31. "Civil Defense Shelter Statement," *BAS* 18 (February 1962): 25–28. Also see "Civil Defense," *BAS* 18 (January 1962): 45–46; and *BAS* 17 (November 1961): 25–28.

32. Gerard Piel, "The Illusion of Civil Defense," *BAS* 18 (February 1962): 2; Gerard Piel, "On the Feasibility of Peace," *Science* 135 (February 23, 1962): 648–52; David Singer, "Deterrence and Shelters," *BAS* 17 (October 1961): 310–15; Don Oberdorfer, "Survival

of the Fewest," advance copy (later published in *Saturday Evening Post*), White House Central Files, Box 597, JFKL; "The Fallout Shelter," *Consumer Reports*, January 1962, 8; Linus Pauling, "Colossal Deception: Why I Am Opposed to Fallout Shelters," *Liberation*, November 1961, 4–6.

33. "Open Letter to President Kennedy"; Foster Haily, "200 Professors Say Shelters Invite War," both in *New York Times*, November 10, 1961. Also see Norman Cousins, "Shelters, Survival and Common Sense," *Saturday Review*, October 1, 1961. James Reston, "Those Sweet and Kindly Shelter Builders," *NYT*, November 12, 1961, E8, said, "The situation, to state it mildly, is a mess."

34. Margaret Mead, "Are Shelters the Answer?" *NYT Magazine*, November 26, 1961.

35. Telephone interview by author, Mark Lane, March 27, 2000.

36. Statement by the Governor to the New York State Assembly Committee on Ethics and Guidance Concerning Fallout Protection Legislation Enacted by the New York State Legislature, February 6, 1962, PPGR.

37. "Only Hope of U.S. Survival Is Shelters, Teller Says," *Albany Times Union*, November 10, 1961, 1; "Rockefeller Asks $100 Million for Shelters Today," *Albany Times Union*, November 9, 1961, 1.

38. Interview, Mark Lane, March 27, 2000.

39. "Carlino Concedes He Got Legal Fees," *NYT*, November 23, 1961, sec. 1, 1; "Albany Report: A Weekly Review of the New York State Legislature," January 1, 1962, in Box 21, SANE, SCPC; Mark Lane, "Serving Two Masters," *Liberation*, January 1962, 12–14; interview, Mark Lane. Also see biography of Lane in "Campaigning Legislator," *NYT*, December 22, 1961, 10.

40. "Carlino Accused on Shelter Bill," *NYT*, November 21, 1961, 30; "The Carlino Symptom," *NYT*, November 24, 1961, 30; "Legislative Ethics," *NYT*, December 2, 1961, 22. Also see Clayton Knowles, "Carlino Accused of Divulging Bill," *NYT*, December 22, 1961, 1. Also see New York State Archives, Albany, Rockefeller Subject Files, containing considerable material pertaining to the fight over civil defense from 1959 to 1973. Record Series nos. 13682–78.

41. Dozens of other stories on the case appeared during the next few months in Albany and New York City newspapers.

42. "Carlino's Inquiry Opens in Albany," *NYT*, December 8, 1961, 1.

43. "Report of the Assembly Committee on Ethics and Guidance," 1962, New York Legislative Documents, vol. 2, no. 12, 33, New York State Library, Albany. Basically, the committee noted that there was not sufficient control over the financial interests of legislators, that he was no more guilty than anyone else, and that special interests were not monitored for anyone. In conclusion, the committee recommended the formation of another committee.

44. "Shelter Bill Foes Picket in Albany," *NYT*, February 13, 1962, 6:4.

45. "Civil Defense and Nuclear War," April 2, 1962, 1226, PPGR; To the Governor from June Goldthwait, April 24, 1962, Governor's Speeches, 15, NAR.

46. Weisner to Bundy, and Raskin to Bundy, July 7, 1961, National Security Files, Box 295, JFKL; Sorenson to JFK, Memorandum to President, November 23, 1961, Sub-

ject: Civil Defense, Box 30, Ted Sorenson Papers, JFKL; Kerr, *Civil Defense in the U.S.*, 125–29; Blanchard, *American Civil Defense*, 308–9; Jerome Wiesner, *Where Science and Politics Meet* (New York: McGraw-Hill, 1965), 293–94; Fred Kaplan, *The Wizards of Armageddon* (New York: Simon and Schuster, 1983), 313–14; Kai Bird, *The Color of Truth: McGeorge Bundy and William Bundy, Brothers in Arms: A Biography* (New York: Simon and Schuster, 1998).

47. Oral history interview of Steuart L. Pittman, September 18, 1970, by William W. Moss, JFKL; Arthur A. Schlesinger, Jr., *A Thousand Days: John F. Kennedy in the White House* (Boston: Houghton Mifflin, 1965), 749.

48. Schlesinger, *A Thousand Days*.

49. Galbraith to JFK, November 9, 1961, Folder 7, Box 295, JFKL.

50. Gordon Christiansen, "CD's Little Yellow Booklet: Fatal Illusion," *Liberation*, March 1962.

51. Kerr, *Civil Defense in the U.S.*, 128–31; Stanley Newman, "Civil Defense and the Congress: Quiet Reversal," *BAS* 16 (November 1962): 33–37. Also see oral history of Theodore Sorenson by Carol Kaysen, March 26, 1964, JFKL.

52. "Fallout Shelter Budget Faces Reduction in House," *NYT*, April 23, 1962, 1.

53. U.S. Congress, House, Committee on Appropriations, Subcommittee on Independent Offices, Appropriations for 1963, 87th Cong., 2d sess., 1962, Hearings, 8, 37, 54, 53.

54. Among the many major publications in opposition to civil defense that were widely read and reprinted, see Seymour Melman, ed., *No Place to Hide: Fact and Fiction about Fallout Shelters* (New York: Grove, 1962); Ronald Steel, "The Cost of Survival," *Commonweal* (October 13, 1961): 63–66; "The Fallout Shelter," *Consumer Reports*, January 1962, 8–14; Sidney Lens, "The Case against Civil Defense," special issue of the *Progressive* (February 1962); Herman Kahn, Erich Fromm, and Michael Maccoby, "The Question of Civil Defense: A Debate," *Commentary* 33 (January 1962): 1–23.

55. Dulles cited in Wittner, *Resisting the Bomb*, 362. Also see Christopher Driver, *The Disarmers: A Study in Protest* (London: Hodder and Stoughton, 1964), 120, 126, 185; Duncan Campbell, *War Plan UK: The Truth about Civil Defense in Britain* (London: Burnett, 1983); Richard Taylor, *Against the Bomb: The British Peace Movement, 1958–65* (Oxford: Clarendon, 1988); Richard Taylor and Colin Pritchard, *The Protest Makers: The British Nuclear Disarmament Movement of 1958–65 Twenty Years On* (New York: Pergamon, 1980).

56. "Civil Defense Cut Backed in Oregon," *NYT*, May 25, 1963, 6; "Civil Defense Called 'Useless,' Is Eliminated by Portland, Ore.," *NYT*, May 24, 1963, 1.

57. "Surprise Vote Kills Civil Defense in the City," *Oregonian*, May 22, 1963, 1; "Deer Hunt Trip Silences Radio during Storm," *Oregonian*, March 10, 1963, 1; "Portland Chided on Civil Defense," *NYT*, June 22, 1963, 23; "Portland Official Led Successful Fight against Civil Defense," *Seattle Times*, June 17, 1963, 1:6; "Oregon Votes End to Civil Defense," *NYT*, May 28, 1963, 15.

58. "Portland Chided on Civil Defense," *NYT*, June 22, 1963, 23; "Oregon Closes Down Its Civil-Defense Organization," *Seattle Times*, June 28, 1963. On Baltimore and Los Angeles, see Box 2, 6, Women Strike for Peace, SANE, SCPC. Interviews by author with Kay Clarke, Libby Mines, Edith Laub, Pam Ford, and Madeline Duckels, 1994, all lead-

ers of Women Strike for Peace in Los Angeles and in the San Francisco area. Also see Clarke's files on anti–civil defense protests, in possession of author.

59. "Brown Meets 250 Women for Peace, Opposing Fallout Shelter Program," *Sacramento Bee*, February 7, 1962; "County CD Appropriation Opposed at Hearing," *Seattle Post-Intelligencer*, October 9, 1963, 3; and 1994 interview by author with Anci Koppel, Seattle. See also her archives on Seattle Women Act for Peace.

60. See Correspondence, Box 5, 22, Citizens Committee to Abolish School Drills, DG17, Box 5, SCPC; James Council, "Civil Defense in the Schools," *Liberation* (January 1963): 25–26. The National Commission on Safety Education of the National Educational Association reported in *Civil Defense Preparedness, 1964–65* (Washington, D.C.: Government Printing Office, 1965) that less than 15 percent of about 25,000 school districts still had air raid drills.

61. Interview with Jackie Goldberg, 1994; "Can Jackie Goldberg Teach L.A. a Lesson?" *Los Angeles Times Magazine*, March 5, 1995, 10–14, 31–36.

62. *NYT*, October 8, 1963; Cannon cited in Blanchard, *American Civil Defense*, 341.

CHAPTER 5

1. Spencer Weart, "History of American Attitudes to Civil Defense," in *Civil Defense: A Choice of Disasters*, ed. John Dowling and Evans M. Harrell (New York: American Institute of Physics, 1987), 24; Thomas Kerr, *Civil Defense in the U.S.: Bandaid for a Holocaust?* (Boulder, Colo.: Westview, 1983), 134; Wayne Blanchard, *American Civil Defense, 1945–1975: The Evolution of Programs and Policies* (Washington, D.C.: FEMA, 1980), 428–29; Henry M. Jackson Papers, General Correspondence and Legislation, Civil Defense, Archives, University of Washington, Seattle; Paul Boyer, "From Activism to Apathy: The American People and Nuclear Weapons, 1963–80," *Journal of American History* 70 (March 1984): 821–44.

2. Cited in Kerr, *Civil Defense in the U. S.*, 132.

3. Morton Halperin, "The Decision to Deploy the ABM: Bureaucratic and Domestic Politics in the Johnson Administration," *World Politics* 25 (October 1972): 62–96. Also see Peter Pringle and William Arkin, *SIOP: The Secret U.S. Plan for Nuclear War* (New York: Norton, 1983); Blanchard, *American Civil Defense*, 369–70.

4. Cited in Janne E. Nolan, *Guardians of the Arsenal: The Politics of Nuclear Strategy* (New York: Basic, 1989), 75–76; Deborah Shapley, *Promise and Power: The Life and Times of Robert McNamara* (Boston: Little, Brown, 1993). Also see Spurgeon M. Keeny, Jr., and Wolfgang K. H. Panofsky, "MAD vs. NUTS: The Mutual Hostage Relationship of the Superpowers," *Foreign Affairs* 60 (Winter 1981–1982): 287–304.

5. Eugene Wigner, ed., *Who Speaks for Civil Defense?* (New York: Scribner's, 1968); Eugene P. Wigner, as told to Andrew Scanton, *The Recollections of Eugene P. Wigner* (New York: Plenum, 1992); Eugene Wigner, *Survival and the Bomb: Methods of Civil Defense* (Bloomington: Indiana University Press, 1969); Eugene Wigner, ed., *Civil Defense: Project Harbor Summary Report* (Washington, D.C.: National Academy of Sciences, 1964). The Eugene Wigner Papers, Mudd Library, Princeton University, provide exten-

sive evidence regarding Project Harbor and his long interest in civil defense issues; see especially Boxes 26–28, 30–34. Also see Princeton Library, Eugene Wigner, Faculty File, for a large collection of clippings about his activities.

6. Paul Dickson, *Think Tanks* (New York: Atheneum, 1971), 106–7, 90–116. Detailed information on the GAO findings, including a reply by Kahn, are in General Accounting Office, *Observations on the Administration by the Office of Civil Defense of Research Study Contracts Awarded to Hudson Institute, Inc.: Report to the Congress on the Department of the Army by the Comptroller General of the United States* (Washington, D.C.: GPO, March 25, 1968). Also see Ronald Steel, "Up the Doomsday Ladder," *New York Review of Books*, July 15, 1963; Basil McDermott, "Thinking about Herman Kahn," *Journal of Conflict Resolution* 14 (March 1971): 55–71; and Jeffrey D. Porro, "The Policy War: Brodie vs. Kahn," *BAS* 18 (June–July 1982): 16–19.

7. Stanley Blumberg and Louis G. Panos, *Edward Teller: Giant of the Golden Age of Physics* (New York: Scribner's, 1990); Edward Teller with Julie Shoolery, *Memoirs: A Twentieth Century Journal in Science and Politics* (Cambridge, Mass.: Perseus, 2001); Dan O'Neill, *The Firecracker Boys* (New York: St. Martin's, 1994); Frank Von Hippel, "The Myths of Edward Teller," *BAS* 39 (March 1983): 6–12; Report 342, System Planning Corporation, 1977, study of civil defense, Edward Teller Papers, Box 20, Hoover Institution, Stanford University, Stanford, California.

8. Cited in Stephen I. Schwartz, ed., *Atomic Audit: The Costs and Consequences of U.S. Nuclear Weapons since 1940* (Washington, D.C.: Brookings Institution Press, 1998), 286. Also see Eugene Rabinowitch and Ruth Adam, eds., *Debate: The Anti-Ballistic Missile* (Chicago: Bulletin of the Atomic Scientists, 1967).

9. John Newhouse, *Cold Dawn: Story of SALT* (New York: Holt, Rinehart and Winston, 1973), 98; Gerard H. Clarfield and William M. Wiecek, *Nuclear America: Military and Civilian Power in the U.S., 1940–1980* (New York: Harper and Row, 1984), 302; Joan Hoff, *Nixon Reconsidered* (New York: Basic, 1994). It wasn't easy to find a name for the Sentinel missile program. The first choices were discarded only after the Pentagon brass realized that the names they proposed had already been adopted for several popular brands of male contraceptives then on the market. The names of rubber condoms emphasized the protective safety and on-guard vigilance promised by the various brands. This naming difficulty associated with missiles and condoms seems to confirm once again the often-noted propensity of early cold warriors to erect sexual imagery when naming or discussing their new weapons.

10. U.S. General Accounting Office, *Activities and Status of Civil Defense in the United States: Report to the Congress by the Comptroller General of the United States* (Washington, D.C.: GPO, October 26, 1971), 14, 23.

11. Schwartz, *Atomic Audit*, 289.

12. U.S. Department of Defense, James R. Schlesinger, *Annual Defense Department Report* (Washington, D.C.: Government Printing Office, 1974), 38. Secretary of State Kissinger was furious because he felt that he had been preempted by Schlesinger in the announcement of the new strategy, leading to the new doctrine being called the Schlesinger, not the Kissinger, Doctrine. Also see Terry Terriff, *The Nixon Administration and the Making of U.S. Nuclear Strategy* (Ithaca, N.Y.: Cornell University Press,

1995); Lynn Davis, *Limited Nuclear Options: Deterrence and the New American Doctrine* (London: IISS, 1976); James Schlesinger, Charles Horner, and Casper Weinberger, *Rebuilding America's Military Strength: Recommendations for the New Administration* (Washington, D.C.: Heritage Foundation, 2001).

13. Richard Nixon, *A Report to Congress: U.S. Foreign Policy for the 1970s: A New Strategy for Peace* (Washington, D.C.: GPO, February 18, 1970), 122.

14. Nolan, *Guardians of the Arsenal*, 26–27. Also see Sidney Drell, Arthur Broyles, and Eugene Wigner, "Civil Defense and Limited War: A Debate," *Physics Today* 29 (April 1976), 46; William Kinkade, "Repeating History: The Civil Defense Debate Renewed," *International Security* 2 (1978): 99–120.

15. Paul Boyer, *Promises to Keep: The United States since World War II* (New York: Heath, 1995), 418. Also see Peter Bourne, *Jimmy Carter: A Comprehensive Biography from Plains to Post-Presidency* (New York: Scribner's, 1997).

16. Frances Fitzgerald, *Way Out There in the Blue: Reagan, Star Wars, and the End of the Cold War* (New York: Simon and Schuster, 2000), 80.

17. William Beecher, "High Level Study Says CIA Understates Extent of Soviet Threat," *Boston Globe*, December 17, 1976; Fitzgerald, *Way Out There in the Blue*, 83, 91; Strobe Talbot, *Master of the Game: Paul Nitze and the Nuclear Peace* (New York: Knopf, 1998), 139–40, 144–47; Robert Scheer, *With Enough Shovels: Reagan, Bush and Nuclear War* (New York: Random House, 1982), 53–65; Paul Nitze, *From Hiroshima to Glasnost* (New York: Grove Weidenfeld, 1989), 352–54; Janne Nolan, *Guardians of the Arsenal: The Politics of Nuclear Strategy* (New York: Basic, 1989); Jerry W. Sanders, *Peddlers of Crisis: The Committee on the Present Danger and the Politics of Containment* (Boston: South End, 1983); Richard Pipes, "Team B: The Reality behind the Myth," *Commentary* 73 (October 1986): 25–41, and "Why the Soviets Think They Can Fight and Win a Nuclear War," *Commentary* 64 (June 1977): 21–34; John Prados, "Team B: The Trillion Dollar Experiment," *BAS* 49 (April 1993), 23, 27–31.

18. The *Philadelphia Inquirer*, March 10, 2001, A1, reported that a recently declassified 1989 CIA study in fact concluded that every CIA major intelligence assessment between 1974 and 1986 had vastly exaggerated the pace of the expansion and modernization of nuclear forces undertaken by the Soviet Union.

19. Robert Scheer, *With Enough Shovels: Reagan, Bush and Nuclear War* (New York: Random House, 1982), 60; Graham quoted in Talbot, *Master of the Game*, 146.

20. Sanders, *Peddlers of Crisis*, 198, 203.

21. Ibid., 183.

22. Ibid., 235–63; also see Charles Tyroler II, ed., *Alerting America: The Papers of the Committee on the Present Danger* (New York: Pergamon-Brassey's, 1984).

23. Talbot, *Master of the Game*; David Callahan, *Dangerous Capabilities: Paul Nitze and the Cold War* (New York: HarperCollins, 1990); Paul Nitze, *From Hiroshima to Glasnost: At the Center of Decision: A Memoir* (New York: Grove Weidenfeld, 1989); Paul Nitze, "Assuring Strategic Stability in an Era of Detente," *Foreign Affairs* 54 (January 1976): 207–32.

24. Cited in Edward Zuckerman, *The Day after World War III* (New York: Viking, 1984), 252.

25. Goure wrote roughly fifteen books and lengthy monographs between 1962 and 1988. Much of this work was funded by civil defense agencies or by the Rand Corporation. Among Goure's books, see especially *Civil Defense in the Soviet Union* (Berkeley: University of California Press, 1962). Even in 1988, Goure was writing in the FEMA newsletter on the value of civil defense to save lives. Also see Goure, testimony before Joint Committee on Defense Production, Civil Defense Panel, Civil Defense Review, February 9–26, March 2–9, 1976, 187; Edward Teller, "On the Brink," *NYT*, February 3, 1980, E21; J. M. Weinstein, "Soviet Civil Defense and the U.S. Deterrent," *Parameters*, March 1982, 70–83; author's telephone interview with Lawrence Vale, November 20, 2001; Louis Rene Beres, "Surviving Nuclear War: U.S. Plans for Crisis Relocation," *Armed Forces and Society* 12 (Fall 1985): 75–94; "Civil Defense Hearings before the Committee on Banking, Housing, and Urban Affairs," U.S. Senate, 95th Cong., 2d sess., 1979.

26. CIA, *Soviet Civil Defense*, was reprinted in U.S. Congress, Senate, Committee on Armed Services, Hearings, Department of Defense Authorization for Appropriations for Fiscal Year, 1981, 96th Cong., 2d sess., 1980. The CIA 1978 study also concluded that in a nuclear war the Soviet casualties would be well over 100 million. In April 1977, the Joint Congressional Committee on Defense Production reported little real evidence of an efficient Soviet civil defense effort. This view was also reported by an Arms Control and Disarmament Agency study in 1978. Also see Lawrence Vale, *The Limits of Civil Defense in the USA, Switzerland, Britain, and the Soviet Union* (New York: Macmillan, 1987), 189–94; Fred Kaplan, "The Soviet Civil Defense Myth," parts 1 and 2, in *BAS* 34 (March 1978): 14–20, and (April 1978): 48–51, with reply by Leon Goure.

27. Vale, *The Limits of Civil Defense*, 175–76; John Burns, "Russians, Too, Joke Sadly on Atom War Survival," *NYT*, June 11, 1982, A2. It was not until 1988 that the American far Right's view of the Soviet Union's civil defense program—touted as second only to Switzerland in its sophistication and effectiveness—finally collapsed completely. When a moderate-size earthquake hit a few villages in Armenia, the *Wall Street Journal* described the chaos: "[R]eports from the area continue to describe masses of soldiers doing little or nothing while freezing survivors dig for relatives with their hands. There also have been reports of heavy equipment standing idle for lack of an organized rescue plan." This, in combination with the 1986 Soviet response to the nuclear disaster at Chernobyl, ensured that any further argument for the superior quality of Soviet civil defense would only elicit amused skepticism.

28. U.S. Congress, House, Committee on Armed Services, Hearings, Civil Defense Review, 94th Cong., 2d sess., 1976. For Jones, see *NYT*, April 1, 1982, 17. Also see *Defense Industrial Base, Industrial Preparedness and Nuclear War Survival: Hearings before Joint Committee on Defense Production*, 94th Cong., 2d sess. (Washington, D.C.: GPO, 1976); W. K. H. Panovsky, *Civil Preparedness and Limited Nuclear War*, congressional testimony before Joint Committee on Defense Production, 94th Cong., 2d sess. (Washington, D.C.: GPO, 1976).

29. See Kerr, *Civil Defense in the U.S.*, 157–59; Jeffrey D. Porro, "The Policy War: Brodie vs. Kahn," *BAS* 38 (June–July 1982): 16–19; Herman Kahn, *On Thermonuclear War* (Princeton, N.J.: Princeton University Press, 1960), and *Thinking about the Unthinkable* (New York: Avon, 1962); Colin Gray and Keith Payne, "Victory Is Possible," *Foreign*

Policy 39 (Summer 1980): 14–27; U.S. Congress, Joint Committee on Defense Production, Hearings, Civil Preparedness and Nuclear War, 94th Cong., 2d sess., 1976.

30. See Nolan, *Guardians of the Arsenal*, 131; Raymond Garthoff, *Detente and Confrontation: American Soviet Relations from Nixon to Reagan* (Washington, D.C.: Brookings Institution, 1985), 787–88; Eric Mlyn, *The State, Society, and Limited Nuclear War* (Albany: State University of New York Press, 1995), 115; Huntington testimony, Civil Defense in the 1980s, Committee on Banking, Housing, and Urban Affairs, U.S. Senate, January 8, 1979.

31. Vale, *The Limits of Civil Defense*, 74–78.

32. Thomas Powers, "Choosing a Strategy for World War III," *Atlantic* 250 (November 1982): 82–110; Zbigniew Brzezinski, *Power and Principle: Memoirs of the National Security Advisor, 1977–1981* (New York: Farrar, Straus and Giroux, 1983); Henry Kissinger, *The Necessity for Choice: Prospects of American Foreign Policy* (New York: Harper and Row, 1961).

33. Nolan, *Guardians of the Arsenal*, 129–39.

34. See Richard Burt, "Carter Adopts a Plan to Bolster Civil Defense," *NYT*, November 13, 1978, A1; Bernard Weinraub, "Carter Plans to Limit Civil Defense Budget," *NYT*, December 28, 1978, A1.

35. John Dowling, "FEMA Programs, Problems, and Accomplishments," in *Civil Defense: A Choice of Disasters*, ed. John Dowling and Evans M. Harrell (New York: American Institute of Physics, 1987), 33–47.

36. Cited in Garthoff, *Detente and Confrontation*, 790 n.111, also see 788–92, 1019–22. On PD-59, see J. Richelson, "PD-59, NS DO-13 and the Reagan Strategic Modernization Program," *Journal of Strategic Studies* 6, no. 2 (1983): 125–46; Louis Renee Beres, "Presidential Directive 59: A Critical Assessment," *Parameters: Journal of the U.S. Army War College* (March 1981): 29–37; Richard Burt, "The New Strategy for Nuclear War: How It Evolved," *NYT*, August 13, 1980, A3.

37. Scheer, *With Enough Shovels*, 105–6. In an interview with Robert Scheer of the *Los Angeles Times* during the 1980 presidential campaign, Reagan made clear his belief that the Soviet Union had practiced civil defense evacuation and that "in one summer alone, they took over 20 million young people out of the cities into the country to give them training in just living off the countryside." Of course no one, including members of the CPD, had ever claimed that the Soviet Union had practiced large-scale evacuation of its cities. Indeed, the evacuation of 20 million, if actually true, would have surely set off a massive American nuclear alert, perhaps even a first strike, based on the assumption that the Soviet Union was emptying its cities in preparation for a first strike on the United States.

38. Fitzgerald, *Way Out There in the Blue*, 107.

CHAPTER 6

1. Frances Fitzgerald, *Way Out There in the Blue: Reagan, Star Wars, and the End of the Cold War* (New York: Simon and Schuster, 2000), 98. Charles Tyroler, ed., *Alerting*

America: The Papers of the Committee on the Present Danger (New York: Pergamon-Brassey's, 1984), lists members of the CPD executive committee and board of directors appointed to Reagan's administration. Rostow is cited in Jerry W. Sanders, *Peddlers of Crisis: The Committee on the Present Danger and the Politics of Containment* (Boston: South End, 1983), 286.

2. Robert Scheer, *With Enough Shovels: Reagan, Bush and Nuclear War* (New York: Random House, 1982), 105.

3. Jennifer Leaning, *Civil Defense in the Nuclear Age: What Purpose Does It Serve and What Survival Does It Promise?* (Boston: Physicians for Social Responsibility, 1982), 5; Scheer, *With Enough Shovels*, 32, 141–42; John Hassard, "Maintaining Perceptions: Crisis Relocation in the Planning of Nuclear War," in *Civil Defense: A Choice of Disasters*, ed. John Dowling and Evans M. Harrell (New York: American Institute of Physics, 1987), 91.

4. John Dowling, "FEMA: Programs, Problems, and Accomplishments," in Dowling and Harrell, *Civil Defense*, 36–38. See Edward Zuckerman, *The Day after World War III* (New York: Viking, 1984), for good general discussion of continuity of government.

5. Unless otherwise cited, the information on CRP is drawn from Zuckerman, *The Day after World War III*, esp. 97–125; and Jennifer Leaning and Langley Keyes, eds., *The Counterfeit Ark: Crisis Relocation for Nuclear War* (Cambridge, Mass.: Ballinger, 1984), which also presents a series of essays to show that many national experts deny the validity of CRP assumptions.

6. Leaning and Keyes, *Counterfeit Ark*, xiv.

7. Mary McGrory, "Heading for the Hills the Hard Way," *Washington Post*, August 1, 1982, B1.

8. Officials in the U.S. Post Office devised an elaborate plan to collect change-of-address cards from the refugee millions fleeing nuclear bombs. During a 1982 congressional hearing, one incredulous senator questioned the post office representative about how postal service might be reestablished in the highly radioactive urban rubble. The postal authority finally admitted that post-attack mail service might have to be centralized in one of three less likely to be bombed areas, that is, in the Florida Everglades, in northern Minnesota, or in the Rocky Mountains. See Lee Clarke, *Mission Improbable: Using Fantasy Documents to Tame Disaster* (Chicago: University of Chicago Press, 1999), 31–33.

9. Jack Anderson, "Nuke Survival Plan 'Bizarre,'" *Orange Coast Daily Pilot*, July 7, 1982, A6.

10. William Raspberry, "There's Nothing Civil about It," *Washington Post*, April 12, 1982, A15.

11. Clarke, *Mission Improbable*; Louis Rene Beres, *Reason and Realpolitik: U.S. Foreign Policy and World Order* (Lexington, Mass.: Heath, 1984), 22.

12. Rejection of this 80 percent figure is prevalent in comments critical of CRP. Many scholars have analyzed the original source of this number and denied its validity. See, for example, Clarke, *Mission Improbable*, 35–37; Leaning, *Civil Defense in the Nuclear Age*, 15–33. Also see Charles F. Estes, Jr., testimony before the Senate Committee on Armed Services, 97th Cong., 1st sess., March 30, 1981, 4380–81; John McConnell, in ibid.,

4382; William F. Chipman, testimony before House Committee on Armed Services, Military Installations and Facilities Subcommittee, 97th Cong., 1st sess., February 27, 1981, 847; Louis Giuffrida, testimony, in ibid., 939.

13. James Ring, "Sheltering from a Nuclear Attack," in Dowling and Harrell, *Civil Defense*, 79.

14. Wiesner cited in Leaning and Keyes, *Counterfeit Ark*, xiv–xv.

15. Nomination of Louis O. Giuffrida, Hearing before the Committee on Governmental Affairs, U.S. Senate, 97th Cong., 1st sess., May 6, 1981, 15, 17. A copy of Giuffrida's forty-seven-page Army War College paper, entitled "National Survival—Racial Imperative," is also in the Senate hearing report.

16. Louis Rene Beres, "Surviving Nuclear War: U.S. Plans for Crisis Relocation," *Armed Forces and Society* 12 (Fall 1985): 84; John Hassard, "Maintaining Perceptions: Crisis Relocation in the Planning of Nuclear War," in Dowling and Harrell, *Civil Defense*, 85–105.

17. Howard Kurtz, "Military Policemen Troop into Highly Paid Government Jobs," *Washington Post*, February 3, 1985; Diana Reynolds, "FEMA and the NSC: The Rise of the National Security State," *Covert Action* 23 (Winter 1990): 54–58.

18. Cited in Kenneth D. Rose, *One Nation Underground: The Fallout Shelter in American Culture* (New York: New York University Press, 2001), 219; cited in Zuckerman, *The Day after World War III*, 105; also see 97–124.

19. "Civil Defense Relocation Plan Said to Be Dropped," *NYT*, March 4, 1985, A9; "City Says No to Crisis Relocation," *NYT*, June 10, 1982, A1; Ben A. Franklin, "Festival Rings with Ridicule of Civil Defense Plan," *NYT*, May 30, 1982, 20.

20. Editorial, "The Shelter Fraud," *NYT*, April 3, 1982, 24.

21. Joel Savishinsky, "Ithaca Won't Do You Much Good," *Columbian* (Vancouver, Wash.), July 18, 1982, 31.

22. Zuckerman, *The Day after World War III*, 108–9.

23. Barry Casper, "Under the Mushroom Cloud," in Dowling and Harrell, *Civil Defense*, 203–6; Clarke, *Mission Improbable*, 122.

24. Jack Vieta, "Marin Opts Out for Nuclear War," *San Francisco Chronicle*, March 17, 1982, 2; Allan Appel, "Burlesque in Burlington," *Progressive* (February 1983): 36.

25. Transcript, "MacNeil-Lehrer Report" episode titled "Civil Defense, Boulder Evacuation," WMET, March 2, 1982.

26. "Civil Evacuation Plan Ill-Advised," *Seattle Post-Intelligencer*, February 6, 1982, A1; Editorial, "Doctors Call Nuclear War Evacuation Plan Rubbish," *Seattle Post-Intelligencer*, April 11, 1983, A4; "Nuclear War Evacuation Plan Riles Island Residents," *Seattle Post-Intelligencer*, June 30, 1982, A3.

27. Fitzgerald, *Way Out There in the Blue*, 149.

28. Robert Scheer, *With Enough Shovels*, 18–26, 138–40; "U.S. Could Survive in Administration's View," *Los Angeles Times*, January 16, 1982.

29. "The Dirt on T. K. Jones," *NYT*, March 19, 1982, A30.

30. "Capitol Commentary," *Journal of Civil Defense* 16 (April 1983): 2.

31. Thomas R. Rochon, *Mobilizing for Peace: The Antinuclear Movements in Western Europe* (Princeton, N.J.: Princeton University Press, 1988).

32. John Minnion and Philip Bolsolver, eds., *The CND Story: The First Twenty-Five Years of CND* (London: Allison and Busby, 1983), 89. Also see E. P. Thompson and Dan Smith, eds., *Protest and Survive* (New York: Monthly Review Press, 1981); Duncan Campbell, *War Plan UK: The Truth about Civil Defense in Britain* (London: Burnett, 1982).

33. John Churcher and Elena Lieven, "Images of War and the Public in British Civil Defense," *Journal of Social Issues* 39 (Spring 1983): 124.

34. John Minnion and Philip Bolsolver, eds., *The CND Story: The First 25 Years of CND in the Words of the People Involved* (London: Allison and Busby, 1983), 90–93.

35. For discussions of the 1980s peace movement and the Nuclear Freeze, see especially Frances B. McCrea and Gerald E. Markle, *Minutes to Midnight: Nuclear Weapons Protest in America* (Newbury Park, Calif.: Sage, 1989); David S. Meyer, *A Winter of Discontent: The Nuclear Freeze and American Politics* (New York: Praeger, 1990); Sam Marrulo and John Lofland, eds., *Peace Action in the Eighties* (New Brunswick, N.J.: Rutgers University Press, 1990); Lawrence Wittner, *Nonprofit Organizations and Nuclear Disarmament, 1971 to the Present*, Working Paper Series, Aspen Institute, Winter 200l. For the conservative perspective, see J. Michael Hogan, *The Nuclear Freeze Campaign: Rhetoric and Foreign Policy in the Telepolitical Age* (East Lansing: Michigan State University Press, 1994); and Adam M. Garfinkle, *The Politics of the Nuclear Freeze* (Philadelphia: Foreign Policy Research Institute, 1984).

36. George Kennan, *The Nuclear Delusion: Soviet American Relations in the Atomic Age* (New York: Pantheon, 1983), 236.

37. Fitzgerald, *Way Out There in the Blue*, 207–8.

38. Ibid., 199.

39. Howard Kurtz, "FEMA Chief, 6 Aides Defy Hill Subpoena," *Washington Post*, December 13, 1984, A1; Pete Early and Myron Struck, "House Panel to Subpoena FEMA Documents," *Washington Post*, October 4, 1984, A17.

40. See the following articles in the *Washington Post*: "FEMA Chief Resigns amid Investigations," July 25, 1985, A23; Howard Kurtz and Pete Earley, "No. 3 FEMA Official Quits amid Charges of Misusing Funds," August 4, 1984, A3; Howard Kurtz and Pete Earley, "Hill Panel Probes FEMA Official," August 1, 1984, A3; Howard Kurtz, "U.S. Paid for FEMA Chief's Attendance at a Fund Raiser," October 25, 1984. Also see in *NYT*, "House Unit Finds Mismanagement at U.S. Emergency Agency," July 5, 1985, A9; in *Seattle Times*, "Probers Blast Emergency Agency's Chief," July 25, 1985, B3; "Fiscal Practices of the Federal Emergency Management Agency," Report of the Committee on Science and Technology, 99th Cong., 1st sess., July 25, 1985, in *Oversight: Federal Emergency Management, Hearing of the Subcommittee on Investigations and Oversight of the Committee on Science and Technology, House of Representatives* (Washington, D.C.: GPO, March 4, 1985), vol. 2.

41. "Civil Defense Plans Said to Be Dropped," *NYT*, March 4, 1985, A9; John Dowling, "FEMA: Programs, Problems and Accomplishments," in Dowling and Harrell, *Civil Defense*, 40.

42. Alfonso Chardy, "Reagan Aides and the 'Secret' Government," *Miami Herald*, July 5, 1987; Pete Earley, "Smith Accuses FEMA of Grab for Power," *Washington Post*,

September 3, 1984, A19; author's telephone interview with Alfonso Chardy, December 10, 1997; William French Smith to Robert McFarlane, August 2, 1984; Edwin Meese III to James C. Miller III, December 13, 1985; George Jett to Bernard Maguire, August 27, 1984; Louis Giuffrida to Robert McFarlane, August 3, 1984; Louis Giuffrida to Edwin Meese, January 2, 1985—all in possession of author, provided by William Cumming, Vacation Lane Group, Arlington, Virginia; Ben Bradlee, *Guts and Glory: The Rise and Fall of Oliver North* (New York: Fine, 1988), 132–35; Steven Emerson, "America's Doomsday Project," *U.S. News and World Report*, August 7, 1989, 26–30; Jack Anderson syndicated columns, *Washington Post*, September 7, 1984, E12; September 5, 1984, E9; October 9, 1984, C12. Also see Richard Perle, Statement before Subcommittee on Strategic and Theater Nuclear Forces, Senate Armed Services Committee, March 17, 1982, in H. M. Jackson Papers, University of Washington Archives, Seattle.

43. Scholars will soon discover that there exists an enormous trove of materials, especially on the Internet, which addresses some of the issues posed by FEMA crisis management, the role of North, and related issues of continuity-of-government planning. Much of this material, from both left- and right-wing sources, is best described as "conspiratorial" in nature; much of it is unsupported by historical evidence and is attempting to convince the reader that vast conspiracies of various sorts exist, which are intent on the destruction of American democracy and which are often centered in current secret plans to take over the government.

44. "New Plan Would Shelter Officials," *Seattle Times*, May 11, 1986, A24; "Civil Defense Diehards Resurrect the Fallout Shelter," *Seattle Times*, June 8, 1986.

45. Retired general Becton came to head the scandal-ridden FEMA after forty years in the army. With a reputation as a troubleshooter, he later became president of the troubled Prairie View A&M in Texas and then became chief executive officer of the District of Columbia school system.

46. By 1987, several states had passed similar laws, including California, Maryland, Wisconsin, Massachusetts, and New Mexico. See "FEMA's Management Controls Need Strengthening," Report to the Chairman, Subcommittee on Military Installations and Facilities, Committee on Armed Services, House of Representatives, December 1987, U.S. General Accounting Office. This subcommittee was headed by Democratic representative Ronald V. Dellums of California, a major progressive figure in Congress. See also Ronald V. Dellums and H. Lee Halterman, *Lying Down with the Lions: A Public Life from the Streets of Oakland to the Halls of Power* (Boston: Beacon, 2000).

47. See *Seattle Times*: "Feds Forcing State into Test of Response to Nuclear War," January 24, 1987, A24; "Biggest Explosion Might Come from Public," January 28, 1987, B1; "State Is Out of N-War Test: Gardner Calls FEMA Plan Overkill, Waste of Money," February 5, 1987, B1.

48. See *Seattle Times*: "Nuclear War Exercises," January 28, 1987, B3; "Oregon Refuses to Join Drill," February 24, 1987, B3; Editorial, December 29, 1987, A7. Also see Pete McConnell, "Anti-Nuclear Groups Praise State's Refusal to Take Part in Attack Drill," *Seattle Post-Intelligencer*, March 3, 1987, D10; Booth Gardner, "Nuclear Civil Defense: Does It Make Sense for States to Prepare for a Nuclear Attack?" *State Government News* (March 1, 1990): 20.

49. Goldschmidt had been elected to head the state in 1986. A Democrat, Goldschmidt was the youngest mayor of a major city when he became mayor of Portland in 1973 at the age of thirty-two. An activist student in the 1960s, he had been president of the student body at the University of Oregon and had worked to register voters in the Freedom Summer civil rights campaign in Mississippi in 1964.

50. In *Seattle Times*, see "State to Lose Federal Emergency Money—$1.4 Million at Stake in Federal Holdout," February 25, 1987, B1; "Tit for Tat: Hatfield Threatens FEMA," March 24, 1987, B3.

51. Editorial, *Seattle Times*, December 29, 1987, A7. By May 1991, Washington state, which had by then lost an estimated $2.8 million in federal grant money during 1988 and 1989, worked out a compromise deal with FEMA in which the state would plan not for evacuation, but for terrorist attacks, with the understanding that those plans could also be used in the event of a nuclear attack. Also see "NW States Can Offer Own Nuclear Attack Drill, Opinion Says," *Seattle Post-Intelligencer*, March 27, 1987, A11; "Disaster Agency Gets Swift Kick," *Seattle Times*, April 9, 1987, D3, all in Judy Turpin Peace Collection, in possession of the author.

EPILOGUE

1. Cited in Lawrence Wittner, *Toward Nuclear Abolition: A History of the World Nuclear Disarmament Movement, 1971 to the Present* (Stanford, Calif.: Stanford University Press, 2003), 370–71.

2. Ibid., 434.

3. Congress never voted to ratify the entire START II package. Russia and the United States attempted to bring portions of the treaty into force until May 2002, when both signed the Strategic Offensive Reductions Treaty, which calls for each country to deploy no more than 1,700–2,200 strategic warheads. In June 2002, the United States withdrew from the ABM Treaty.

4. The monument, dedicated in April 2002 in honor of volunteers in civil defense and emergency management, was built with private and some state donations. Its creation was sparked by the civil defense supporters in the American Civil Defense Association. The group, first formed in the early 1960s, still functions today, currently selling radiation counters, anti-anthrax pills, and other emergency supplies.

5. "FEMA Accused of Dwelling on Nuclear Wars," *San Francisco Chronicle*, December 26, 1989, A1; "Lag in U.S. Aid Angers Hugo Victims: Relief Centers Open but Applicants Face Long Waits," *Washington Post*, October 4, 1989, A1; Michael Kranish, "Amid Disasters, FEMA Has Its Own Problems," *Boston Globe*, October 25, 1989, 25; Mike Royko, "Too Bad Hugo Didn't Flatten FEMA," *Seattle Times*, October 15, 1989, A18; Martin Weil, "Violent Earthquake Strikes Northern California, Killing Dozens, Causing Widespread Damage: Sections of Bridge, Highway Collapse in Rush Hour," *Washington Post*, October 18, 1989, A1; "FEMA Disaster Coordinator Took Leave Day after Quake," *Seattle Times*, October 31, 1989, A2.

6. Leo Bosner, "A Whistleblower's Story," *Government Executive* 23 (May 1, 1991): 36;

telephone interview with Leo Bosner, July 8, 2002; interview with Leo Bosner, Washington, D.C., January 9, 2004.

7. Judith Haveman, "Finding More Fault at FEMA," *Washington Post*, October 26, 1989, 25; Henry Bedford, *Seabrook Station: Citizens, Politics and Nuclear Power* (Amherst: University of Massachusetts Press, 1990); Rick Eckstein, *Nuclear Power and Social Power* (Philadelphia: Temple University Press, 1997); "Sununu Picks Ex-Aide as FEMA Chief," *Washington Post*, March 23, 1990, A21; "Patronage Jobs Go Sour at FEMA," *Seattle Times*, September 12, 1992, A1; "Emergency Mismanagement," *Portland Oregonian*, May 23, 1992, E8.

8. "Homosexual Tells of Pressure at FEMA," *Seattle Times*, May 7, 1992, D2; "Vigilantism's Victory at FEMA," *Washington Post*, May 16, 1992, A24; "FEMA Employee Says Agency Destroyed Gay List to Save Face," *Portland Oregonian*, May 20, 1992, A10; Dana Priest, "Staff Questions Latest FEMA Moves: Schism between Political Appointees, Career Employees Widens," *Washington Post*, June 11, 1992, A25; "Appropriations Report Calls FEMA 'a Political Dumping Ground,'" *Washington Post*, July 31, 1992, A21; "GAO Urges Major Changes at FEMA," *Washington Post*, July 23, 1993; interview with Leo Bosner, January 9, 2004.

9. "What Went Wrong?" *Newsweek* (September 7, 1992): 22–27; "Andrew Is Brutal Blow for Agency," *Congressional Quarterly Weekly Report* (September 12, 1992): 2703; "FEMA Doesn't Work," *Seattle Post-Intelligencer*, September 16, 1992, A15; "Patronage Jobs Go Sour at FEMA: Report Calls Agency a Turkey Farm," *Seattle Times*, September 12, 1992, A1; "FEMA Fights Mounting Criticism," *San Francisco Chronicle*, September 15, 1992, A3.

10. *Managing the Federal Government: A Decade of Decline: A Majority Staff Report to the Committee on Government Operations*, House of Representatives, 102d Cong., 2d sess. (Washington, D.C.: GPO, 1993).

11. Larry Lipman and Elliot Jaspin, "Disaster Agency Ready for War," Cox News Service, February 21, 1993. Also see, for example, "Unmasked: FEMA's Eyes Are on Doomsday," *Oregonian*, February 23, 1993, A1; Larry Lipman and Elliot Jaspin, "Disaster Agency FEMA Shields Ultrasecret Program," *Seattle Post-Intelligencer*, February 22, 1993, A1; "Fiscal Disaster: Secret Project to Protect Politicos Aired," *Columbus Dispatch*, March 6, 1993, 6A; "FEMA's Unnatural Disasters," *St. Petersburg Times*, February 25, 1993, 18A; "FEMA's Focus Found to Be on Armageddon," *St. Petersburg Times*, February 23, 1993, 1A.

12. William Claiborne, "FEMA's Clarification Muddies Budgetary Waters," *Washington Post*, February 23, 1993, A17.

13. Ted Gup, "The Doomsday Plan," *Time*, August 10, 1992, 32–39; Ted Gup, "How the Federal Emergency Management Agency Learned to Stop Worrying," *Mother Jones* (January–February 1994): 28–31.

14. Daniel Franklin, "The FEMA Phoenix," *Washington Monthly* (July 1995): 38–46; Mark Murray, "FEMA Administrator Wins Management Kudos," *Government Executive Magazine*, January 16, 2001; Richard T. Sylves, "Ferment at FEMA: Reforming Emergency Management," *Public Administration Review* 54 (May–June 1994): 303–7; Gary Warmsley and Aaron Schroeder, "Escalating in a Quagmire: The Changing Dy-

namics of the Emergency Management Policy Subsystem," *Public Administration Review* 56 (May–June 1996): 235–57.

15. Patrick Brogan, "Armageddon Off: Third World War Canceled: Official," *Herald* (Glasgow, Scotland), April 19, 1994, 4; Tim Weiner, "Pentagon Book for Doomsday Is to Be Closed," *NYT*, April 18, 1994, A1.

16. Thomas B. Cochran, Robert S. Norris, William R. Arkin, and Matthew G. McKinzie, "The U.S. Nuclear War Plan: A Time for Change," Natural Resources Defense Council, available at http://www.nrdc.org/nuclear/warplan. Also see Desmond Ball and Jeffrey Richelson, eds., *Strategic Nuclear Targeting* (Ithaca, N.Y.: Cornell University Press, 1986); Scott D. Sagan, *Moving Targets: National Strategy and Nuclear Security* (Princeton, N.J.: Princeton University Press, 1989); Steven T. Ross, *American War Plans, 1945–1950* (London: Cass, 1996); Aaron L. Friedberg, "A History of the U.S. Strategic Doctrine, 1945–1980," *Journal of Strategic Studies* 4 (December 1980): 37–71; Janne E. Nolan, *An Elusive Consensus: Nuclear Weapons and American Security after the Cold War* (Washington, D.C.: Brookings Institution Press, 1999).

17. Brett Lortie, "A Do It Yourself SIOP," *BAS* 57 (July–August 2001): 22–29; Brian Hall, "Overkill Is Not Dead," *NYT Magazine*, March 15, 1998, 42. In 1992, the Strategic Air Command became the Strategic Command, which Butler headed until his retirement. In that year, he was a candidate for chair of the Joint Chiefs of Staff, but Colin Powell was chosen instead. Butler retired at age fifty-four.

18. Paul Richter, "Plan Ordered for Nuclear Arms Use: Smaller Weapons Part of Deterrence," *Los Angeles Times*, March 9, 2002, A3.

19. Butler cited in Jonathan Schell, *The Gift of Time: The Case for Abolishing Nuclear Weapons Now* (New York: Holt, 1998), 208.

20. "Allbaugh Confirmed as Chief of FEMA," *Los Angeles Times*, February 16, 2001, 15; James Risen, "Emergency Flight Draws Criticism," *NYT*, June 28, 2001, A20; http://www.newbridgestrategies.com.

21. Bradley Graham, "Poindexter Resigns, but Defends Program," *Washington Post*, August 13, 2003, A2.

22. Philip Shenon, "Threats and Responses: Wartime Economy; U.S. Tries to Ease Jitters on Terror," *NYT*, February 15, 2003, A1; Frank James, "Critics Unglued by Government's Advice on Duct Tape," *Chicago Tribune*, February 13, 2003, 23.

23. Quoted in appeal for funds sent by Emergency Committee of Atomic Scientists, Inc., to Dear Friends, January 20, 1947, Department of Special Collections, University of Chicago Library.

Index